# Scalix

## Linux Administrator's Guide

Install, configure, and administer your Scalix
Collaboration Platform email and groupware server

**Markus Feilner**

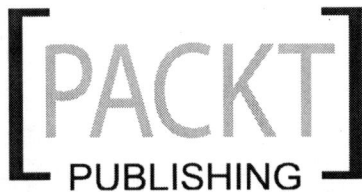

[PACKT]
PUBLISHING

BIRMINGHAM - MUMBAI

# Scalix
## Linux Administrator's Guide

First published: April 2008

Production Reference: 1210408

Published by Packt Publishing Ltd.
32 Lincoln Road
Olton
Birmingham, B27 6PA, UK.

ISBN 978-1-847192-76-9

www.packtpub.com

Cover Image by Mrs Webby (mrs.webby@googlemail.com)

# Credits

**Author**

Markus Feilner

**Reviewers**

Braam van Heerden

Kevin Anderson

**Senior Acquisition Editor**

Priyanka Baruah

**Development Editor**

Nikhil Bangera

**Technical Editor**

Ajay Shanker

**Editorial Team Leader**

Mithil Kulkarni

**Project Manager**

Abhijeet Deobhakta

**Project Coordinator**

Patricia Weir

**Indexer**

Monica Ajmera

**Proofreader**

Camille Guy

**Production Coordinator**

Aparna Bhagat

**Cover Work**

Aparna Bhagat

# About the Author

**Markus Feilner** is a Linux author, trainer, and consultant from Regensburg, Germany, and has been working with open-source software since the mid 1990s. His first contact with UNIX was a SUN cluster and SPARC workstations at Regensburg University (during his studies of geography). Since the year 2000, he has published several documents used in Linux training all over Germany. In 2001, he founded his own Linux consulting and training company, Feilner IT (http://www.feilner-it.net). Furthermore, he is an author, currently working as a trainer, consultant, and systems engineer at Millenux, Munich, where he focuses on groupware, collaboration, and virtualization with Linux-based systems and networks.

He has also written *OpenVPN: Building and Integrating Virtual Private Networks* in 2006 for Packt. Since 2007, he is an editor at the German *Linux-Magazin*, where he is writing about Open-Source Software for both printed and online magazines, including the *Linux Technical Review* and the *Linux Magazine International*. He regularly holds speeches and lectures at conferences in Germany.

He is interested in anything about geography, traveling, photography, philosophy (especially that of open-source software), global politics, and literature, but always has too little time for these hobbies.

Markus Feilner supports Linux4afrika—a project bringing Linux computers into African schools. For more information please visit http://www.linux4afrika.de.

I'd like to thank all the people at Scalix and Xandros for their help, especially Florian von Kurnatowski for his proofreading and correcting many mistakes. A big thank you goes to Dirk Ahrnke of It25.de, who helped me with his know-how on administering large Scalix-installations with several thousand users. I want to thank everybody at Packt, especially Louay, Patricia, Ajay, Nikhil, Jimmy, Sagara, Priyanka, and Viraj; everybody at NoMachine and SEP; and everybody whom I might have forgotten now.

A very big thank you goes to Norbert Graf for providing so many Windows and Scalix screenshots and know-how, and Arne Baeumler for a lot of research work.

*For Agnes*

# About the Reviewers

**Braam van Heerden** obtained a B.Sc. (Hons) from the Rand Afrikaans University in Johannesburg in 1995. He has been playing with Linux and related technologies like Linux security, PHP, Perl, and Linux System and Network Administration since 1993; and with HP OpenMail, Samsung Contact, and Scalix since 2000. He is employed at Conversant Systems, a Linux consultancy company.

**Kevin Anderson** was born and raised in Winnipeg, Manitoba, Canada, moving to Calgary, Alberta in 1999. The oldest of four brothers, he was introduced to a Commodore 64 by his mom in grade 6 and has been resolving people's technical issues since teachers started coming to him in junior high. From assisting teachers, he progressed to administering national and multinational networks, such as Palliser Furniture and Seminole Canada Gas Company.

Combining MCSE and CNE training with a decade of Linux experience, Kevin brings a vast skill set to any technical discussion. Familiarity and experience with the integration of all of these networking systems allows a depth of knowledge rarely found in the industry today.

President of Digital Adrenaline IT Services since 2003, Kevin's focus is on providing reliable trouble-free solutions for dozens of businesses across North America. Focused on Linux and other open solutions such as Scalix, Samba, and Asterisk, Digital Adrenaline has seen explosive growth as Linux proves to be the solution for the growing demands of system reliability and scalability.

In 2001, Kevin was introduced to the packages that eventually were developed to become Scalix. Immediately recognizing the need for this software, Kevin has been involved with Scalix ever since. Active in the community support forums or presenting Scalix to companies and Linux User Groups across the continent, Scalix is a product he believes in and promotes actively.

Kevin can be contacted by email at support@digital-adrenaline.com.

I'd like to thank my wife Nicole, for her love and her support throughout our marriage. You make everyday a great day. Thank you for being my wife. Thanks also to my daughters, Melanie and Gina, who have had their dad pulled away to assist with downed servers and networks far more often than is fair. My mom, for blowing the budget to get us that first Commodore 64, and my dad, for skiing, fishing, camping, and help with the TR7. Loren, Mike, Lyle, Mark, Larry, Al, Jerret, Brett, Jay, and Johnny for great memories and great times growing up.

# Table of Contents

# Preface

Scalix email and calendaring, HP OpenMail, and Samsung Contact: these three names stand for some of the most powerful open-source-based groupware solutions available. This book sets out to explain their fundamentals to Linux administrators.

Since the early 90s, Hewlett Packard had earned many awards for its mail server, and OpenMail was said to be more scalable, reliable, and better performing than any other mail and groupware server. After only a few years, the product had managed to conquer the United States' fortune 1000 almost entirely. Scalix Inc., a member of the Xandros family, has continued this story in the last years: several reviewers claim that it has better Outlook support than MS Exchange.

With the right know-how, Scalix can be easily managed. Several thousand mailboxes are possible on a single server; Web-GUIs and command line tools help the administrator; and Scalix integrates easily with other professional tools, be it OpenVPN, Nagios monitoring or others.

During its history of almost 20 years, many tools and programs were developed for Scalix to help the admin in his/her daily work. While the official documentation has several thousand pages, which are not all up-to-date, this book tries to give a detailed overview from installation to advanced setups and configuration in big companies.

With this book, I want to provide both a concise description of Scalix' features and an easy-to-use introduction for the inexperienced. Admins, consultants, and teachers will all find this book a helpful base for daily work and training. Though there are many other possible ways to success in the described scenarios, the ones presented have been tested in many setups and have been selected for simplicity reasons.

High-end email and groupware is a domain where only few vendors can provide solutions. This is not the realm of Microsoft, and it has never been. It is where companies like HP, Novell or Scalix offer reliable and scalable products. And, Scalix is the only one that has licenced parts under a free and open-source licence. The software is free for up to 10 users, easy-to-use, and offers a lot of possible features ranging from caldav or syncml to clusters.

# What This Book Covers

*Chapter 1* will cover how email became a communication standard, what RFCs are, and where you can find the relevant ones. After a short glance on how email works, the related protocols: SMTP, POP, IMAP, and MAPI are explained in brief as well as LDAP, X500, MIME, and SOAP. An overview of the groupware market, including the various definitions of the latter by different vendors closes the chapter.

*Chapter 2* will start with the history of Scalix groupware. We'll see what a mail node is and where to get more information on Scalix terms like the indexing server, daemons, and services. The chapter will also deal with the protocols supported by Scalix, the license involved, and the packages offered by Scalix.

*Chapter 3* describes the standard installation of Scalix software on OpenSUSE 10.2 and Fedora Core 5.

*Chapter 4* deals with advanced installation techniques. First, you will learn about how to get the graphical installation on Windows systems by using NoMachine NX Terminal software. The second part of this chapter shows a typical text-based installation. As an example, we show how the graphical installer is used to correctly uninstall a Scalix server. The last example shows upgrading and reconfiguration of the Scalix server.

*Chapter 5* deals with the Scalix Administration Console (SAC). We will take a short tour through the interface, add a first user, and have a closer look at the available configuration options.

*Chapter 6* will cover how to deploy Scalix Connect for Microsoft Outlook, to your Windows clients. After that, the integration of the supported Scalix groupware client Evolution and other IMAP mail clients is shown.

*Chapter 7* covers the most important configuration files and commands of Scalix.

*Chapter 8* deals with standard Scalix monitoring tools and the integration of Scalix in your centralized Nagios monitoring. After some details on Scalix administration programs like omstat and omlimit, we see how Outlook clients can be monitored. In the end, some of our Nagios scripts and configuration files serve to add another host to an existing Nagios configuration.

*Chapter 9* will deal with several recommendations that make your Scalix server safe—like minimizing the number of services running and listening. We will set up a firewall that allows Scalix users to connect. After that we will set up Stunnel to provide SSL-encrypted Scalix services. Then, we will use OpenVPN to protect the server. Last but not least, we will have a look at the services running and discuss advanced possibilities of securing the server.

*Chapter 10* will discuss how to backup and restore a Scalix mail server—for small and large environments.

*Chapter 11* will cover how to administrate Scalix in sync with data stored in remote directories. This chapter starts with an explanation of how Scalix delivers its information in LDAP-style and rounds up with a guide on how to integrate Scalix with an external Microsoft Active Directory.

*Chapter 12* starts with questions that you have to ask yourself before you set up any multi-server environment with Scalix. After that, we see two examples as to how a High Availability (HA) setup might look like.

*Chapter 13* will cover how to integrate measures against spam and viruses in Scalix.

*Bibliography* contains a comprehensive list of all the links used through out the book.

# Who is This Book for

This book is written for Linux Administrators who wish to set up an email server for businesses or those who wish to switch to Scalix from another email server. Scalix can be used very easily by beginners; however, strategies and administrative tasks are difficult to learn and this book will help you master them all.

# Conventions

In this book, you will find a number of styles of text that distinguish between different kinds of information. Here are some examples of these styles, and an explanation of their meaning.

There are three styles for code. Code words in text are shown as follows: "We can include other contexts through the use of the `include` directive."

A block of code will be set as follows:

```
# Generic host definition template
define host{
    name                generic-host    ; The name of this host template
    notifications_enabled      1    ; Host notifications are enabled
```

**New terms** and **important words** are introduced in a bold-type font. Words that you see on the screen, in menus or dialog boxes for example, appear in our text like this: "clicking the **Next** button moves you to the next screen".

[ Important notes appear in a box like this. ]

[ Tips and tricks appear like this. ]

# Reader Feedback

Feedback from our readers is always welcome. Let us know what you think about this book, what you liked or may have disliked. Reader feedback is important for us to develop titles that you really get the most out of.

To send us general feedback, simply drop an email to feedback@packtpub.com, making sure to mention the book title in the subject of your message.

If there is a book that you need and would like to see us publish, please send us a note in the **SUGGEST A TITLE** form on www.packtpub.com or email suggest@packtpub.com.

If there is a topic that you have expertise in and you are interested in either writing or contributing to a book, see our author guide on www.packtpub.com/authors.

# Customer Support

Now that you are the proud owner of a Packt book, we have a number of things to help you to get the most from your purchase.

# Errata

Although we have taken every care to ensure the accuracy of our contents, mistakes do happen. If you find a mistake in one of our books—maybe a mistake in text or code—we would be grateful if you would report this to us. By doing this you can save other readers from frustration, and help to improve subsequent versions of this book. If you find any errata, report them by visiting http://www.packtpub.com/support, selecting your book, clicking on the **Submit Errata** link, and entering the details of your errata. Once your errata are verified, your submission will be accepted and the errata are added to the list of existing errata. The existing errata can be viewed by selecting your title from http://www.packtpub.com/support.

# Questions

You can contact us at questions@packtpub.com if you are having a problem with some aspect of the book, and we will do our best to address it.

# 1

# Email and Groupware:
# History and Basics

This book starts with a short history of email and related protocols. In this chapter, you will learn how email became a communication standard, what RFCs are, and where you can find the relevant ones. After a short glance on how email works, the related protocols: SMTP, POP, IMAP, and MAPI are explained in brief as well as LDAP, X500, MIME, and SOAP. An overview of the groupware market, including the various definitions of the latter by different vendors closes the chapter.

## A Brief History of Email

In the last 20 years, email has become one of the pillars of Internet. Today, almost everyone has at least one or more email addresses, but nobody realizes that the mail system was born as soon as the early 1960s. The community grew in the '70s, matured to big companies and institutes in the '80s, and the commercialized mail system in the '90s. In the last decade, spam and viruses have been endangering our trust in the whole mail system.

Though initially designed for plain text messages, today's mail programs enable users to send messages in HTML or RTF with multimedia documents attached. Modern systems have made sending emails an easy job, but at the same time few people understand what their PC is doing at this moment. This is a pity, because the basic email protocols use very simple processes.

# The 1960s—CTSS and MIT

In 1961, a multi-user system called **CTSS** (Compatible Time-Sharing System) was introduced at MIT, with which remote users could log in and work together on a central server. Working together also included storing files on this machine and exchanging information. Tom van Vleck, then a young programmer at MIT described the situation:

> *"When CTSS users wanted to pass messages to each other, they sometimes created files with names like TO TOM and put them in "common file" directories, e. g. M1416 CMFL03. The recipient could log into CTSS later, from any terminal, and look for the file, and print it out if it was there."*

"The History of Electronic Mail" by Tom Van Vleck: `http://www.` `multicians.org/thvv/mail-history.html`.

Needless to say, the programmers at MIT saw the need for a more sophisticated solution. Thus, the first mail program was developed during the following years. Tom and his colleague, Noel Morris, programmed an early version of "mail" for the CTSS during the summer of 1965. This tool had already been used as a privileged program that could add the message to a file in the recipient's directory. Unlike earlier versions, now there was no need for a common directory with write-access for both sender and recipient. Maybe this was the birth of a mail server daemon. When invoked, the mail command took two arguments:

- The first of these represented the problem.
- The second represented the programmer, that is, the recipient.

Some wild cards were also possible, a command like `mail m1416 *` would send a message about problem `m1416` to all the programmers on your project. Only a few users could send mail to arbitrary amounts of recipients. Regarding spam, this system was better than our mail system today.

Another feature was implemented later — delivering mail created a file called "MAIL BOX", and the user logging in was informed about new mail with a line printing "YOU HAVE MAIL BOX "or "YOU HAVE URGENT MAIL" if these files existed. What a pity no one thought of a copyright for such sentences then. The mail program would add mail to the MAIL BOX file or, if the mail was tagged as urgent, to a file called URGENT MAIL in the user's home directory.

Noel Morris and Tom Van Vleck wrote several other programs, including the first chat or instant messaging feature. They also tried to find out what the US Post Office would say about this new mailing procedure. Would the monopolist expect postage? A talk between a MIT professor and a US Post representative ended with the words "Don't worry.", which was maybe bad luck for the monopolist, but luck for us all.

Other computer systems like SDC or SDS also had mail commands until the fall of 1965, a speed pretty normal in the '60s. There were neither software patents nor non-disclosure agreements on code; they were unfortunate inventions of the '80s. Until then, large parts of the computer community freely shared their code.

# The '70s—From MULTICS to RFC Standards

In 1969, the first **MULTICS** `mail` command was created as a reimplementation of CTSS `mail`. Again, Tom van Vleck was the programmer who did it, and one of the things that got lost during transition from CTSS to Multics was the concept of a privileged command. Multics could not offer privileges like CTSS did, and programming a real daemon would cause too much load. Therefore, Van Vleck passed a momentous decision:

> "*The only design I could find was one that depended on the good behavior of the users.*"

The Mailbox of the users was treated as a shared memory segment with a keyword preventing simultaneous writes from corrupting the file. Multics mail is much like our modern mail systems: insecure, forgeable, and trashable. At that time, knowing the user's real name was necessary for delivery. A command `mail firstname.lastname` would store the message in the recipient's mail box. The Multics mail program was redesigned in the early '70s to an early server style, including a set of permissions for the mail box file.

According to Van Vleck, that was also the time when the very first spam message was sent. Using MIT's CTSS Mail, the first mass mailing was sent in 1971. It was the time of the Vietnam war and the political mood had inspired a privileged user, a programmer of Van Vleck's team, who sent this mail to all the mail users of CTSS:

*THERE IS NO WAY TO PEACE. PEACE IS THE WAY.*

According to Brad Templeton, the first commercial spam mail was sent later, in 1978, by a marketer for DEC. ("Reflections on the 25th Anniversary of Spam" by Brad Templeton: `http://www.templetons.com/brad/spam/spam25.html`.)

In 1968, John Licklider of the ARPA contacted Tom Van Vleck with the idea of connecting the various ARPANETs to one big network, one of the birthdays of the Internet. One of the topics discussed most was how to enable mail communication between these networks, because they all had different mail systems. The ideal place for such a standard is an RFC, a "Request for Comments", and as a consequence, in 1971, for the first time a RFC, # 0196 (RFC 196 – "A Mail Box Protocol": `http://www.faqs.org/rfcs/rfc196.html`) with the title "Mail Box Protocol" dealt with electronic mail, specifying how mail had to be delivered to a ARPANet site.

According to techtarget.com, "A Request For Comments (RFC) is a formal document from the Internet Engineering Task Force (IETF) that is the result of committee drafting and subsequent review by interested parties." (http://whatis. techtarget.com/definition/0,,sid9_gci214264,00.html.)

A RFC is the ultimate place for administrators who need to find out definitions, standards, and how some things should work theoretically. A RFC-defined standard is commonly accepted and remains unchanged for long periods of time. Whenever you're stuck in a technical discussion, picking the right RFC will back you up.

## The Story of @

By 1971, every site could handle mail with its own system. The system indicated a combination of username and host at a site for the destination. The computer engineer, Ray Tomlinson, had written a mail program called READMAIL—a mailer that was designed to send and receive mail from a local host. However, it was not designed to deal with mail from, or to, other hosts. Connecting the machines in his office made it necessary for a distinguisher between email addresses and hosts. Tomlinson says why he chose the @-sign:

*"I am frequently asked why I chose the at sign, but the at sign just makes sense. The purpose of the at sign (in English) was to indicate a unit price (for example, 10 items @ $1.95). I used the at sign to indicate that the user was "at" some other host rather than being local."* ("The First Network Email" by Ray Tomlinson http://openmap.bbn.com/~tomlinso/ray/firstemailframe.html.)

On March 8, 1973, the @-sign was defined as the distinguishing character between username and host RFC 469 (RFC 469 - "Network Mail Meeting Summary": http://tools.ietf.org/html/469).

The '70s became the time of standardization of electronic mail. Many RFCs continued to specify various aspects of email throughout the 1970s and '80s. The new medium "mail" became more and more popular. It soon became obvious that the ARPANET was becoming a human-communication medium with very important advantages over normal mail and telephone calls. The formality and perfection that most people expect in a typed letter did not become associated with network messages, probably because the network was so much faster, and so much more like the telephone. (J.C.R. Licklider, Albert Vezza, "Applications of Information Networks", Proc of the IEEE, 66(11), Nov 1978, as quoted by Dave Crocker: http://www.livinginternet. com/e/ei.htm.

# RFCs—Request for Comments

Obviously, the lack of form was an important aspect that made the Internet and mail appealing for a growing number of people. Totally underestimated by its creators, email became more and more popular. As soon as 1971, more traffic in the ARPANET was generated by Email than from FTP or telnet. With the increasing amount of mail, it became important to have messages sorted and ordered. Tomlinson's README was rewritten and the mail program RD was developed. NRD, BANANARD, and MSG followed until the mid-'70s. According to Dave Crocker, initiator of several RFCs concerning Email and Domain Name System, MSG was the first Email program that provided an "Answer" function. In 1975, an early mail client was developed by Steve Walker at RAND, it was named MS and is said to have been "very powerful, and very, very slow". After several drafts, for the first time, RFC 733 standardized mail formats under the title of "Standard for the format of ARPA network text messages". (RFC 733 - Standard for the format of ARPA network text messages: `http://tools.ietf.org/html/733`.)

Three years later, the next milestone followed with RFC 772, "Mail Transfer Protocol". Until then, network mail had been a component of FTP, according to RFC 385. RFC 772 defined the Mail Transfer Protocol and set the path for the Simple Mail Transfer Protocol SMTP (RFC 821, August 1982), which we still use today. RFC821 is still the most read RFC of all times. The website `www.faqs.org` ( The Top 50 RFCs: `http://www.faqs.org/rfc-pop1.html`) offers a complete and up-to-date list of all RFCs and is a very helpful location, offering searches, listings, and lots of links. According to the chart on this site, there are four RFCs concerning mail in the top twenty of the most viewed RFCs. These papers are definitely the best place to go to whenever you are unsure of some technical specifications, if you need to impress your boss or colleagues, or simply want to prove a point. The following descriptions in this chapter will contain a lot of links to such RFCs, simply because they are the commonly accepted authority throughout the Internet.

If you are using KDE, Konqueror has a neat function to help you search for RFCs: an Internet shortcut is provided, with which you can search the apt RFC for a keyword. Simply type "`rfc SMTP`" in the address bar, and Konqueror takes you to the results of the IETF's RFC search. Of course, most of today's browsers support similar shortcuts.

# Mailing Lists, Sendmail, X.400, BBS, and More

In the late '70s, Email usage began to soar and reach more and more people. The very first mailing list was created. According to Howard Rheingold, it was called "SF-Lovers" and enabled the ARPANET mail users to exchange information about their favorite literature: science fiction (Howard Rheingold on the very first mailing list: `http://www.rheingold.com/vc/book`.) Rheingold says:

*"In computer technology, playgrounds often are where real innovations emerge."*

During the early 1980's, Sendmail was programmed. It later became the (in)famous dinosaur among all mail servers. Still in use today, though there are many replacements, Sendmail is both hated for the syntax of its configuration files and loved for its stability (once properly configured). Sendmail's origin lies in Berkeley, California. A free UNIX operating system called BSD was being developed at Berkeley University, and Sendmail was its mailer. In the beginning, the mail command used UUCP (UNIX to UNIX Copy Protocol) to copy files from one UNIX system to a different vendor's system. After RFC 821, Sendmail became the first and most common SMTP mail program. Today, Sendmail still lives on in different flavors, both commercial and free, and it is still delivered with many Linux distributions. There is also a Sendmail daemon running Scalix SMTP services.

Nevertheless, the classic email system soon became competitors: In 1984, the mail standard X.400 was developed by CCITT, Comité Consultatif International Téléphonique et Télégraphique, which is today the International Telecommunication Union, (ITU) located in Geneva ( X.400 Message handling services: `http://www.itu.int/rec/T-REC-X.400/en.`). X.400 became ISO standard 10021, and was called Standard Message Oriented Text Interchange System (MOTIS). In contrary to standard Email, the X.400 Mail System is transparent. Origin, path, and receiver of every message are traceable, which is why X.400 is still being used in many military or security environments. Other competitors like Mailbox Systems, X.25, BTX or Bulletin Board Systems (BBS) were overtaken by the success of the Internet in the 1990s, and are practically non-existent today. However, especially BBS's, left lots of traces on the Web—the idea of blogs, chat, and more can easily be traced back to these systems. Citadel ( Citadel BBS: `http://www.citadel.org`), an open source BBS and SMTP-Mailserver shows how alternative concepts can work.

## The '90s: Groupware, the WWW, and Microsoft

In the late '80s and early '90s, collaboration software for enterprises like HP OpenMail, IBM Domino/Notes (Lotus), and Novell GroupWise emerged. The term groupware was created and comprised basically of everything related to email, contacts, and calendaring within a team of colleagues. From the very beginning, each vendor followed his own path.

At the end of the 1980s, CompuServe had started the first commercial Email service, and in the early '90s, providers like AOL connected their networks, providing the World Wide Web (WWW) for everyone. Late, but powerful, Microsoft (MS) finally entered the scene with its Exchange Server, Outlook and Internet Explorer. Until the end of the millennium, MS achieved a market leader's role and is today still almost a monopolist in the groupware market. If you are interested in the history of MS Exchange, go to "A history of MS Exchange": `http://blogs.brnets.com/michael/archive/2005/02/07/347.aspx`. For many Windows users, Outlook, Exchange, and Mail have become a synonym for the same concept. But the monoculture of Microsoft's products, made spam, viruses, and other threats flourish. Of course, some causes lie in history, openness, and design failures of the mail protocols, but another big burden can be found in severe, conceptual security issues of the Windows operating system, the email software, and a software design that focuses more on usability than security, thereby opening the system for intruders. Mail has become a nuisance because spam, viruses, phishing, and other threats make us spend more and more time dealing with our emails. Time for a change!

# How does Email Work?

So what is behind email? We have learnt that in per-network-mail, files on a server were created and the user was informed upon login. This does not seem like the way we are using mail today. The following pages show, what is working behind the scenes of sending and retrieving emails. We are watching two users, Norbert and Arne, and we will dive into it deeper and deeper, step by step.

In an example, our user Arne notices that his friend Norbert has his birthday today and decides to send him an email. After composing it in his mail client, Arne hits the Send-button and the message is put on its way to Norbert. Some hours later, Norbert reads his new email and replies to Arne with a short "Thank you!". This is how everybody knows email. But what is really happening in the background?

## Sending Mail—the User View

Arne composes an email: A text message is being written. His mail client uses a special format to "wrap" the message text inside with additional information that is needed by the mail servers involved. Such information contains the sender's and the recipient's address, a time stamp, and more. The email with the metadata is transferred to Arne's mail server, which looks up the recipient's mail server in the Domain Name System's (DNS) database. Among other useful things, DNS servers hold paired lists of the name and IP of servers in the Internet. Furthermore, an MX (Mail Exchanger) entry in this database tells a client which mail server provides mail to a recipient's domain.

After having found Norbert's mail server's IP, the message is transferred using SMTP. The receiving mail server notices that the Email is destined for Norbert and stores it in its local storage. Sometime later, Norbert is switching on his PC and retrieving Email with his mail client. The server hands over the new mails, including Arne's best wishes. Norbert now presses reply and hacks in his "Thank you". Once he clicks on **Send**, the same procedure runs again. That's how everybody uses email today. But what's happening in the background?

# The Protocols Involved

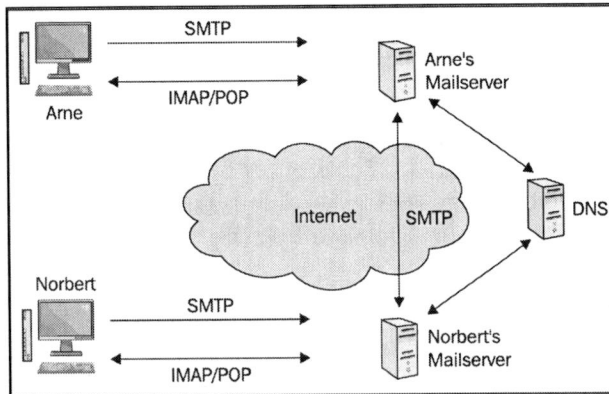

In detail: Arne's mail client contacts his mail server using SMTP. A Mail Transfer Agent (MTA) like Sendmail takes the mail, maybe performing some checks on it. At first, the mail will be put in the MTA's mail queue. After having found the IP of Norbert's mail server in the Domain Name System (DNS), Arne's server uses SMTP to transfer the mail to Norbert's server. The latter recognizes that the mail is for a local user and hands it over to the local Mail Delivery Agent (MDA) who stores the mail locally and hands it to Norbert's mail client via a protocol like POP, IMAP or an interface like MAPI. POP and IMAP are protocols only used to retrieve mail or other data by a Mail User Agent (MUA), who we know as mail client or mail program. SMTP, however, is being used for sending mail both by servers and by clients. Thus, after having received his new mail by using POP or IMAP, Norbert will send the reply by SMTP to his mail server, who hands it to Arne's mail server using the same protocol.

| The acronym... | ...means |
| --- | --- |
| MTA | Mail Transfer Agent |
| MDA | Mail Delivery Agent |
| MUA | Mail User Agent |

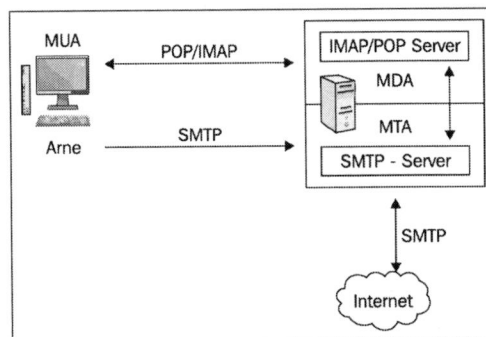

# SMTP

SMTP stands for "Simple Mail Transfer Protocol" and is used for sending mail. It is defined in RFCs 821, 876, 1047, 1090, 1425-1427, 1651-53, 1830, 1845, 1846, 1854, 1869, 1870, 2197, and many others later on. Whereas a SMTP server sends and receives email via SMTP, clients only use this protocol for sending mail. Alternative standards are UUCP and X.400. Standard SMTP uses TCP port 25 (as defined in /etc/services on Linux machines). Because SMTP is a plain text protocol, Arne could have sent his birthday greetings also with the help of telnet. The following command can be used to send emails in a telnet session.

The correct syntax is: telnet <hostname> <portnumber>.

A typical SMTP session thus looks like the following example.

```
arne@localhost :~> telnet scalixbook.org 25
Trying 127.0.0.1...
Connected to localhost.
Escape character is '^]'.
220 scalixbook.org ESMTP Postfix
helo localhost
250 scalixbook.org
mail from: <arne.baeumler@scalixbook.org>
250 2.1.0 Ok
rcpt to: <norbert.graf@scalixbook.org>
250 2.1.5 Ok
data
from: arne.baeumler@scalixbook.org
to: norbert.graf@scalixbook.org
subject: Happy Birthday, Arne!
354 End data with <CR><LF>.<CR><LF>
Hello Norbert,
Happy Birthday!
Arne
.

250 2.0.0 Ok: queued as A335540A08B1
quit
221 2.0.0 Bye
Connection closed by foreign host.
arne@localhost :~>
```

The command `telnet scalixbook.org 25` opens a telnet session to port 25 on the machine `scalixbook.org`. In the following lines, a SMTP session takes place. After the initial greeting with `helo <yourhostname>` or `ehlo <yourhostname>` (the latter invokes extended SMTP features), Arne has typed `"mail from:"` and `"rcpt to:"` to specify sender and addressee. Following the keyword `"data"`, we find the content of the message as it will appear in the mail client later.

The lines "to:" and "from:" are necessary for correct display of the message in the mail client. If the line "to:" is left out, the mail client will display "undisclosed-recipients:" in the "to:" field. If you are using a spam filter, such a mail would probably be tagged as spam, dropped or rejected. The "data" block is finished with a new line followed by a single dot and another new line, this is what the `"<CR><LF>.<CR><LF>"` means.

Famous open-source SMTP servers are Sendmail, Postfix, Qmail, and Exim.

# POP

POP3 (The Post Office Protocol Version 3) is the abbreviation for Post Office Protocol, currently in version 3, and is used by an MDA. It has been defined in 1984 in RFC 937, enabling a first standard for mail clients who have temporary Internet access only. POP was further specified in RFCs 937, 1081, and 1939 — and several later RFCs. Together with SMTP, POP has become the most common mail protocol on the Internet.

A POP server accepts and stores mails in a local storage. If a POP-enabled client connects, the POP server delivers the mail to the client. Normally, the client simply receives all new messages that are deleted from the server after fetching. Nevertheless, most POP servers also provide server-side deleting of mails without delivery, which can be very useful when a low bandwidth client connects and does not want to download a mail with a 100MB attachment.

Norbert is now fetching his mail. He is also using telnet:

```
norbert@localhost:~> telnet scalixbook.org 110
Trying 62.116.156.xx ...
Connected to scalixbook.org.
Escape character is '^]'.
+OK Qpopper (version 4.0.5) at scalixbook.org starting.
<24773.1174162756@scalixbook.org>
user norbert
+OK Password required for norbert.
pass mybirthday2day
+OK norbert has 1 visible message (0 hidden) in 538 octets.
list
+OK 1 visible messages (538 octets)
```

```
1 538
.

retr 1
+OK 538 octets
Date:  xx yy zzzz 21:16:58 +0100
From: Arne Baeumler <arne.baeumler@scalixbook.org>
Subject: Happy Birthday, Norbert!
Message-ID: <1174162618@scalixbook.org>
Status: RW

Hello Norbert,
I just wanted to say: Happy Birthday!
Enjoy your Party.
Arne

.

quit
+OK Pop server at scalixbook.org signing off.
Connection closed by foreign host.
norbert@localhost:~>
```

The POP syntax is as simple as the SMTP Syntax. After an initial login with the "user" and "pass" command, Norbert can read his mail using "list" and "retr". After having read his birthday greetings, the logout is done with "quit". The following table gives an overview of common pop commands:

| The POP Command... | ... lets you... |
| --- | --- |
| user | enter your username. |
| pass | enter your password. |
| stat | list status, incl. the number of new mails. |
| list | list number and length of the emails. |
| retr <n> | retrieve email number <n>. |
| dele <n> | delete mail <n>. |
| noop | test server. The Server should respond with „Ok". |
| rset | reset all "dele" commands. |
| quit | exit the pop session. |

Famous open-source POP servers are Cyrus, Qpopper, Dovecot, and Uwimap. Standard POP uses TCP port 110, SSL-encoded POP is using port 995.

# IMAP

IMAP stands for *Internet Message Access Protocol*. This protocol has been standardized through RFCs 1731, 1732, 1733, and many more until RFC 3501 from 2003 defined the standard IMAP Version 4 that we are still using today. It was invented in the '80s at Stanford University, has been steadily improved and has become rather complex

today. With IMAP, a mail client can access a mail server's mail storage without downloading a single mail. IMAP offers the possibility of centralizing the storage. Clients only connect to read and manage mail. All the action takes place only on the server, the client does not need a local mail storage. With a POP-based mail system, the local administrator would have had to backup every local PC, but with IMAP a backup of the server's mail storage is sufficient for a whole company.

The central mail storage makes mail accessible from different locations. A user can access his email with an IMAP client from everywhere, given access to the server. Furthermore, a client no longer needs to download the complete email. Especially in low-bandwidth networks, this concept has had great success, and modern mobile services like Blackberry still use similar concepts. A client can connect to the IMAP server and retrieve only the metadata of the new emails, like sender, size, and subject. The user selects the mail he wants to read and has his mail client download it, whereas the other mails stay untouched. However, with large mailboxes, this protocol will use much more network bandwidth, because the communication between client and server is far more complex.

IMAP supports access rules, creation of folders on the server, sharing these folders between users, and searches for and in messages—before the client really has read their content. Many servers use indexing services that speed up searches significantly. Arbitrary flags like "**new**" or "**unread**" can now be set by the users, who can also subscribe to or unsubscribe from shared folders.

As in the examples before, Norbert now uses telnet to fetch the birthday email from Arne, using some commands of the IMAP protocol.

```
norbert@scalixbook.org:~# telnet localhost 143
Trying 127.0.0.1...
Connected to localhost.
Escape character is '^]'.
OK scalixbook.org Cyrus IMAP4 v2.2.12-Debian-2.2.12-4ubuntu1 server
ready
. login norbert xxxxxxxxxxxxx
. OK User logged in
. list "" "*"
* LIST (\HasChildren) "." "INBOX"
* LIST (\HasNoChildren) "." "INBOX.Bestellungen"
(...)
. status INBOX (messages)
* STATUS INBOX (MESSAGES 6)
. OK Completed
. select INBOX
* FLAGS (\Answered \Flagged \Draft \Deleted \Seen)
(...)
```

```
. fetch 1 rfc822.header
* 1 FETCH (RFC822.HEADER {1240}
Return-Path: <a>
Received: from scalixbook.org ([unix socket])
        by scalixbook.org (Cyrus v2.2.12-Debian-2.2.12-4ubuntu1)
        with LMTPA;
        Wed, xx xxx 2007 21:40:43 +0000
X-Sieve: CMU Sieve 2.2
(...)
Message-ID: <1174162618@scalixbook.org>
Date: Wed, xx xx 2007 21:40:43 -0000 (UTC)
From: Arne Baeumler <arne.baeumler@scalixbook.org>
Subject: Happy Birthday, Norbert!
Message-ID: <1174162618@scalixbook.org>
Status: RW
(...)
. fetch 1 rfc822.text
* 1 FETCH (RFC822.TEXT {633}
Hello Norbert,
I just wanted to say: Happy Birthday!
Enjoy your Party.
Arne
(...)
. OK Completed (0.000 sec)
. logout
* BYE LOGOUT received
. OK Completed
Connection closed by foreign host.
. logout
norbert@scalixbook.org:
```

All IMAP commands in this telnet session begin with an initial ".". After logging in with the command `. login`, followed by his username and password, Norbert types ". list "" "*"" to have the IMAP server display all his mail folders. A ". status INBOX (messages)" displays all new messages in the folder INBOX, which is where new mail goes per default. Norbert uses the command ". select INBOX" to switch his context to the Inbox and types ". fetch 1 rfc822.header" ". fetch 1 rfc822. text" to receive the header and the content of the first new email, which is the happy-birthday Email from Arne. A final ". logout" quits his IMAP session.

The following table shows some IMAP commands:

| The IMAP command ... | means: |
| --- | --- |
| . login <name> <password> | Enter your username and password. |
| . list | List mailbox and folders. |
| . status <folder> | List status of current folder. |
| . examine <folder> | Display information on folder |
| . select <folder> | Select folder as context for next commands. |
| . create <folder> | Create a folder. |
| . rename <folder> | Rename a folder. |
| . delete <folder> | Mark a folder for deletion. |
| . expunge | Delete the messages marked for deletion. |
| . close | Expunge messages and exit the session. |
| . fetch <message number><options> | Access the information on Email <number>,<br>- the headers of the mail #1, |
| . fetch 1 rfc822.header | - the text of mail #2. |
| . fetch 2 rfc822.text | |
| . getacl <folder> | List the access rules for <folder>. |
| . store <message number> <flags> | Change flags and access rules of messages and folders. |
| . copy <message> <folder> | Copy a message to a folder. |

A special way of dealing with IMAP is the so-called "cached IMAP": The client connects to the server, fetches all mail folders and data and stores it in its local file system. Every time the user triggers the "Check mail" button, the local mail storage is synchronized with the server. By doing so, a user with a client that is only temporarily connected to the IMAP server can still work with his email. This method is often called "Offline-Sync(hronization)" and is only used with desktop email clients, mainly on mobile devices like laptops. Offline Sync combines the advantages of classical POP and IMAP.

Famous open-source IMAP Servers are Courier, Cyrus, UWImap, and Dovecot. Standard IMAP uses TCP port 143. SSL-encoded IMAP is using TCP Port 993.

## MAPI—IMAP, the Microsoft Way

First of all: there is no RFC on MAPI. It is not an open protocol, but a vendor-specific interface for Microsoft clients and servers. MAPI is an abbrevation for Messaging Application Programming Interface. Programs that are MAPI-compliant can directly send application data attached to emails and retrieve information stored in MAPI mail servers. Even though there are some free projects developing MAPI implementations, there is no free MAPI version around.

Microsoft was a little late at discovering the importance of the Internet and especially of the mail system. However, in 1987, the company decided to develop a proprietary mail system plus API on their own, and it has been integrated in all Microsoft applications and operating systems since 1995. Its origins can be found in the late '80s. MAPI version 0 originally contained functions that were X.400-based; a "Simple MAPI" interface followed and was removed from Exchange 2003, and replaced by the Extended MAPI Interface.

Since MAPI was developed at a time when open and free standards like SMTP and IMAP had been running successfully for more than a decade, Microsoft has always been under suspicion of trying to use its operating system monopoly to establish a nonstandard mail protocol. The details of the MAPI protocol are proprietary and intellectual property of Microsoft. According to techtarget.com, MAPI consists of:

"a standard set of C language functions that are stored in a (...) dynamic link library (DLL)." (MAPI definition at techtarget.com: `http://searchexchange.techtarget.com/sDefinition/0,,sid43_gci214084,00.html`.)

Open-source projects like Samba and companies like HP (or later Scalix) have acquired great knowledge of Microsoft's protocols. A common rumor suggests that the Samba guys know more about the network behavior of Windows systems than the MS engineers do, and Scalix is said to have the best MAPI implementation, even better than Microsoft's own.

The Microsoft Developer's Network, (MSDN) is probably the best official place to get information on MAPI (Microsoft's MAPI documentation: `http://msdn2.microsoft.com/en-us/library/ms879918.aspx`). If you intend to dive into reengineering MAPI, go to the wiki of the OpenChange project ( Openchange Projekt: `http://www.openchange.org`), where open source Samba and Groupware specialists share their knowledge in order to create a free MAPI implementation for a free MAPI server. Until then, we have to work with Outlook plugins connecting the MAPI client to a non-MAPI server. Standard MAPI uses TCP port 135.

# MIME

Multipurpose Internet Mail Extensions are of a standard (RFCs 2045, 2046, 2047, 2048, and 2077) that define how application data, normally non-ASCII-text, is sent via email. As you may have noticed, the email protocol is a text-based protocol that supports US-ASCII only. MIME-types specify encoding styles and content types for binary data formats within Emails (and other www-related protocols). MIME Encoding helps to send arbitrary data with protocols like SMTP that only supports 7-bit ASCII code. Thus for example German umlauts or 8-bit binary content can be wrapped within the 7-bit ASCII code of a standard email. MIME encoding is

something most people hardly ever know or care about. Since the mail clients have always been doing this work for the user transparently, no interaction is needed. MIME adds a subset of email headers to an email that define the parameters of the encoding and the MIME type of the file attached. Such a message is also called a Multipart/MIME message.

This example shows how an image would be embedded in an email using MIME:

```
Subject: MIME message
MIME-Version: 1.0
Content-type: multipart/mixed; boundary="------content"
Content-type: text/plain; charset=utf-8

Hello Arne,
I have attached a nice picture from my birthday party!
Best regards,
Norbert
------content
Content-type: image/jpg; name="party01.jpg"
Content-Transfer-Encoding: base64

asdf12312d//fADWERD34212424SFVFDGSG...
------content
```

The Wikipedia page on MIME (`http://en.wikipedia.org/wiki/MIME`) is a very good start. Examples for typical MIME types are:

| Documents with the file name extension ... | ... usually are of the Mime type |
| --- | --- |
| `.doc` | `application/msword.` |
| `.dot` | `application/msword.` |
| `.zip` | `application/x-compressed.` |
| `.zip` | `application/x-zip-compressed.` |
| `.zip` | `application/zip` |

The extensions S/MIME and PGP/MIME allow safe encryption and digital signing of mails and attachments; they are defined in RFC 2015 and 3156.

# Headers—What Does an Email Look Like?

RFC 2822, RFCs 2045, and the following ones define in detail how an email has to be structured. In some parts of this chapter, we have already seen what that means. A standard email is split in two big parts: the headers and the body. The header fields contain the metadata of the email like sender and recipient, the body contains the message text, and eventually MIME blocks. Here is the Multipart Mail from Norbert to Arne containing the birthday picture:

```
From: norbert.graf@scalixbook.org
To: arne.baeumler@scalixbook.org
Subject: Images from my party
Date: Sun, xx xx 2007 01:29:14 +0100
User-Agent: KMail/1.9.6
MIME-Version: 1.0
Content-Type: Multipart/Mixed;
  boundary="Boundary-00=_bfI/FxN8p5hMpLk"
X-KMail-Recipients: arne.baeumler@scalixbook.org
Message-Id: <200703180129.15195.norbert.graf@scalixbook.org>
Status: R
X-Status: NQ
X-KMail-EncryptionState:
X-KMail-SignatureState:
X-KMail-MDN-Sent:

--Boundary-00=_bfI/FxN8p5hMpLk
Content-Type: text/plain;
  charset="utf-8"
Content-Transfer-Encoding: quoted-printable
Content-Disposition: inline

Hello Arne,

I have attached a nice picture from my birthday party!

Best regards,
Norbert
--

--Boundary-00=_bfI/FxN8p5hMpLk
Content-Type: image/jpeg;
  name="party01.jpg"
Content-Transfer-Encoding: base64
Content-Disposition: attachment;
    filename="party01.jpg"
```

```
/9j/4AAQSkZJRgABAQEASABIAAD/4RT5RXhpZgAASUkqAAgAAAAJAA8BAgAGAAAAegAAA
BABAgAXAAAAgAAAABIBAwABAAAAAQAAABoBBQABAAAAmAAAABsBBQABAA
AACgBAwABAAAAgAAADIBAgAUAAAAqAAAABMCAwABAAAAAQAAAGmHBAA
BAAAAvAAAAIQJAABDYW5vb
(...)
DcMxiA3ky4MYozYLzRjEDAMYDIKMYAGMYIDdGMYKxupjAbqYxgMbo
YwGB1MYAm6GMBrMjGAzdBi7
wYxFE15MYI//2Q==
```

```
--Boundary-00=_bfI/FxN8p5hMpLk--
```

The ISO Standard X.500 (ISO/IEC 9594) includes several subsets of directory standards like DAP, the Directory Access Protocol. X.500 was originally developed to accomplish the needs of the X.400 Mail standard. X.400 has unique identifiers for every member of the communication, thus the need for a central directory was obviously stronger and rose much earlier than for common email services. One disadvantage of DAP was that the Network infrastructure had to be adapted to its X.400 roots. Few scenarios could provide the full OSI protocol stack needed for DAP, and consequently the Lightweight Directory Access Protocol was developed. LDAP has since then had tremendous success and is standardized in RFC 4510 in its current version 3.

The communication between a LDAP Server and his client comprises authentication, adding, deleting, modifying, and searching. The data in the directory is arranged in the form of a tree with branches and leaves. A leaf may represent a person, one of this person's attributes is his or her name, a small branch of the tree could be the department where she works, a thicker branch might stand for the company's American branch with the tree representing the company. Thus a distinguishing name for a person might be:

```
Germany, Regensburg, Feilner-IT, Markus Feilner.
```

If we want to make clear the meaning of each of these words, we might need to add:

```
Country=Germany, City=Regensburg, Company=Feilner-IT, Name="Markus
Feilner"
```

This is almost a perfect description in LDAP syntax. LDAP uses abbreviations as well. Another correct example could be:

```
cn=Markus Feilner, o=Feilner-IT, ou="Regensburg Division", c=Germany.
```

In this example, "cn" stands for common name,CN "o" for organization, "ou" for organizational unit, and "c" for country. LDAP is highly configurable, thus the structure of such a "dn" (Distinguished Name) is almost completely up to the administrator. He can add schemata, including object descriptions and extra attributes, and thus build a directory tree from scratch.

LDAP is the standard directory service today. Data can easily be imported and exported from an LDAP directory via ".ldif" (LDAP Data Interchange Format) files. Command line tools and GUIs import, export, and manage the data in the directory, and almost every mail client's address book can be bound to a LDAP Server.

The listing leaves out large parts of the encoded JPEG picture. After the 15 lines with initial headers, the body of this Email is composed of two parts, a text part with the message, and a longer part with the MIME-encoded picture.

The following table explains the used headers and shows more standard headers:

| Header: | Explanation: |
| --- | --- |
| From: | Sender of the Email |
| To: | Recipient (as specified in the SMTP protocol) |
| CC: | Carbon Copy |
| Bcc: | Blind Copy |
| Subject: | The subject line of the mail |
| Date: | The date when this Email was sent |
| Received: | The path the Email took (every standard SMTP server will add an header here) |
| Content-Type: | The MIME type of the Email's content |

A complete list of common email headers can be retrieved from the Internet Assigned Numbers Authority (IANA, Permanent Message Header Field Names List by the IANA: http://www.iana.org/assignments/message-headers/perm-headers.html), including links to the corresponding RFCs. As the listing shows, there are also headers generated by the mail client. Obviously, Norbert has composed this mail using KMail, and the KDE mail program has left its traces.

# Storing the Groupware Data

As far as Email is concerned, classical SMTP, POP and IMAP offer anything an Internet user might expect. Mails can be sent and retrieved, and stored on a central server or on a local machine. Nevertheless, one more issue leads us directly to groupware: How does an email user know the address of the recipient? There has to be some kind of address book. In companies, this has to be stored, dispatched, and backed up from a central server.

# Directory Services—DAP and LDAP

A standard way to accomplish this is a *directory service*. A directory is a kind of database where data is stored in a read-optimized manner. Whereas changes to an address book occur rather seldom (that is, writing to the database), reading the contact data is happening all the time. Like in a telephone book, the arrangement of data is optimized for quick searches.

# VCAL, ICAL, GroupDAV, CalDAV, WebDAV, ...

Another very common way of storing address book data are databases or standardized text files. An interchangeable standard for such files is vcard (RFC 2426). But the file format is only one side: The address book data has to be stored in the network and made accessible to clients. Several projects, servers, and protocols have risen to accomplish this: users of GroupDAV, WebDAV, and CalDAV share their addresses via an HTTP-based server with write access. Groupware solutions like Kolab store XML or VCAL text files within Emails in specially tagged folders on an IMAP server. Other Groupware solutions use databases—mostly PostgreSQL or MySQL—for storing the contact data. However, LDAP is the de facto standard, to which every groupware solution, client and server software has to be compatible. Almost all groupware solutions fulfill this demand; the others usually have import/export tools.

One of the biggest challenges for all groupware solutions is storing and providing calendar data. Although it is obvious that free standards and open formats like iCAL, vCAL, CalDAV, and GroupDAV will dominate the future, today there are no solutions that provide interchangeable data and that can cooperate with groupware clients and servers from other vendors. Even worse, only few groupware solutions can export calendar data. Almost every software package has its own different model and the communication between server and client is mostly proprietary and closed-source. A lot of calendaring and scheduling is done by the client, especially if group calendars are involved and dates must be scheduled in teams. The exchange of free/busy lists and the definition of recurring events are the biggest problems for groupware coexistence. The only perspective I see is the development around the CalDAV standard (RFC 4791), and more and more vendors seem to adopt this standard.

In a nutshell, a server simply ought to publish both free/busy lists and calendar data for a client. The client is supposed to authenticate to the server, retrieve the dates, calculate schedules, and present group calendars to the user. Although that sounds easy, there is only one Windows program capable of this task and merely two Linux programs that partly manage that. The first is Microsoft Outlook, the latter two are KDE Kontact and Novell Evolution (GNOME).

A lot has been written about the dangers of using Outlook, about viruses, spam and phishing attacks. Linux evangelists argue, that Outlook and Window's flaw only made that possible. But still there is no replacement. The open-source groupware clients are far from enterprise-ready when run with a groupware server. AJAX (Asynchronous Java And XML)-enabled Web Clients are cheaper to develop and obviously sufficient for the Linux desktop. That is why all groupware projects still focus on the Microsoft client. And so does Scalix.

## Groupware Definitions

Apart from Microsoft Exchange and Scalix, there are many groupware products, both open source and proprietary available. And there are as many definitions of "groupware" as there are solutions. Products like openXchange and eGroupWare include wikis, document management, project management, and even CRM options. The typical setup for Microsoft's environment includes fax and telephony software integrated in your client's address book. Novell's GroupWise comes with a full featured instant messaging and IBM's Lotus maps your whole company's work flow in the groupware system.

Famous groupware solutions are:

- IBM Domino Server with Lotus Notes
- Novell GroupWise
- HP OpenMail, that became Samsung Contact and then Scalix
- Microsoft Exchange
- OpenXchange
- Kolab
- Zarafa
- Zimbra
- Citadel
- eGroupWare

And many more...

Scalix calls its product a "mail and calendaring solution", avoiding the term groupware in its marketing. Nevertheless, the scope of Scalix fulfills my favorite definition of groupware: email, contacts, group calendaring plus optional features.

# Summary

In this chapter, you have learnt how email became the communication standard we are using today. You now know why some things are not perfect, and where to look up the RFC that may contain the information you need. You know what's happening when you send an email and what servers and daemons are necessary for sending and retrieving email. Furthermore, LDAP, iCAL, and vCAL are not cryptical abbreviations anymore.

# 2
# Scalix Groupware

This chapter will start with the history of Scalix Groupware. Invented as HP OpenMail, both Samsung and Scalix bought licenses from HP and provided their own "interpretation" of the product. In the end, it ended up a part of the Xandros Family. A technical overview introduces Scalix concepts and terms along with a description of the different servers and features. This chapter closes with detailed information about getting help about and from Scalix.

## The History of Scalix: Why HP Won the "Bury The Gold" Award

The history of Scalix is a mix of fascinating comic and thriller features. A big company is afraid of the success of its own product and decides to stop it.

In the 1980s, Hewlett Packard developed a mail server software for large enterprises and institutions. It was to be called HP OpenMail. This product soon became famous for its multi-protocol support, stability, and performance. Unlike other solutions, it could interchange data with almost every other mail system in the universe—X.400, SMTP, POP; IMAP; even Microsoft's MAPI Protocol were supported. OpenMail worked on HP UX, AIX, Solaris, Linux, and Windows NT. Although the product received very positive reviews and feedback, HP never seemed to truly back up Openmail.

Nevertheless, the release on Windows NT and the presentation of a browser front-end is reported to have shocked competitors. In 1999, HP published OpenMail for Linux and a WAP-interface followed as early as the year 2000.

However, at the beginning of the new millenium, HP had gotten closer to Microsoft and therefore decided to stop OpenMail. Microsoft is reported to have been worried about the success and stability of HP's groupware solution. Thus HP officials decided to stop OpenMail so as to not burden the relationship with MS. Infoworld wrote in January 2000:

> *"The "bury the gold" award goes to Hewlett-Packard, which makes HP OpenMail 6.0. HP is sitting on a potential gold mine, but it is afraid to start digging. OpenMail runs on a variety of platforms, including Red Hat Linux, Sun Solaris, IBM AIX, and HP-UX. OpenMail is not only a drop-in replacement for Microsoft Exchange, it is faster, more scalable, more stable, less expensive, and performs some tasks more intelligently than Exchange. But HP won't market OpenMail as an Exchange replacement. HP is petrified of what Microsoft might do in retaliation."*
> "And now announcing the General Protection Fault award "winners" for 1999", Nicolas Petreley on Infoworld: `http://www.infoworld.com/ articles/op/xml/00/01/17/000117oppetreley.html`).

One year later, HP had decided to sell OpenMail, Nicolas Petreley comments in Linuxworld:

> *"Unwanted buyers*
> *(...) I'm guessing that until now HP figured it could get by with a product like OpenMail, in spite of the fact that it threatened Exchange, because OpenMail was nearly invisible. But HP would risk damaging its relationship with Microsoft far more if it were to sell the OpenMail division to a company that might market the product properly."*
> "Closing down OpenMail: It's not about profit", Nicolas Petreley on Linuxworld: `http://www.itworld.com/App/325/lw-03-penguin_2`).

# Abandoning OpenMail

It was clearly a tactical decision that forced HP to abandon OpenMail in 2001. The final press release from HP can be found here: `http://www.hp.com/softwarereleases/ releases-media2/discon/B2298-80060.htm`. On Nov 13, 2001, HP declared that Samsung SDS had bought licenses for further development of HP OpenMail. This is how HP describes the features of the software that it just decided to stop:

> *"Initially released in 1990, OpenMail software has been used by more than 60 percent of Fortune 1000 companies. As the only e-mail server apart from Microsoft® Exchange to support a wide range of important Microsoft Outlook features, OpenMail software provides a cost-sensitive enterprise solution allowing deployment of thousands or even millions of users on a single server. SDS has used OpenMail software as the basis of its own internal communication system for five years, providing reliable communications across the company's 230,000 users."*

HP's Press Release on selling Openmail to Samsung: `http://www.hp.com/hpinfo/newsroom/press/2001/011113a.html`)

HP OpenMail was obviously very reliable and stable, because almost two third of the Fortune 1000 were using it. Samsung continued to develop and use OpenMail under the new name Samsung Contact and won several prices for it. Samsung Contact became famous for being: "more compatible with Outlook than Exchange" ("Samsung Contact: More compatible with Outlook than Exchange?" Robin 'Roblimo' Miller on Linux.com: `http://trends.newsforge.com/article.pl?sid=02/11/01/1827249&tid=138&tid=29&tid=30&tid=31`). But history seems to have repeated itself when on December 22, 2005, Samsung declared that there was no need for this perfect and reliable MS Exchange replacement and they stopped Samsung Contact. (Samsung Contact retreats from its Mailserver: `http://samsungcontact.com/documents/Samsung%20Contact%20Announcement%20Letter.pdf`)

Luckily, another company had bought licenses from HP in the meantime—Scalix Inc. Scalix Inc. continued developing HP OpenMail under the name of Scalix. The company began to add features to its new product. A full-featured Webmail client was added, and a Linux server became the standard operating system. Outlook support was enhanced and optimized for newer versions. The support for open protocols like LDAP, IMAP, and POP was improved and third-party-products were integrated. And what HP had not dared in 2001, Scalix did in 2006—large parts of the software became open source.

However, history repeats itself again, and so does the Scalix history. In July 2007, the Linux distributor Xandros, who had been under heavy criticism from the open source community for patent deals with Microsoft, announced that he had bought Scalix Inc. According to Xandros, Scalix will remain a product of its own, and Microsoft has no power over Scalix or Xandros.

# Scalix at First Glance—SAC and SWA

Most of Scalix administration takes place in the browser. A web GUI enables the Admin to perform all typical tasks like adding, modifying or deleting users; checking, monitoring or restarting server processes; and creating and managing resources or groups.

The Scalix administration console is the central place where the Admin works with the groupware server. It looks like this:

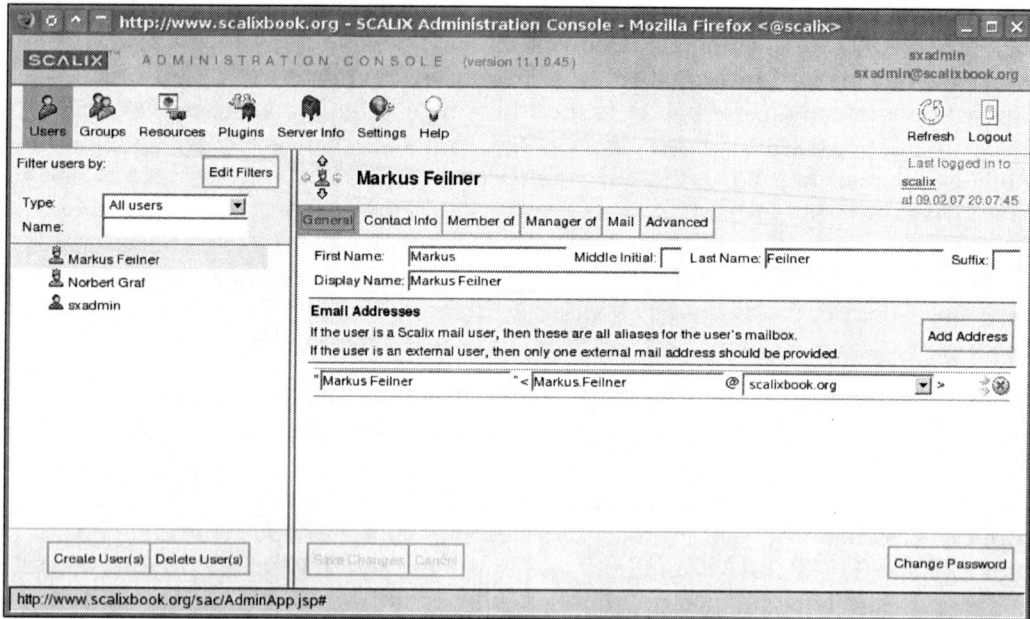

The mail user will either have contact with Scalix via Outlook, the Webmail client or a simple mail program with IMAP/POP-support. A Microsoft Outlook client connected to a Scalix server works in exactly the same way as it does with Microsoft Exchange, due to the native MAPI support that Scalix offers. On the other hand, the web client is how most Linux users will get into contact with Scalix groupware. Although there are plug-ins for Evolution and Kontact, they are not yet to be found in productive environments.

# Scalix Web Access—the Web Client

The web client offers email, calendar, group scheduling, notes, and address book features. The following screenshot shows a session of the user Markus Feilner logged into the webmailer. In the background, we see the SWA window, with the mailbox info, upcoming appointments, and the current month in an overview.

Markus has opened his calendar and double-clicked on a time slot on the day chosen. Then he chose the tab **Scheduling** to make a date with one of his colleagues. To invite another user on the Scalix server, he clicked on the button **Add from addressbook** and selected **Norbert Graf** in the list of the available users.

By clicking on **OK**, Scalix will show Norbert's calendar with the time slots available for a meeting. Please note: it is necessary for Norbert to have logged in once, made at least one entry in his calendar, and added Markus to the list of allowed users for his calendar folder.

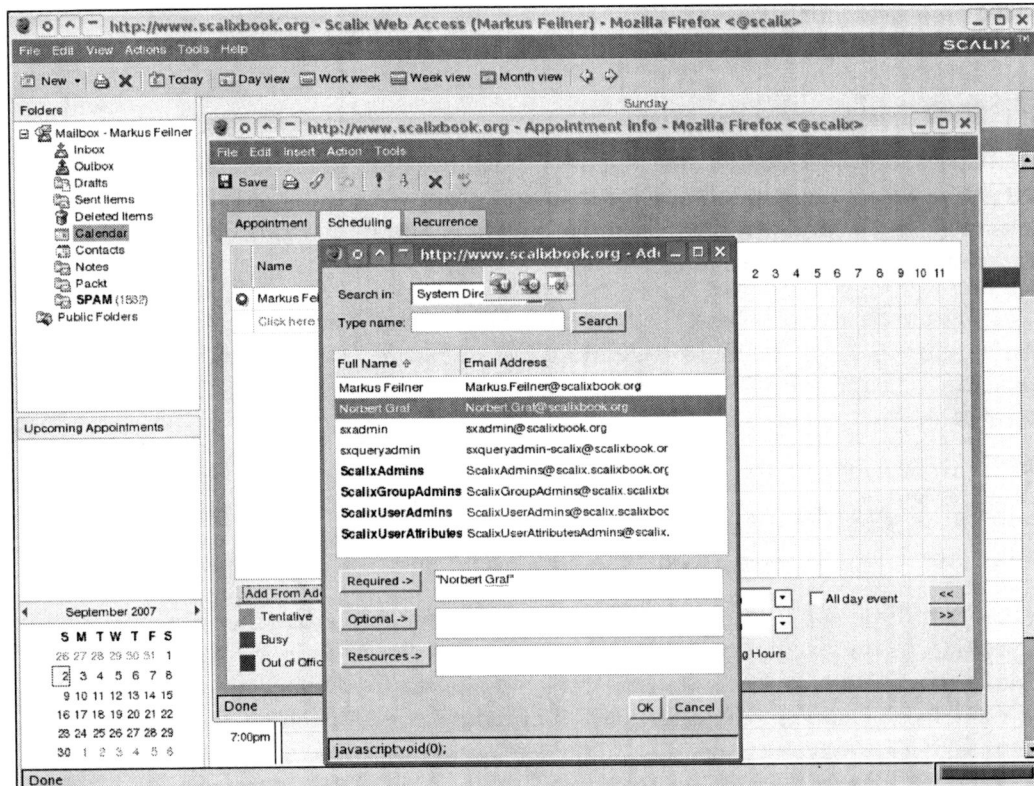

The design of the web client is clearly aimed to copy Outlook. Outlook Users will have no problem working with SWA. Linux mail users may have to learn a little. However, POP, IMAP, and SMTP can be used from any mail client, only groupware data is restricted to MAPI enabled clients like Outlook or SWA. But Scalix has been working on support for free standards like CalDAV. On the mailing list of the KDE Project, there has been some promising conversations, and obviously there is a cooperation between Xandros, Trolltech, and Scalix working on Kontact support. Beginning in January 2008, the Scalix connector has been integrated in the enterprise-branch of the KDE-PIM-project.

# Scalix Architecture and Protocols

Every Scalix documentation has a complete glossary on its last pages, thus this book will only reference the most important and striking terms connected with Scalix administration. If you need more information on one or more Scalix terms, take a look at the online PDF-documentation.

## Protocols

Scalix uses standard IMAP4 and POP3 for email transfer. Microsoft clients address the native MAPI implementation for mail and groupware data. SMTP is done by Sendmail, and a configuration file in the "horrible" Sendmail syntax is provided, but no Admin needs to make changes here.

Whereas the directory behind Scalix is an X.400 directory, most directory services can be addressed via the built-in standard LDAP Server. Scalix provides several tools to synchronize the internal directory with external services like OpenLDAP or Active Directory.

## User Types

Scalix knows two types of users: "Standard Users" and "Premium Users".

A Standard User can use the email functions of Scalix and access the webmail client. A Premium User also has access to groupware data. Because the number of Standard Users is not limited in Scalix, the email service is open to any local user with a working POP/IMAP and SMTP client. MAPI and Groupware however is limited to Premium Users, which means that only these users have free/busy lists and group calendars. Furthermore, public folders and wireless email and PIM are only possible for Premium Users. The licensed model of Xandros differs a little from Scalix' own, but only the number of Premium Users available in the cheaper version is affected.

## Mailnodes

Scalix calls a mailnode a "logical structure used to organize users into administrative groupings". Because users are located by the mailnode attributes of their Scalix entries, there can only be one mailnode of a certain name in a network, and this name has to be resolvable in the local DNS.

Every user has a mailnode responsible for him. In every network with Scalix servers, there will be a primary mailnode, though the whole system works on a p2p basis. Every Scalix server has to be associated with a mailnode. There is no direct connection between a mailnode and an Internet domain, but many sites will have one mailnode for one Internet domain. A Scalix mailnode can administrate several domains, and automatically create and manage multiple Internet mail addresses per user. The mailnodes are installed and configured by the Scalix installer and are administrated by the Scalix Admin console and the command line tools.

In a nutshell: If you set up your first Scalix server, this will automatically be the primary mailnode in your network, and at the same time the local mailnode for all your users. If you later decide to add more Scalix servers, you may have to spend some thoughts on your mail infrastructure, with special regards on how to arrange mailnodes, users, and mail routing.

# Services

Like common UNIX/Linux servers, Scalix offers various services. Among others, client access, mail delivery, indexing, POP, SMTP, and directory services can be stopped and started by the administrator at any time. Both the Admin GUI and the command line offer various tools to check, control, start, and stop these services.

# Daemons

The concept of daemons is also known to UNIX/Linux administrators. Daemons are background processes that spend most of their living "asleep" and "listening". When a client process requests information from a daemon, the latter wakes up, starts a child process, and goes back to sleep. The newly started process deals with the client and serves the requests. After complete communication, the child process is terminated. Scalix has several server daemons running and listening on external and internal interfaces. Some of these daemons serve only for internal requests; others like the IMAP or the LDAP server daemon directly interact with the user's mail client. Most of the server daemons can also be started, stopped, and managed both from the Admin console and the CLI.

# Queues

The Scalix processes, daemons, and services communicate with each other through queues. Every message passing through the Scalix system is queued before a server daemon passes it on. The daemon process takes the message, performs its work with or on it, and places it in the queue of the following next service, daemon or process. The next daemon or service will do the same, until the message reaches the user's message store or is sent to a different mail server. Thus, if one of the processes fails or hangs, the mail will still be in the appropriate mail queue, and can be restored and processed the next time the service runs. This concept is very sophisticated within Scalix, and adds a great deal to the stability and reliability of the system. Like services and daemons, queues can be managed from the Admin GUI and the CLI.

# The Message Store

Unlike other open-source IMAP servers, Scalix has a rather complex, but very efficient model of storing messages on the server. Its design with flat Linux files in a hierarchical structure composed of "Container Items", "Basic Items" and "User Folders" speeds up searches and lookup processes. Redundancies are successfully avoided by referencing message data rather than storing single messages several times. Ideally, a message sent to ten users on a Scalix server will only be stored once, but referenced ten times. Furthermore, the Scalix Search and Index Service (SIS) speeds up changes significantly by indexing all objects stored in the message store. SIS processes the complete mail store and builds search indexes that speed up searches and lower resource consumption by connected clients. Command line tools empower the administrator to control or fix the message store in case of corruptions.

HP designed OpenMail for large companies and institutions, the heritage of this time can be found here. According to Scalix Inc., a Scalix server can serve up to 15,000 (!) mail boxes on a single system. Furthermore, Scalix marketing promises 99.9% availability.

# Scalix Versions and Packages

- Scalix recently changed the numbers of allowed users in several versions, especially beginning with 11.3.0, so a small look at the Scalix website can be helpful here. Today (early 2008), Scalix comes in three different editions: Community (CE), Small Business (SBE), and Enterprise Edition (EE). The free CE comprises all standard Scalix Features.

- Beginning with version 11.3, Scalix introduced new limits. Scalix community shows a limit of 10 Premium Users (older versions allowed 25 users) and unlimited Standard Users. Scalix SBE limits Standard Users to 3 times the number of Premium Users, and Scalix EE limits Standard Users to 5 times the number of Premium Users.

- The Small Business Edition (SBE) adds Active Directory and Exchange integration, migration tools, recovery folders, an interface for wireless email access via Notify Link, and support by means of an extra software subscription. The Enterprise Edition (EE) is for IT departments in need of high availability, multiple server modes, clustering, and multiple instances. An unlimited number of Standard Users have been free of charge before, but beginning with version 11.3, Scalix also introduced limits here (3:1 or 5:1 Standard to Premium Users). The SBE brings 20 or 50 Premium Users at a fixed price, and the business model of the EE is a per-user charge, beginning with 20 Premium Users.

- Any version of Scalix can be upgraded to a higher version; a license key entered in the installation and configuration dialog validates your subscription and activates the extended features. But in reality, only systems installed on enterprise distributions like Red Hat Enterprise (RHEL) or SUSE Linux Enterprise Server (SLES) can be upgraded to higher versions, because the free Linux distributions are not supported for more than two or three Scalix editions.
- The source code provided contains the following Scalix components (Scalix Management Console for Administration):
    - Management services that offer SOAP-based automation and integration with other non-Scalix services
    - Management plug-ins and script-based automation of administration tasks
    - An indexing service speeding up complex searches in the mail store
    - Messaging service interfaces to other software like CRMs
    - The standard Scalix Mobile Webclient
    - The graphical or text-based Scalix installer
    - Localization kits for many countries

The Outlook MAPI Connector, several parts of the Scalix server, and the webmailer are unfortunately not open source. Scalix says they are currently reimplementing all parts of the software that are closed-source or subject to licenses of third parties. Let's see what the Xandros deal means for that.

# Licenses

Scalix Community Edition is free of charge and partly open source. Unfortunately, it is not licensed under the GPL, but the "Scalix Public License SPL", which can be retrieved from The License of the Scalix Community Edition: `http://www.scalix.com/community/opensource/licensing.php`. Here are the first lines of it:

```
Scalix Public License (SPL)
The Scalix Public License Version 1.1 ("SPL") consists of the Mozilla
Public License Version 1.1, modified to be specific to Scalix, with
the Additional Terms in Exhibit B. The original Mozilla Public License
1.1 can be found at: http://www.mozilla.org/MPL/MPL-1.1.html
(...)
```

As we can see, the SPL claims to be based on the Mozilla Public License. It is an open-source license, in that the user is allowed to change, add, and distribute the software. However, there are terms concerning commercial use that maybe infringe the possibility of reselling a modified version of Scalix. And the SPL resembles SUN's CDDL and other commonly used open-source licences. It states that any changes made to the software must be licensed again under the SPL. Some lines in this license concerning statistical data that Scalix is collecting from installed CEs have provoked bad comments and suspicion.

# Platforms and Hardware Requisites

The Community Edition runs on Red Hat Enterprise Linux 4 or 5, SUSE Linux Enterprise Server 9 or 10. Fedora Core and OpenSUSE are supported with limitations. There are also many howto's and packages available for Scalix on Debian and other distributions. However, no support from Scalix will be provided for these setups. Exceptions to this rule are, of course, partner projects like Scalix for Univention, a German, Debian-based distribution with full directory service integration at enterprise level, or Xandros where Scalix is integrated in a desktop management software. Both partners offer enterprise grade support. The support for the free SUSE and Red Hat distributions may be considered as a temporary one, because Scalix is supporting only one or two of the recent versions, thus you may run into trouble with updates.

Scalix Connect for Outlook is provided for Outlook 9, 10, and 11, which are commonly known as Outlook 2000, 2002/XP, and Outlook 2003. The Windows Operating System must be Windows 2000 or XP and SmartCache technology adds offline capabilities for the Outlook user. The Webmail Client is being tested for Mozilla Versions 1.7.x, Firefox 1.x and 2.x (both on Windows and UNIX/Linux), and Internet Explorer 5.5 SP2, 6 SP2 and 7 on MS Windows. Palm OS, Windows Mobile, and Blackberry are supported by the mobile client.

Scalix recommends 1 GB of RAM and 200 MB hard disk space for the base installation, not including space for users, mailboxes or cache. During installation, a test is performed and the installation will stop on systems with less than 512 MB RAM. By the way, Scalix 11 server needs a PostgreSQL database of version 7.4 or newer.

# Packages

Scalix 11 consists of more than 100 MB Software. The download contains:

- Scalix Installer
- Scalix Server
- Management Interface

- Messaging Services
- Web Mail Client
- Mobile Client
- Indexing Services
- PostgreSQL Database
- Java Application Server Tomcat and Connector
- Scalix Connect for Outlook

The latter one is to be found in an extra package for the Community Edition. All of these services are configured automatically during installation. The EE and SBE contain further software like the tools for Active Directory integration and more.

# Add-Ons

A long list of Scalix add-ons are offered from technology partners for the Scalix architecture. Some of them are:

- Anti-Spam and Anti-Virus: Spamassassin, Clamav, McAfee, and Trend Micro
- Single-Mail-Backup and -Restore by SEP
- Clustering with Red Hat and SUSE
- CRM by SugarCRM
- Integration for various Directory Services: Active Directory, Novell eDirectory, Red Hat Directory Server
- Monitoring with Nagios
- Wireless e-mail: Notify Link, Blackberry, Windows Mobile, Palm OS

There are many more solutions available, an up-to-date list can be found on the Scalix Ecosystem — Add-ons and related software projects:
`http://www.scalix.com/enterprise/ecosystem/applications.php`.

# Getting Help

Scalix offers many resources for help. In fact, there is so much documentation and sources of help around, that in many cases a user may probably not find what he is looking for. Since the software base is more than 15 years old, there will be only few cases where there really is no information on a problem. The Scalix community is big, the OpenMail heritage provides a lot of documentation and resources on enterprise level.

# The Scalix Website

Always the first place to go when in need of help is http://www.scalix.com. In the community area of the website, is a link called "Resources" (Scalix Community Resources on the Web: http://www.scalix.com/community/resources) with a huge amount of information, and in most cases a solution to a problem has already been described by someone else here. The following URLs are active in April 2008 and should work even if the website frontend has been changed.

| URL | Information contained |
| --- | --- |
| http://www.scalix.com/forums | User-generated Q&As, often moderated by Scalix employees. |
| http://www.scalix.com/documentation | Some hundred of pages of manuals and howtos for various tasks. Ideal for advanced reading. |
| http://www.scalix.com/knowledgebase | Tech Notes, Howtos, FAQs, written by technicians. |
| http://www.scalix.com/wiki | The Scalix Wiki. Lots of Howtos, Answers and cool ideas. |
| http://www.scalix.com/faq | The Scalix Frequently Asked Questions section. |
| http://www.scalix.com/blog | The Blog of Scalix employees. Here sometimes thoughts emerge that become features months later. |
| http://www.scalix.com/bugzilla | The bug tracking system. Bug reports can be posted here. |

# Manual Pages

Besides the website, Scalix provides man pages for almost all of the more than 200 command line tools and an online help. Like other UNIX/Linux man pages, they can be viewed simply by typing:

```
man <command>
```

The command man omshowu will display the man page of the omshowu program. This program lists details of users on a Scalix server. Here are the first lines of this manual page:

```
OMSHOWU(8)
                                    OMSHOWU(8)

NAME
       omshowu - list users or display details about a specific user
SYNOPSIS
       omshowu -m mailnode | all [-a] [-l] [-e] [-I] [-t Y|N] [-i]
       omshowu -n authentication-id [-G] [-S] [-f]
       omshowu -n name[/mailnode] [-G] [-S] [-f]
       omshowu -U unix-login [-G] [-S] [-f]
       omshowu -O scalix-id [-G] [-S] [-f]
       omshowu -r Y|N
       omshowu -v { gtN | ltN | eqN | neN | >N | <N | =N | !=N }
DESCRIPTION
       omshowu lists all users on a local mailnode (or all users on
the local system), or displays details about specific users.
OPTIONS
       -m mailnode
               Lists all users on mailnode.  If the mailnode name all
is specified, all local users are listed.
       -a      List only users with admin capability.
       -l      Lists only those users whose accounts are locked.
       -e      Lists only users with expired or pre-expired passwords.
       -I      Displays  the  internet address of the user along with
the normal details.  Multiple addresses are separated by the '='
 Manual page omshowu(8) line 1
 (...)
```

Many manual pages show the HP heritage and still bear the copyright from
OpenMail times. There are about 200 Scalix command line tools and to almost every
single one there is a man page. This could serve as a good example for some other
open-source projects.

# Online Help

Both the Scalix web client and the administration console offer online help within a browser window. In the Scalix Administration Console (SAC), a click on the bulb icon called "Help" starts a pop up window that is split in two regions:

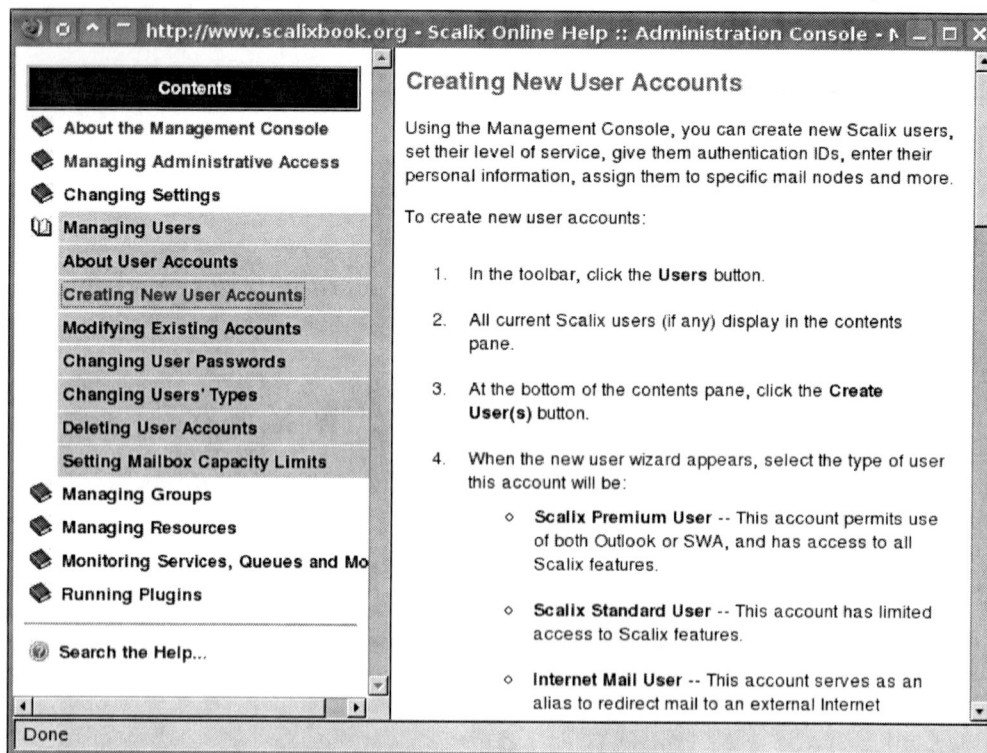

On the left side, categories of topics offer a guided introduction to the Admin GUI. The right part of the window shows detailed information on the selected topic. The last entry in the list on the left-side takes the user to the search engine provided with SAC. Managing users, groups, and resources is explained as well as how to control services, queues, and setting preferences of the administration console.

The same applies to the webmail client Scalix Web Access (SWA): After selecting the menu item "help" in the outlook-style mail window, a popup will appear showing a list and the content of the selected help topic. Whereas the SAC help deals with common administration issues, the SWA help is designed to help the end user:

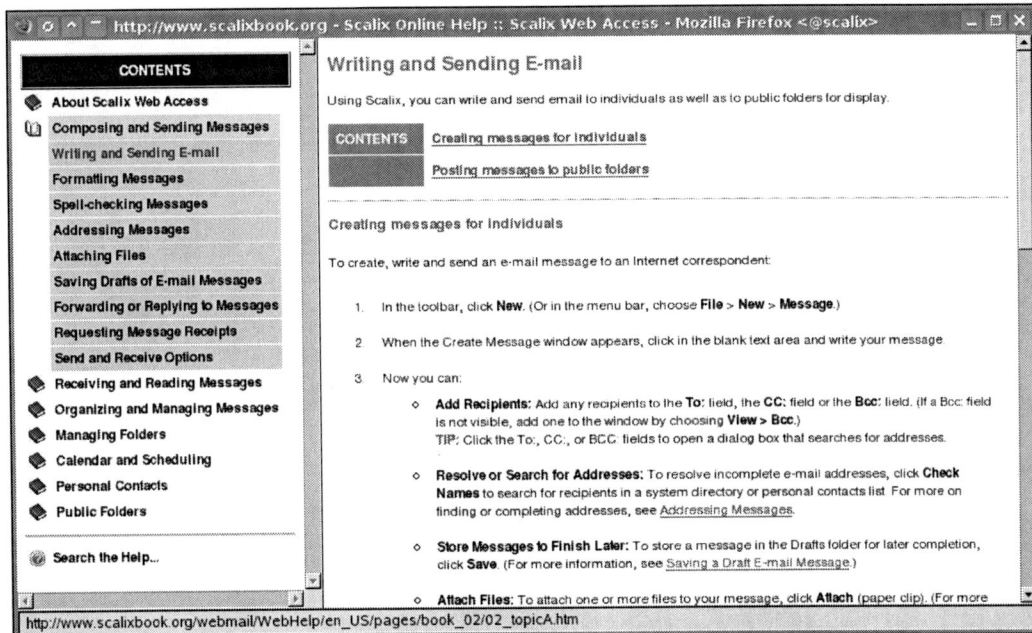

Composing, sending, and receiving messages is explained as well as organizing your data and tips on folder, calendar, and contact management. The information reached with last item in the list deals with public folders, an easy way to share information with other users. Of course, the end-user help also provides a search function. Scalix Connect for Outlook also offers concise online help.

# Summary

In this chapter, we dealt with a brief history of Scalix. You now know about companies like HP, Samsung, Scalix, and Xandros, and why HP didn't want to hurt Microsoft Exchange. We have learnt what a mailnode is and where to get more information on Scalix terms like the indexing server, daemons, and services. The chapter also dealt with the protocols supported by Scalix, the license involved and the packages offered by Scalix. Finally, we have learnt where to get help using the man pages, the online help and the abundance of information on the Scalix website.

# 3
# Installing Scalix

This chapter describes the standard installation of Scalix Software on OpenSUSE 10.2 and Fedora Core 5. Installation is done by downloading the packages from the Scalix website, starting the installation program, and fixing the operating system to meet the requirements of the groupware server.

## Installing Scalix on OpenSUSE

Scalix installation is pretty straightforward. Unlike other groupware servers, Scalix comes with an enterprise-ready, graphical installation toolbox guiding the new user through basic setup. This installer works on Red Hat Enterprise, SUSE Linux Enterprise Server, Fedora Core, and OpenSUSE. Scalix 11 will be the last version that supports RHEL 3. Apart from the graphical installation, there is also a text-based installation and the option to install Scalix manually. These features are explained in *Chapter 4, Advanced Installation*.

You should not use an installation on a community distribution like OpenSUSE and Fedora in a productive environment. The common versions of these operating systems will not be supported by Scalix after more than one or two subsequent Scalix versions. The Enterprise distributions like SLES or RHEL, however, are usually supported for several years.

# Download Community Edition from the Scalix Website

Point your favorite Browser to the URL: http://www.scalix.com/community/downloads/index.php, click on **Download Community Edition** and fill out the registration form available there. Read the license agreement and click on **I agree**.

The Debian installation is not officially supported, and the source packages are far from complete. Scalix is working on making further parts of the software open source. But because there are third-party products and code not licensed by Scalix or HP involved, Scalix is currently rewriting these parts of the software that cannot be released under an open-source license right away.

Click on the version for your operating system and download it to your server. Open a terminal with X-Windows Support on the soon-to-be Scalix server.

> X-Windows is the graphical system on Linux and many UNIX machines. Because it is a complex and big piece of software, many administrators hesitate to have the X-Windows libraries installed on a server. I leave it up to you to decide. But because the standard installation tool of Scalix is a graphical X-Windows application, we will proceed with these libraries installed — which is the default on all the systems listed above — apart from minimalistic setups.

Start a Terminal session on the Scalix server. I recommend you use SSH — the standard, encrypted shell under Linux. On a Linux client, type: `ssh -X root@your-scalixserver` to connect with X-Forwarding enabled.

The following session shows how to download Scalix server software to your server after registration. If the download with wget does not work, download Scalix to your local machine and copy the `tar.gz` file to your server with SCP or Konqueror's built-in **fish-protocol** for SSH file transfer.

```
mfeilner:~> ssh -X root@scalixbook.org
Password:
/usr/X11R6/bin/xauth:  creating new authority file /root/.Xauthority
Last login: Sat Apr 14 19:54:47 2007 from xxx
Have a lot of fun...
scalix:~ # wget http://downloads.scalix.com/.community/11.2/scalix-
11.2.0-GA-core-SUSE102-intel.tgz
scalix:~ # ls -l
-rw-rw-r-- 1 root root 91881314 Mar 26 23:24 scalix-11.2.0-GA-core-
SUSE102-intel.tgz
```

After the download is completed, extract the file with the `tar -xzf` command:

```
scalix:~ # tar -xzf scalix-11.2.0-GA-core-SUSE102-intel.tgz
scalix:~ # ls -l
drwxr-xr-x 6 root root     240 Mar  8 01:00 scalix-11.2.0-GA
-rw-rw-r-- 1 root root 91881314 Mar 26 23:24 scalix-11.2.0-GA-core-
SUSE102-intel.tgz
scalix:~ #
```

A directory name `scalix-11.x.x-GA` has been created. GA stands for **General Availability**. Change to that directory and list its contents:

```
scalix:~/scalix-11.2.0-GA # ls -l
total 1105
drwxr-xr-x 2 root root   4096 2007-09-20 23:12 admin_resource_kit
```

```
drwxr-xr-x 2 root root    4096 2007-09-20 23:13 documentation
-rw-r--r-- 1 root root   42444 2007-03-01 01:35 LICENSE.txt
-rwxr-xr-x 1 root root  273661 2007-09-20 22:56 scalix-installer
drwxr-xr-x 4 root root    4096 2007-09-20 23:11 software
drwxr-xr-x 5 root root    4096 2007-09-20 23:12 third_party
scalix:~/scalix-11.2.0-GA #
```

There are some directories, a license file, and the installer program `scalix-installer`. The `LICENSE.txt` file is known to you because you read the EULA (End User License Agreement) online—did you?. In the directory `software`, lies the Evolution connector and the Scalix software that is to be installed. Furthermore, we find documentation and third-party-software like Libical, Java, and Lynx, which we will get to know during installation.

Now let's fire up the Scalix installer:

```
scalix:~/scalix-11.2.0-GA # ./scalix-installer
```

On some systems, you will immediately receive the following error:

```
scalix:~/scalix-11.2.0-GA # ./scalix-installer

Scalix Installer - extracting archive, please wait...
Scalix Installer - starting version 11.2.52...
Scalix Installer - using Python 2.5 (/usr/bin/python).
Error: 'No module named pygtk'.
 Please install RPM package python-gtk >= 2.0.  This package can
usually be found on the distribution CD or on the vendor web site.
Scalix Installer - cleaning up...
Scalix Installer – done.
scalix:~/scalix-11.2.0-GA #
```

The Scalix installer needs Python-gtk in order to present its graphical user interface. On the SUSE minimal system, these python bindings for the GTK+ widget set are not installed by default, but the standard installation source has a suitable package. Start YaST, change to the **Add or Remove Software**, and install the package Python-gtk:

```
YaST @ scalix                                              Press F1 for Help

[Filterv]           [Actionsv]          [Informationv]          [Etc.v]

     Name                Avail. Vers.  Inst. Vers. Summary
     dbus-1-python       0.60                      Python bindings for D-BUS
  i  kdebindings3-python 3.5.1         3.5.1       Python Bindings for KDE
     libxml2-python      2.6.23                    Python Bindings for libxml2
     postgresql-pl       8.1.3                     The PL/Tcl, PL/Perl, and PL/Python
  i  python              2.4.2         2.4.2       Python Interpreter
     python-cairo        1.0.2                     Python Bindings for cairo
     python-curses       2.4.2                     Python Interface to the (N)Curses L
     python-devel        2.4.2                     Include Files and Libraries Mandato
     python-elementtree  1.2.6                     Fast XML parser and writer
     python-fcgi         2000.09.21                Python FastCGI Module
     python-gnome        2.12.3                    Python bindings for GNOME
     python-gnome-extras 2.12.1                    Python bindings for GNOME
     python-gtk          2.8.2                     Python bindings for the GTK+ widget
     python-imaging      1.1.5                     The Python Imaging Library - PIL
     python-ldap         2.0.11                    Python LDAP interface
     python-numeric      24.2                      A Numerical Extension to Python
     python-openssl      0.6                       Python wrapper module around the Op
     python-orbit        2.0.1                     Python bindings for ORBit
     python-pam          0.4.2                     Python bindings for PAM
     python-pygame       1.7.1release              A Python Module for Interfacing wit
  i  python-qt           3.5.1         3.5.1       Python Bindings for Qt
     python-serial       2.2                       Python Serial Port Extension
     python-sqlite       1.1.6                     Python bindings for sqlite
     python-tk           2.4.2                     TkInter - Python Tk Interface
     python-twisted      2.1.0                     Event-driven networking framework i

Filter: Search Results                    Required Disk Space: 50.5 M

python-gtk - Python bindings for the GTK+ widget set
Version: 2.8.2-21 Size: 4.3 M Media No.: 1
License: LGPL
Package Group: Development/Libraries/Python
Provides: pango.so, gobject.so, pangocairo.so, atk.so, python-gtk == 2.8.2-21, _gtk.so,
glade.so

[Helpv]        [Search]     [Disk Usage]              [Cancel]        [Accept]
```

Searching a package in YaST in detail: Start YaST by typing yast, change to the **Software**, hit the key *ALT-F* and enter "python". You will be provided a list like the one in the previous screenshot. Hit the arrow keys to go up and down in the list, until the green bar highlights the Python-gtk package, and then hit **Enter** to select this package for installation. Click on **Accept** or hit *CTRL-A* twice to accept your selection and have YaST install the package. Depending on the scope of your installation, YaST may ask you to confirm some missing dependencies, that is packages that are going to be installed because they are required by Python-gtk or by its dependencies.

After installation of these packages, YaST asks you whether you want to install further ones. If you hit **Yes** here, Yast will stay open and you can continue to search and install software. But then you will need to open another SSH-shell to the Scalix server for the Scalix installation. Nevertheless, because there are some packages that need to be installed and exchanged, I suggest that you work with two SSH-sessions from now on. If you cannot start the graphical installation, because your client is Windows or your server has no X libraries installed, have a look at the *Advanced Installation* chapter of this book.

Now open a X-enabled SSH-session to the Scalix server and start the installer again:

```
scalix:~/scalix-11.2.0-GA # ./scalix-installer

Scalix Installer - extracting archive, please wait...
Scalix Installer - starting version 11.2.0....
Scalix Installer - using Python 2.4.2 (/usr/bin/python).
Scalix Installer - audit log file is /var/log/scalix-installer-
20070326.log
```

It seems like we managed to start the installer at least, since it recognized our python-gtk installation. Now, Scalix welcomes us with a screen like this:

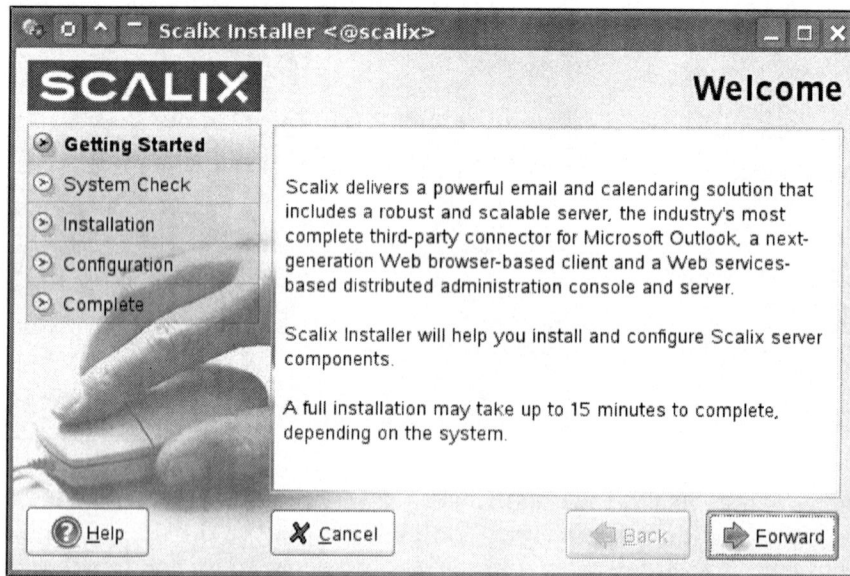

This is the graphical interface of the Scalix installer. It can be used for updates, reconfiguration, and more issues around the Scalix installation. A step-by-step menu on the left consisting of five buttons shows the progress of the installation, four buttons at the bottom offer help, cancellation, and navigation. Clicking on **Next** leads you to the third chance of reading the license agreement that you accepted. Accept the license by checking the box **I have read and accept the above license agreement** and clicking on **Forward**.

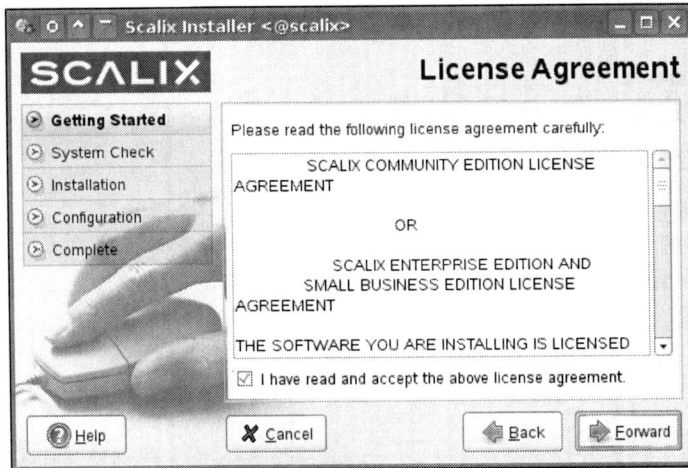

A small window with a bulb informs you that Scalix is now gathering information about your system.

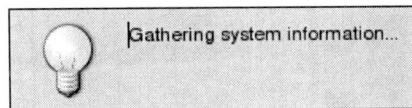

After that, the Scalix installer welcomes you to the Wizard Mode. If there is no Scalix server installed on the local machine, two of the options presented are deactivated. However, if you start the Scalix installer later on, you can reconfigure or uninstall the server from this dialog.

Select **Install all Scalix components (typical)** and hit the button **Forward**.

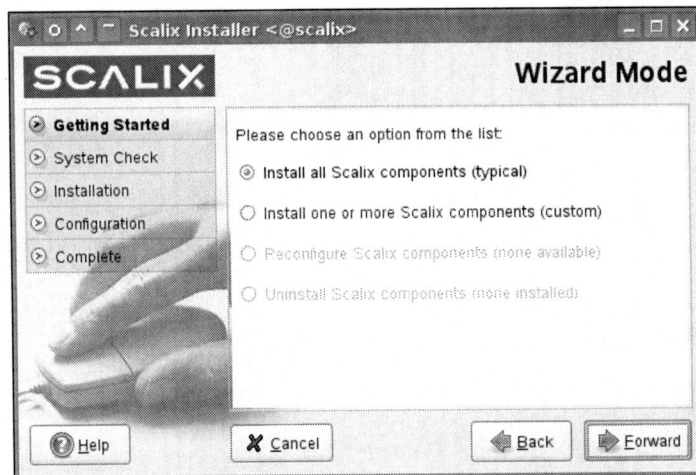

This standard installation will enable all the components that Scalix delivers:

- Scalix Server
- Scalix Database
- Apache/Tomcat Connector
- Messaging Services
- Management Agent
- Web Access
- Management Services
- Search and Index Services
- Mobile Client

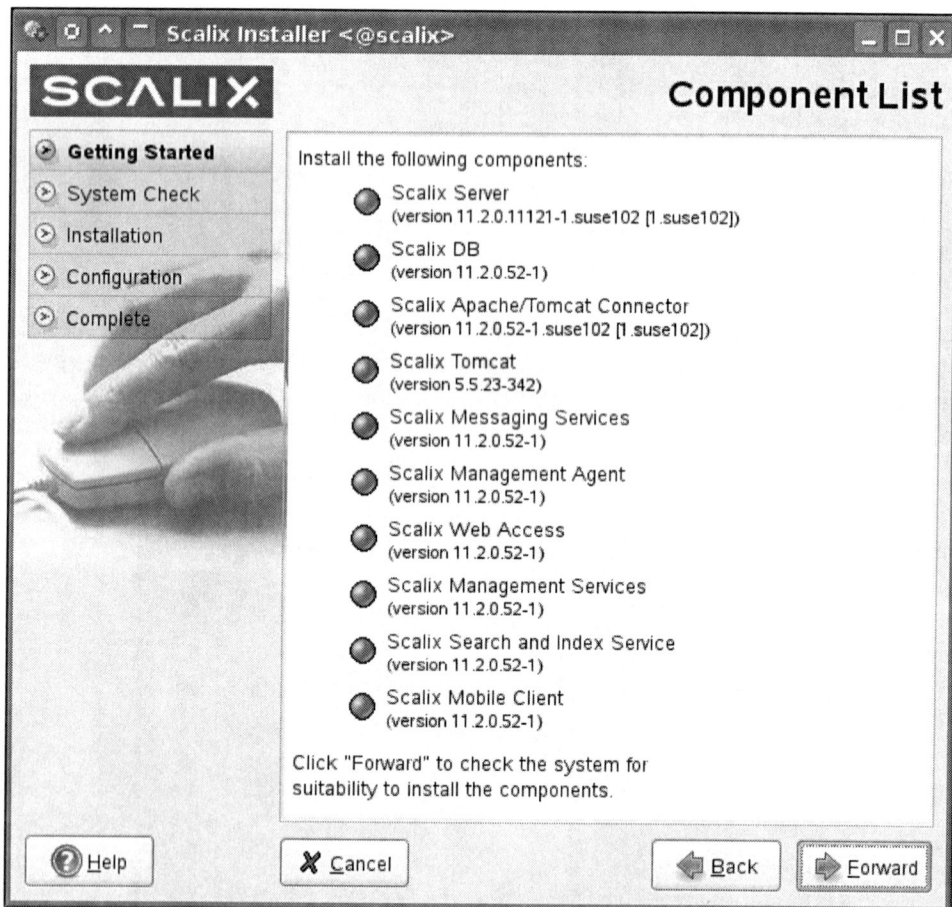

Click on **Forward** to proceed to the **System Check**.

# Checking and Troubleshooting the System Before Installation

One great advantage of the Scalix installation system is the fully automatic checking and reporting of system configuration errors or incompatibilities with the groupware. If your system does not meet the requirements of the Scalix server, this dialog will show. Or the other way around: if this dialog does not show any errors, your Scalix system will most likely work.

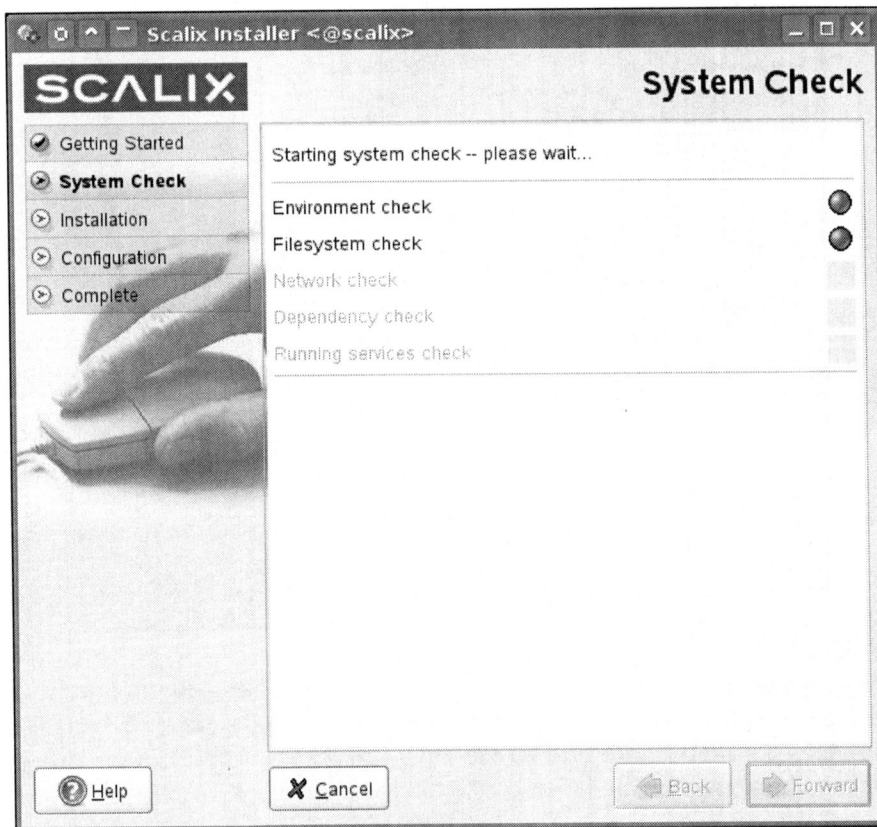

Scalix checks for five groups of dependencies:

- Operating System Environment
- File system consistency
- Network availability and correctness of parameters
- Software dependencies
- Running services

In a nutshell, Scalix checks if your system is if the file system allows correct installation, if network is set up correctly (e.g. regarding DNS), if the software installation is suitable for the server and if there are running services that might collide with Scalix.

A typical **System Check** on a SUSE System will look like this:

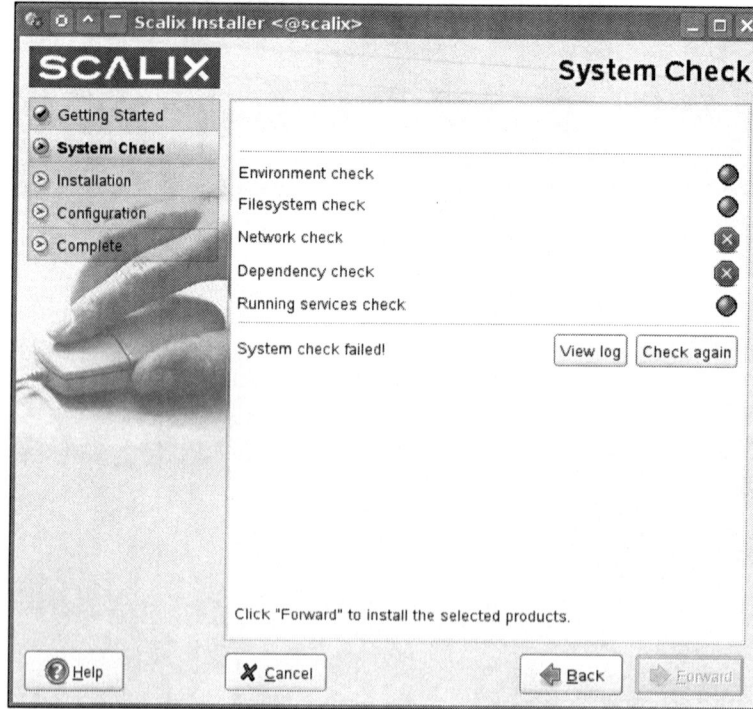

The Scalix newbie will think this is grave, but relax—this is absolutely normal. I do not believe that there is a default setup on any supported distribution where this check does not report any errors. Even on a full install of RHEL, you still get a warning for Libical and for the incorrect /etc/hosts file.

If you don't trust Scalix, hit the button **Check again** to have the installer perform the check once more. The button **View Logs** offers details on the reasons for the red flags, and gives good advice on how to solve the problems:

**Scalix Installer Log <@scalix>**

Messages from the installer log:

Environment check passed.
Filesystem check passed.
Network check failed -- Could not find a host
name in DNS that matches an IP address
Network check failed -- IP address '127.0.0.2'
associated with host name 'scalix.scalixbook.org' in
DNS cannot be confirmed as this host's IP address
Dependency check failed -- The cyrus-sasl-plain
package is needed by the Scalix Server.
Dependency check failed -- The cyrus-sasl-digestmd5
package is needed by the Scalix Server.
Dependency check failed -- The cyrus-sasl-crammd5
package is needed by the Scalix Server.
Dependency check warning -- The following
packages will be installed next to resolve conflicts:
                    libical and lynx
Dependency check failed -- Please resolve the following
package conflicts and re-run the system checks:
                sendmail >= 8.12 is needed by
scalix-server-11.2.0.11121-1.suse102.i586
                    /usr/lib/sasl2/libcrammd5.so is
needed by scalix-server-11.2.0.11121-1.suse102.i586
                    /usr/lib/sasl2/libdigestmd5.so is
needed by scalix-server-11.2.0.11121-1.suse102.i586
                    /usr/lib/sasl2/libplain.so is
needed by scalix-server-11.2.0.11121-1.suse102.i586
                    apache2 is needed by scalix-
tomcat-connector-11.2.0.52-1.suse102.noarch
                    postgresql >= 7.4 is needed
by scalix-postgres-11.2.0.52-1.noarch
                    postgresql < 9 is needed
by scalix-postgres-11.2.0.52-1.noarch
                    postgresql-server >= 7.4 is
needed by scalix-postgres-11.2.0.52-1.noarch
                    postgresql-server < 9 is needed
by scalix-postgres-11.2.0.52-1.noarch
Dependency check failed -- Apache 2.x is not installed,
it is required by the components you have selected
Running services check passed.

✕ Close

The typical failures on a SUSE system are:

1. DNS and hostname failures detected by the network check
2. cyrus-sasl-plain is missing
3. cyrus-sasl-digestmd5 is missing
4. cyrus-sasl-crammd5 is missing
5. libical will be installed
6. sendmail is needed
7. apache2 is needed
8. postgresql is needed
9. postgresql-server is needed

Whereas the first error is caused by the network check scripts that we will correct later, the latter seven are software issues that can easily be addressed by YaST — which is still open in our other terminal, remember? Switch to the other terminal and search for the software packages containing **cyrus**. You will receive the following list:

```
YaST @ scalix                                                    Press F1 for Help

[Filterv]            [Actionsv]            [Informationv]         [Etc.v]

      Name                     Avail. Vers. Inst. Vers. Summary
      cyrus-imapd              2.2.13                    An IMAP and POP Mail Server
   i  cyrus-sasl               2.1.22       2.1.22       Implementation of Cyrus SASL API
   +  cyrus-sasl-crammd5       2.1.22                    cyrus-sasl plugin for the CRAMMD5 mechanism
      cyrus-sasl-devel         2.1.22                    Cyrus SASL API Implementation, Libraries and He
   +  cyrus-sasl-digestmd5     2.1.22                    cyrus-sasl plugin for the DIGESTMD5 mechanism
      cyrus-sasl-gssapi        2.1.22                    cyrus-sasl plugin for the GSSAPI mechanism
      cyrus-sasl-otp           2.1.22                    cyrus-sasl plugin for the OTP mechanism
   +  cyrus-sasl-plain         2.1.22                    cyrus-sasl plugin for the PLAIN mechanism
   i  cyrus-sasl-saslauthd     2.1.22       2.1.22       The SASL Authentication Server
      cyrus-sasl-sqlauxprop    2.1.22                    cyrus-sasl SQL auxprop plugin
      gyrus                    0.3.7                     Gyrus - IMAP/Cyrus administrator
      perl-Authen-SASL-Cyrus   0.12                      SASL Authentication Framework - Cyrus Plugin
      perl-Cyrus-IMAP          2.2.13                    Cyrus IMAP Perl Module
      perl-Cyrus-SIEVE-managesieve 2.2.13                A Perl Module for Cyrus SIEVE



Filter: Search Results                    Required Disk Space: 116.3 M

cyrus-sasl-crammd5 - cyrus-sasl plugin for the CRAMMD5 mechanism
Version: 2.1.22-28 Size: 17.8 K Media No.: 1
License: BSD License and BSD-like, Other License(s), see package
Package Group: Development/Libraries/C and C++
Provides: cyrus-sasl-crammd5 == 2.1.22-28, libcrammd5.so.2, cyrus-sasl2:/usr/lib/sasl2/libcrammd5.so,
cyrus-sasl:/usr/lib/sasl2/libcrammd5.so

[Helpv]        [Search]        [Disk Usage]                   [Cancel]        [Accept]
```

Cyrus is a group of software packages containing a POP/IMAP server and offering some standard libraries needed for many other modern mail applications. Among those are the de-facto standard encryption tools in the cyrus-sasl packages. Scalix needs the libraries plain, digest-md5, and crammd5.

Next on our list, is the web server Apache2:

```
YaST @ scalix                                                         Press F1 for Help

[Filterv]              [Actionsv]              [Informationv]           [Etc.v]

   │ Name                   │Avail. Vers.│Inst. Vers.│Summary                          │
 + │ apache2                │2.2.3       │           │The Apache Web Server Version 2.0│
   │ apache2-doc            │2.2.3       │           │Additional Package Documentation.│
   │ apache2-example-pages  │2.2.3       │           │Example Pages for the Apache 2 Web Server│
   │ apache2-mod_fcgid      │1.10        │           │Alternative FastCGI module for Apache2│
   │ apache2-mod_perl       │2.0.2       │           │Embedded Perl for Apache         │
   │ apache2-mod_php5       │5.2.0       │           │PHP5 Module for Apache 2.0       │
   │ apache2-mod_python     │3.2.10      │           │A Python Module for the Apache 2 Web Server│
 a+│ apache2-prefork        │2.2.3       │           │Apache 2 "prefork" MPM (Multi-Processing Module)│
   │ apache2-worker         │2.2.3       │           │Apache 2 worker MPM (Multi-Processing Module)│
   │ apachetop              │0.12.6      │           │Top-like Realtime Apache Connection Monitor│
   │ gadminhttpd            │0.0:5       │           │An easy to use gtk+ user interface for the Apache HT│
 a+│ libapr-util1           │1.2.7       │           │Apache Portable Runtime (APR) Library│
 a+│ libapr1                │1.2.7       │           │Apache Portable Runtime (APR) Library│
   │ perl-Apache-AuthCookie │3.10        │           │Apache/Perl Authentication and Authorization via coo│
   │ perl-Apache-AuthNetLDAP│0.29        │           │use Net::LDAP for user authentication in Apache│
   │ perl-Apache-DBI        │1.03        │           │Apache authentication via perl DBI│
   │ perl-Apache-Session    │1.81        │           │persistent storage for arbitrary data│
   │ perl-Apache-SessionX   │2.01        │           │Persistent Storage for Arbitrary Data (for Embperl)│

Filter: Search Results                          Required Disk Space: 120.2 M

apache2 - The Apache Web Server Version 2.0
Version: 2.2.3-20 Size: 2.8 M Media No.: 1
License: The Apache Software License
Package Group: Productivity/Networking/Web/Servers
Provides: suse_help_viewer, mod_authn_alias.so, mod_asis.so, mod_auth_basic.so, mod_auth_digest.so, httpd,
http_daemon, apache_mmn_20051115, mod_authn_dbd.so, apache, mod_actions.so, mod_alias.so,

[Helpv]        [Search]        [Disk Usage]                    [Cancel]          [Accept]
```

In YaST, search for all packages called Apache. OpenSUSE 10.2 offers Apache2 in version 2.2.3 and automatically selects the prefork module for multiprocessor mode and some other libraries. In the same way, the problem with PostgreSQL is solved. The very robust and renowned PSQL is not used as a DB back end for the mailstore, but as a header cache for IMAP and the Scalix API. OpenSUSE 10.2 brings two packages that are needed: Postgresql-server and Postgresql, both in version 8.1.3. Toggle them for installation.

```
YaST @ scalix                                                    Press F1 for Help

[Filterv]              [Actionsv]           [Informationv]           [Etc.v]

      Name                  Avail. Vers. Inst. Vers. Summary
      Io-language-postgresql 20070528                Io postgresql bindings
      PgTcl                 1.5                       Tcl Client Library for PostgreSQL
      libdbi-drivers-pgsql  0.8.1                     PostgreSQL Database Driver for libdbi
      libpqxx               2.5.5                     C++ Client Library for PostgreSQL
      libqt4-sql-postgresql 4.2.1                     Qt 4 PostgreSQL plugin
      mono-data-postgresql  1.1.18.1                  Database connectivity for Mono
      perl-DBD-Pg           1.49                      DBD::Pg - DBI driver for PostgreSQL
   +  postgresql            8.1.9                     Basic Clients and Utilities for PostgreSQL
      postgresql-contrib    8.1.9                     Contributed Extensions and Additions to PostgreSQL
      postgresql-devel      8.1.9                     PostgreSQL development header files and libraries
      postgresql-docs       8.1.9                     HTML Documentation for PostgreSQL
   i  postgresql-libs       8.1.9        8.1.9        Shared Libraries Required for PostgreSQL Clients
      postgresql-pl         8.1.9                     The PL/Tcl, PL/Perl, and PL/Python Procedural Languag
   +  postgresql-server     8.1.9                     The Programs Needed to Create and Run a PostgreSQL Se
      qt3-postgresql        3.3.7                     A PostgreSQL Plug-In for Qt
      rekall-postgresql     2.2.6                     Rekall PostgreSQL Database Backend


  Filter: Search Results                       Required Disk Space: 134.4 M

  postgresql-server - The Programs Needed to Create and Run a PostgreSQL Server
  Version: 8.1.9-2.1 Size: 10.2 M Media No.: 1
  License: BSD License and BSD-like
  Package Group: Productivity/Databases/Servers
  Provides: libeuc_jp_and_sjis.so.0, postgresql-server == 8.1, libcyrillic_and_mic.so.0,
  libascii_and_mic.so.0, postgres:/usr/lib/pgsql/bin/postmaster, pg_serv, libeuc_cn_and_mic.so.0,

[Helpv]        [Search]         [Disk Usage]                  [Cancel]        [Accept]
```

Last but not least, we have to install Sendmail. This might be a little tricky and cause some irritation. BSD Sendmail is a very old and reliable mail server daemon that has been said to have security issues and a fairly complex configuration. However, if it is configured properly, Sendmail works fine and does a good job on many big installations — UNIX, Linux, and Scalix.

Since SUSE Linux 8, postfix has become the standard mail server daemon on SUSE systems. However, both SUSE and Novell have always included up-to-date versions of Sendmail in their installation repositories. OpenSUSE 10.2 comes with Sendmail 8.13.6.

Use YaST to search for Sendmail and activate it for installation. If you hit return now or confirm with the **Accept** button, YaST will pop up an error dialogue. The problem displayed is: On standard SUSE systems, you cannot have postfix and Sendmail installed parallel without errors. Though there are procedures that work, ignoring these errors is not supported. Thus the mail server Sendmail will replace the package postfix. Select the entry **Delete Postfix** and click on the button **Solve**.

YaST is now installing the packages required for Scalix:

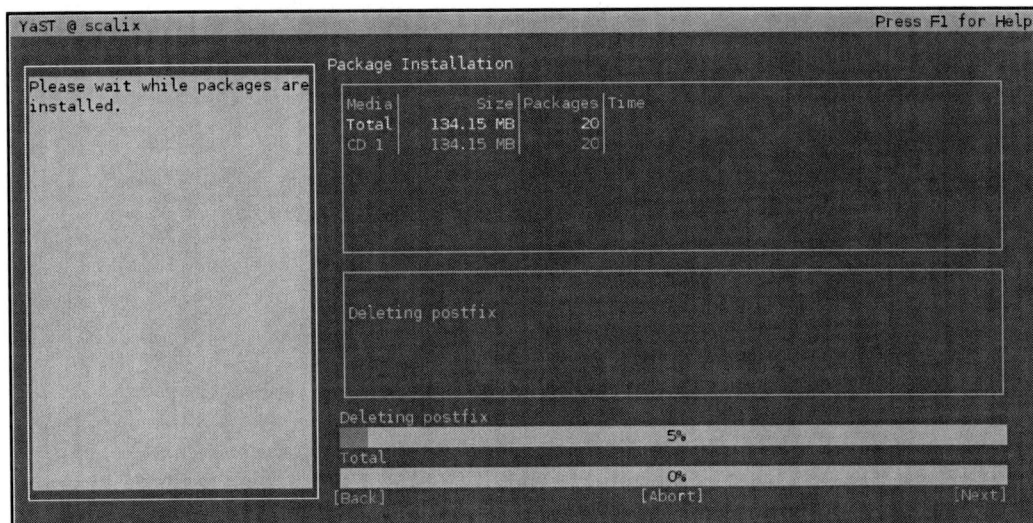

```
YaST @ scalix                                                    Press F1 for Help
┌──────────────────────────────────────────────────────────────────────────────┐
│                          Package Installation                                  │
│ Please wait while packages are                                                 │
│ installed.                   ┌─────────────────────────────────────────────┐   │
│                              │ Media      Size Packages Time               │   │
│                              │ Total   134.15 MB      20                   │   │
│                              │ CD 1    134.15 MB      20                   │   │
│                              │                                             │   │
│                              │                                             │   │
│                              │                                             │   │
│                              └─────────────────────────────────────────────┘   │
│                              ┌─────────────────────────────────────────────┐   │
│                              │ Deleting postfix                            │   │
│                              │                                             │   │
│                              │                                             │   │
│                              └─────────────────────────────────────────────┘   │
│                               Deleting postfix                                 │
│                              ┌──────────────────────5%─────────────────────┐   │
│                               Total                                            │
│                              ┌──────────────────────0%─────────────────────┐   │
│                              [Back]            [Abort]             [Next]       │
└──────────────────────────────────────────────────────────────────────────────┘
```

If everything works fine, you receive the progress bar dialog shown in the previous screenshot. After finishing, YaST will prompt again with a window asking whether you want to install more packages. Now, you can close YaST by clicking on the **No** button. You will find yourself back in the command line.

# DNS Integration

Let's address the last issue that the System Check complained about during installation check: DNS integration. Scalix detected that the host's name could not be resolved via DNS. If your host received its IP via DHCP, there has probably also been a warning about that. Scalix wants your server to have a fixed IP and to be resolvable in the Domain Name System. Thus, it might be a good idea to set up the DNS integration properly for this server. Depending on your setup, there may be several ways to reach that goal:

- Add a host entry to your local DNS server if you own one.
- Set up a full-featured DNS server on the Scalix host.
- If you're running an Internet site, add or correct the entry in your provider's DNS management tool.
- If you are only setting up a local Scalix server without local DNS services, edit your local host file.

Despite the Scalix documentation, most cases require the entry in the hosts-file. This last suggestion works always, but please note that no other server will know your server's host- or domain name. You will need to keep the host files up-to-date manually. It is far better to really fix your DNS setup. However, a quick fix is adding a line to your /etc/hosts file:

```
127.0.0.1          localhost
# special IPv6 addresses
::1                localhost ipv6-localhost ipv6-loopback
fe00::0            ipv6-localnet
ff00::0            ipv6-mcastprefix
ff02::1            ipv6-allnodes
ff02::2            ipv6-allrouters
ff02::3            ipv6-allhosts
192.168.1.175      scalix.scalixbook.org scalix scalixbook.org
```

This last line tells the local system that the server names scalix.scalixbook.org, scalixbook.org and scalix all point to the IP 192.168.1.175, which is the IP of your first Ethernet card. If you need to test a local setup before firing up your Internet host, that may be appropriate.

# Continuing Installation

Back in the Scalix installation window, close the warning window from the last check and click on **Check again**. All the bullets should be green now, with only one warning left. Click on **View Log** to see the details:

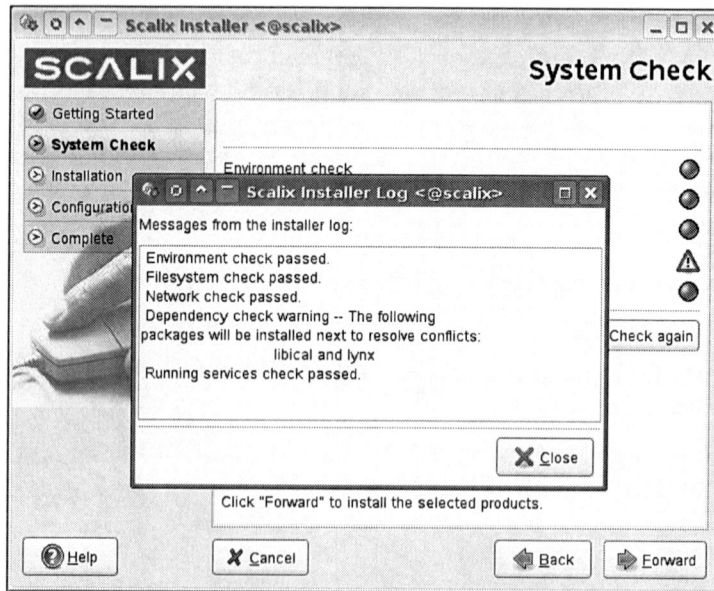

Everything is fine now, the warning about the dependency check tells only about the missing package libical that will be automatically installed by the Scalix installer. You can also find this package in the software directory of the Scalix software package. Click on **Close** and then hit the **Forward** button.

Now, we have left behind the tricky part and the real installation progress is starting. A window called **Installing** shows a progress bar and gives feedback on the components, checks, and tasks that are completed.

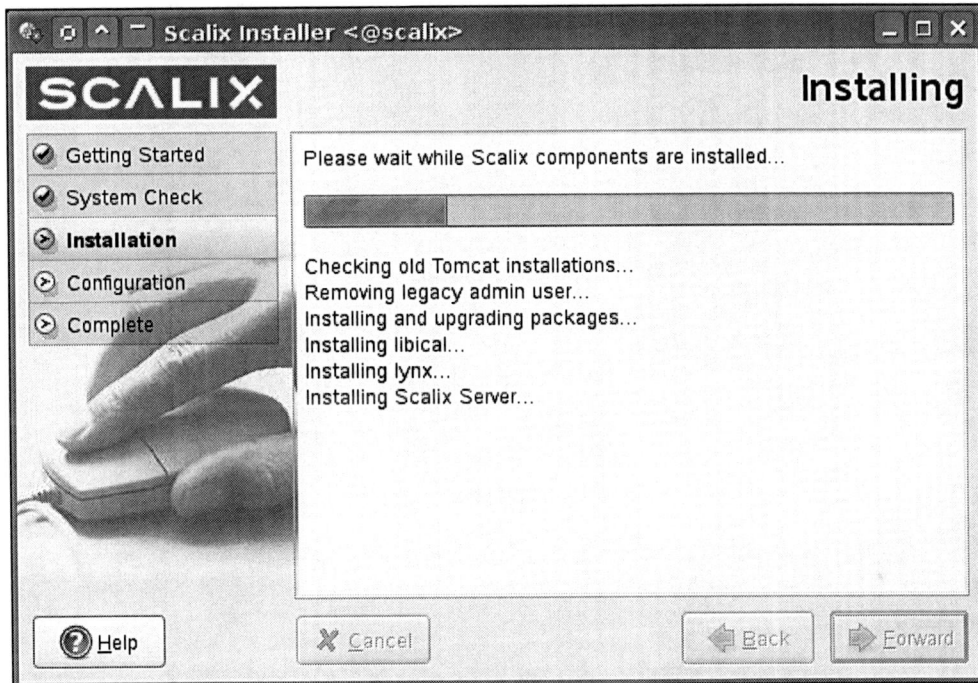

On a modern system, this will take a few minutes and have a Scalix System ready for initial configuration.

# Three Steps for Initial Configuration

There are only three dialogs necessary for initial configuration of your Scalix system:

First, enter the name of the mailnode. This is the name that the Scalix mailnode will use for administrative purposes and in multiserver environment as the default mailnode. Scalix automatically suggests our hostname as the name for the primary mailnode, and we can leave this as is.

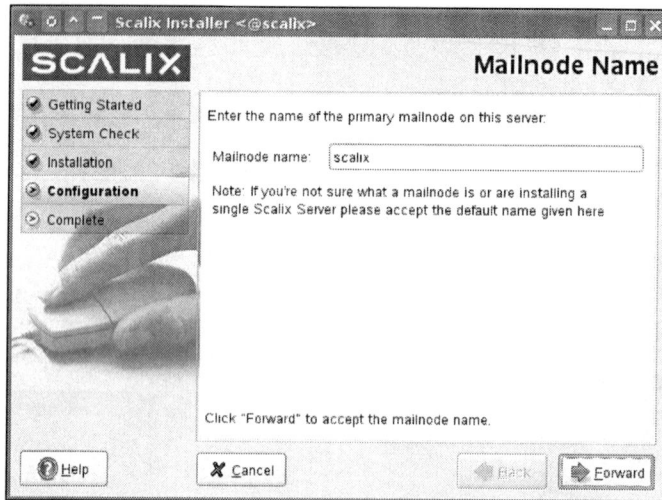

The second step is of particular interest: Here, the Administrator enters the domain name and default address format that Scalix will use for email addresses after creation of users.

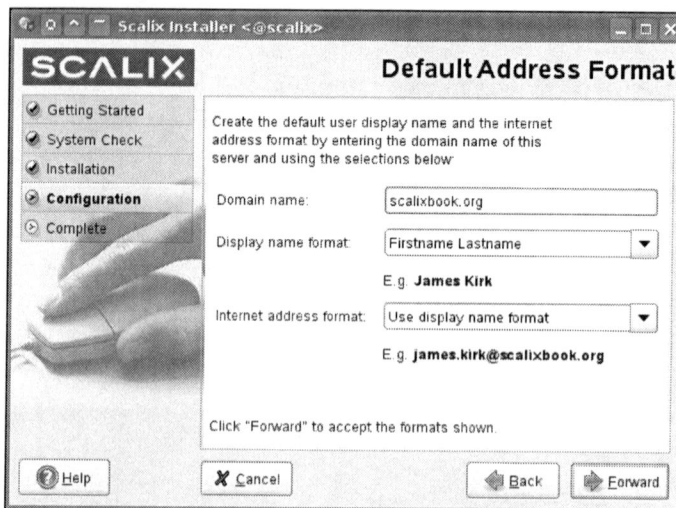

The default setting is the domain that the DNS resolution gave the Scalix system upon initial checks, followed by the standard format for display and user names. For a user with the name Markus Feilner, the default setting will be to display his real name "Markus Feilner" and use Markus.Feilner@domainname as the email address. Feel free to change this, but there is no need to. Click on the **Forward** to continue.

Let's create an Administrator now:

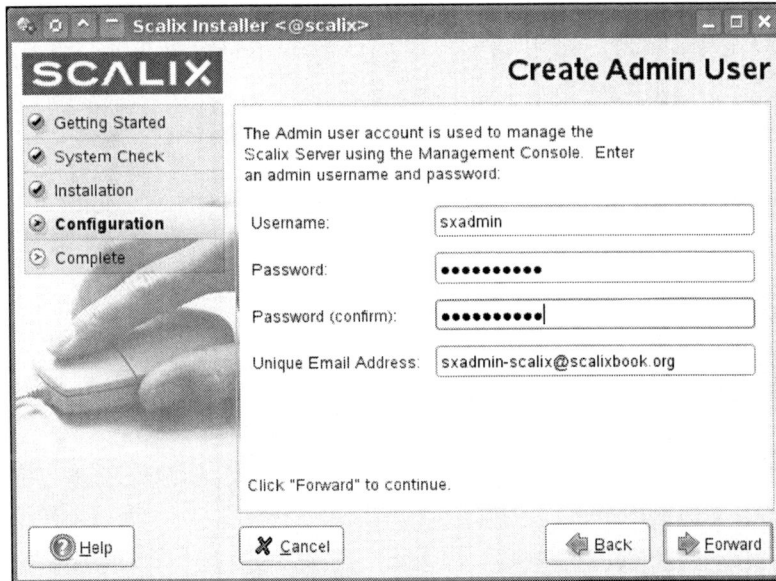

In this third dialog, you can enter the username, password, and email address of the Scalix administrator. Type your password twice (as usual) and click on **Forward** to continue. Now, Scalix is initializing its message store, and configuring the various servers, which may take a few minutes. A small progress bar keeps you informed about the procedure.

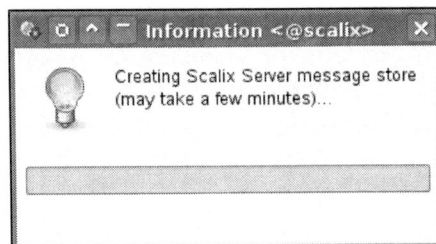

# Setting Up the Server

After some time, you are asked to enter your Scalix License key. If you own one, copy and paste the key into the field saying **Click here and paste license key.** If you want to use the free version of Scalix, click on the button **Forward** and continue without a license.

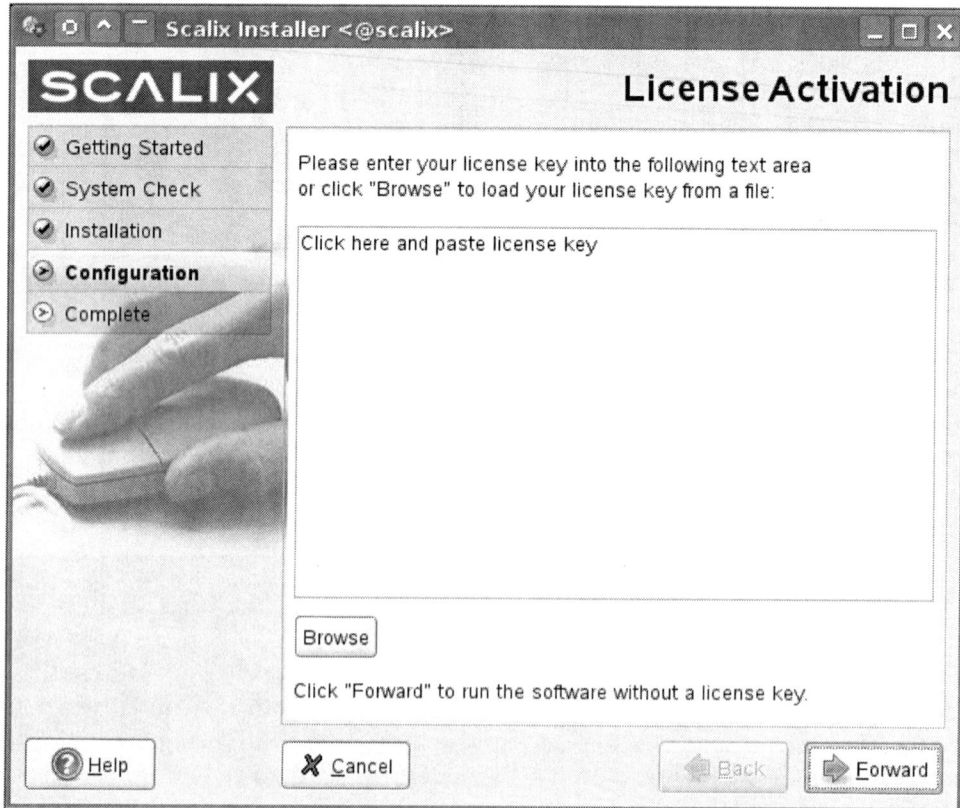

Click **OK** to continue without a licence key and confirm the warning by clicking on **OK**. The Scalix installer will continue by installing third party components like the Java Runtime Environment. Though there may be Java installed on your system, Scalix may install its own package from the software directory.

Click on **Forward** to continue installation. Now a dialog window lets you choose the Java Environment you want the Scalix server to use. You can choose the path to the JRE, browse and search for it in your local file system or install the Java version deployed with Scalix.

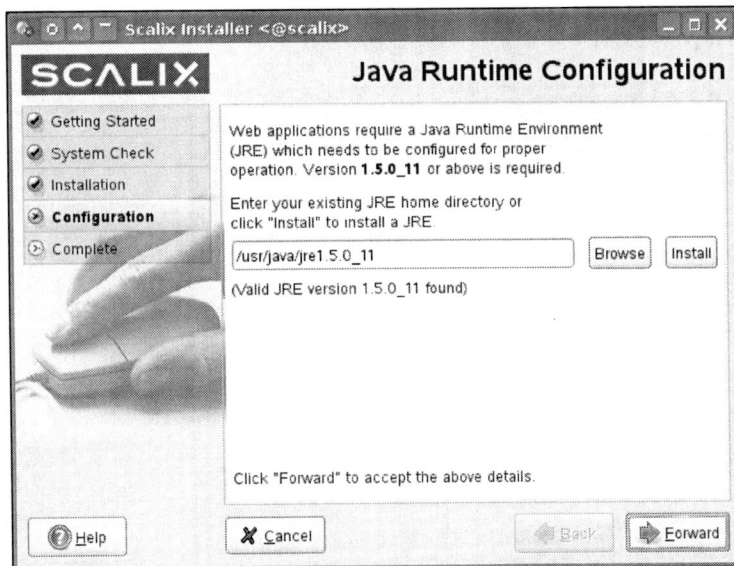

Normally, it is the best solution to accept the installation of the JRE that comes with Scalix, so click on **Install** and then **Forward** to proceed.

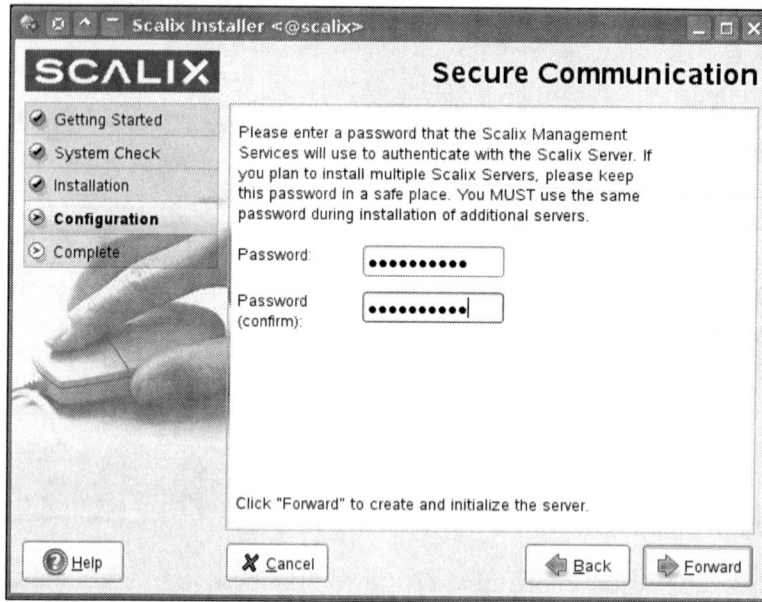

This dialog offers two fields for a password that services and servers will use in their communication. Unless you set up several Scalix servers, you will probably never need this password again. This alone may be a reason to store it in a secure place. Enter your password twice and click on **Forward**.

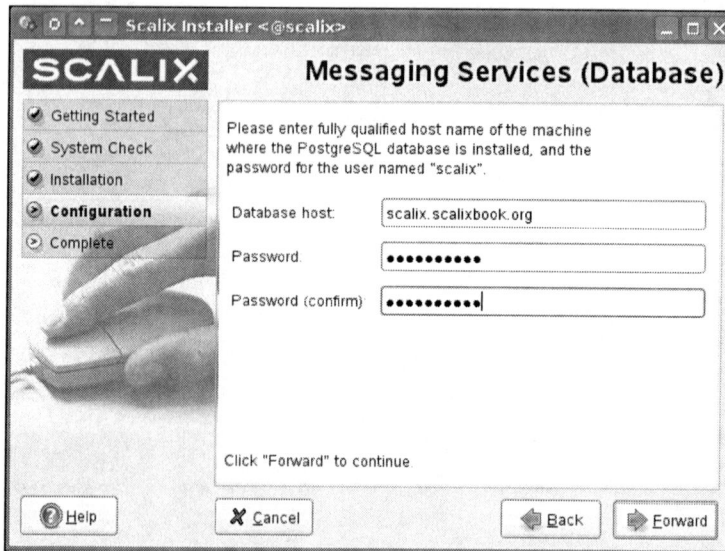

The account data for the database host should also be kept in a safe place. In most cases, the postgres database is running on the same server as the Scalix groupware. However, a different host can be specified here. A user named scalix is to be created in the database. Enter the password this user shall use in this dialog. Click on **Forward** to complete your installation.

Now Scalix is configuring and starting the following services:

- Database
- Management and Indexing services
- Tomcat application server
- Scalix services

Enjoy the congratulations, Scalix is completely installed and you can start the Management console now—if there is a browser installed on your Scalix server. Click on **OK** to leave the installer and have Scalix (try to) start the browser.

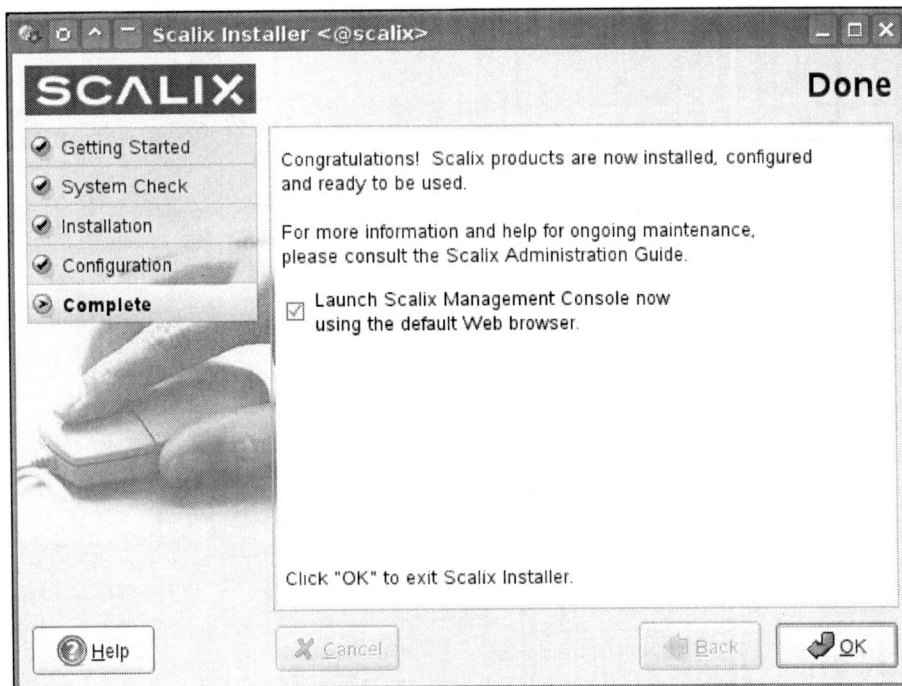

# Testing the Installation

If there is no browser on your Scalix server, start a local Firefox and point it to the URL http://scalixbook.org/sac. Replace **scalixbook.org** with your domain. You should receive a Firefox window like the following.

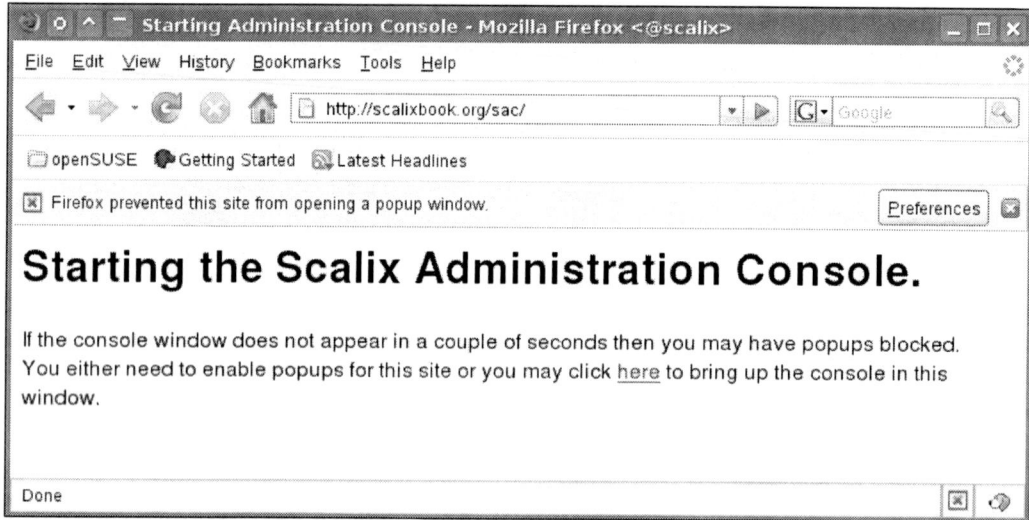

After enabling pop ups for the Scalix host, the standard login window will appear. Check the box **Not using a secure https connenction**, type in your Administrator's name—**sxadmin**—and password and click on **Login**.

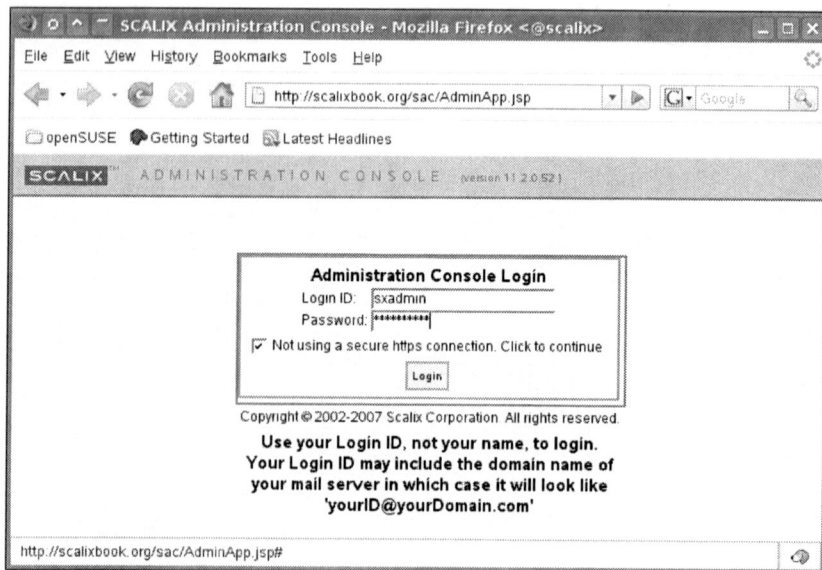

After successful login, the Scalix Administration console is available:

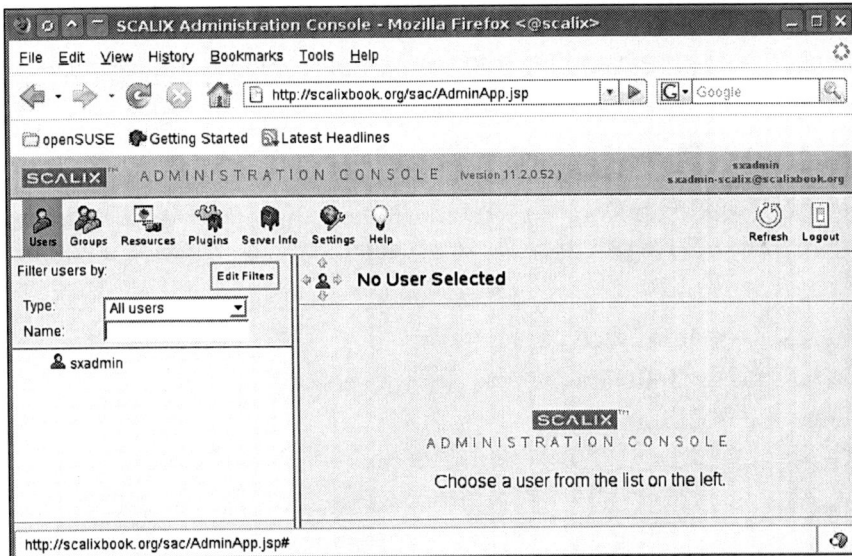

It may be a good idea to check if Scalix is still reachable after a restart of your server. First, make sure that the Scalix services are going to be restarted after a reboot. For that purpose, take a look in the YaST Runlevel Editor. Type `yast runlevel` at a root terminal.

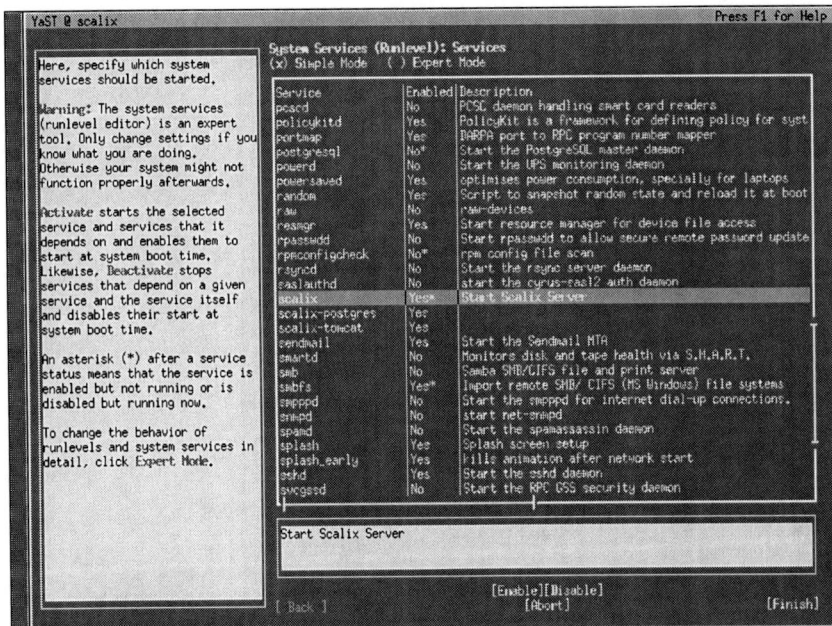

Scroll down and check the lines starting with **scalix**. All of them should have an entry **Yes** in the second column. If your installation has succeeded, this is the case. If not, type *ALT-n* for each of these services. Leave the Runlevel Editor by clicking on **Finish**. Reboot your system and log into the Administration console again.

# Installing Scalix on Fedora Core

Installing Scalix on Fedora Core is pretty much the same as above, there are only slight differences with respect to package management. The required steps are the same:

1. Start an X-enabled shell on the server.
2. Download the software for your Fedora version.
3. Untar the Scalix file.
4. Change to the Scalix-xxx-GA directory.
5. Start the installer with ./scalix-installer.

The Scalix installer also looks like it does on SUSE, and there are only slight differences in some icons.

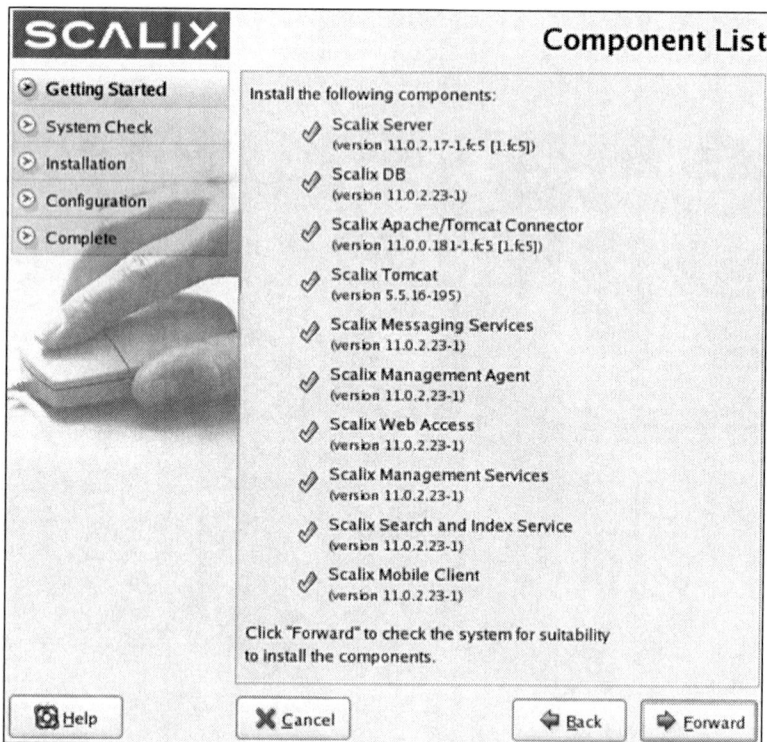

As you can see, there are arrows where buttons used to be on SUSE. The whole procedure is identical, but on Fedora there is no YaST to install software—some may say fortunately... . The standard software management tool on Fedora is Yum. This is a powerful command line tool that can be used to install packages from online repositories. The following code shows the output of Yum installing the required package Sendmail-cf, while dynamically updating its repositories:

```
[root@scalix ~]# yum install sendmail-cf
Loading "installonlyn" plugin
Setting up Install Process
Setting up repositories
core
 [1/3]
core                         100% |=========================| 1.1 kB
00:00
updates
 [2/3]
updates                      100% |=========================| 1.2 kB
00:00
extras
 [3/3]
extras                       100% |=========================| 1.1 kB
00:00
Reading repository metadata in from local files
primary.xml.gz               100% |=========================| 403 kB
00:11
updates    : ##################################################
1164/1164
Added 15 new packages, deleted 16 old in 4.81 seconds
primary.xml.gz               100% |=========================| 1.4 MB
00:03
extras     : ##################################################
4354/4354
Added 69 new packages, deleted 9 old in 15.35 seconds
Parsing package install arguments
Resolving Dependencies
--> Populating transaction set with selected packages. Please wait.
---> Downloading header for sendmail-cf to pack into transaction set.
sendmail-cf-8.13.8-1.fc5. 100% |=========================|  49 kB
00:01
---> Package sendmail-cf.i386 0:8.13.8-1.fc5 set to be updated
--> Running transaction check

Dependencies Resolved

======================================================================
========
```

```
   Package                  Arch       Version           Repository
 Size
 ================================================================
 ========
 Installing:
  sendmail-cf             i386       8.13.8-1.fc5      updates
 311 k

 Transaction Summary
 ================================================================
 ========
 Install      1 Package(s)
 Update       0 Package(s)
 Remove       0 Package(s)
 Total download size: 311 k
 Is this ok [y/N]: y
 Downloading Packages:
 (1/1): sendmail-cf-8.13.8 100% |=========================| 311 kB
 00:06
 Running Transaction Test
 Finished Transaction Test
 Transaction Test Succeeded
 Running Transaction
   Installing: sendmail-cf                   #########################
 [1/1]

 Installed: sendmail-cf.i386 0:8.13.8-1.fc5
 Complete!
 [root@scalix ~]#
```

Yum has checked the online and local repositories for new packages, resolved dependencies, and downloaded the packages required, prompting the administrator before actually downloading and installing.

After Sendmail-cf, we need to install Postgres, Cyrus-sasl and the library Compat-libstdc in the same way:

```
[root@scalix ~]#yum install postgresql-server
(...)
Complete!
[root@scalix ~]#yum install cyrus-sasl-md5
(...)
[root@scalix ~]#yum install compat-libstdc++-296.i386
(...)
```

Once you have installed these packages, your Fedora-based Scalix server will be installed easily, following the guidelines in this chapter.

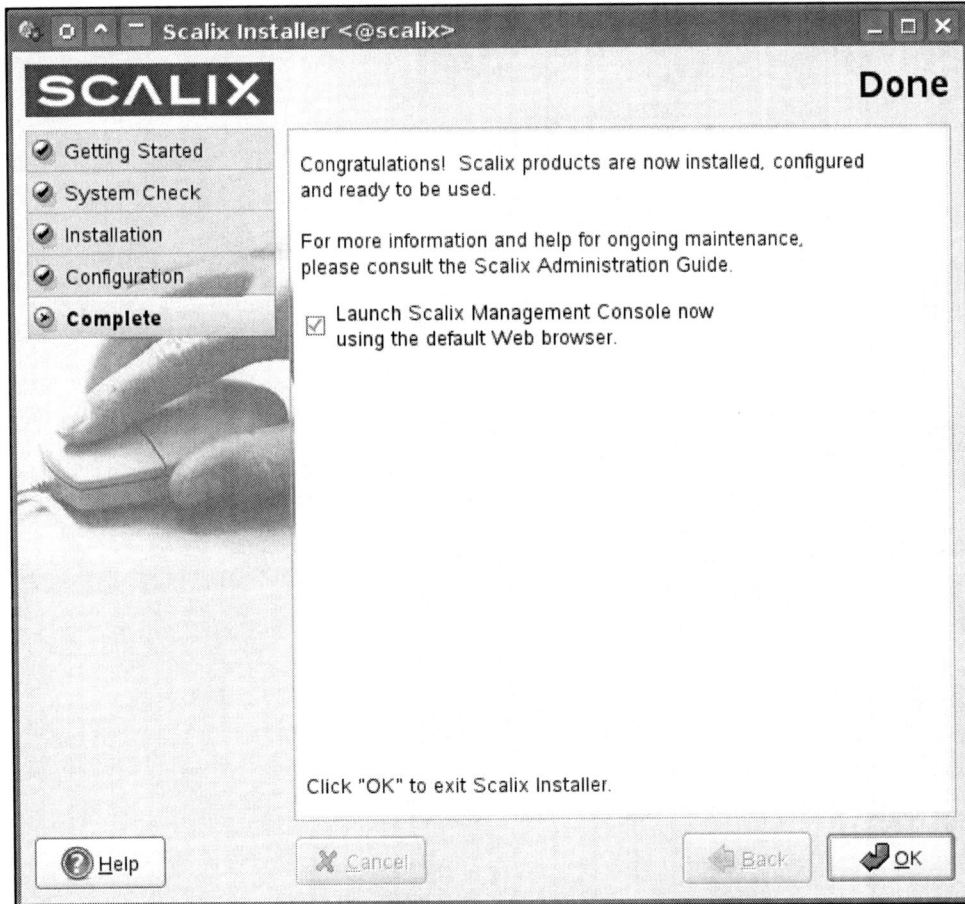

## Summary

In this chapter, we have learned how to install Scalix and cope with the normal procedures that the installation requires. We used the graphical installer to walk through the steps of the installation and used YaST to prepare the system for Scalix simultaneously. After a detailed description of the installation on SUSE 10.2, a short glance on the installation process on Fedora Core followed.

# 4

# Advanced Installations

This chapter deals with advanced installation techniques. First, you will learn about how to get the graphical installation on Windows systems by using NoMachine NX Terminal software. The second part of this chapter shows a typical text-based installation. As a third example, we show how the graphical installer is used to correctly uninstall a Scalix server. The last example shows upgradation and reconfiguration of the Scalix server. What follows is an outlook on how to set up Scalix in a multiserver environment with clustering and replication between servers. This chapter closes with some hints on troubleshooting the installation and some advice for installation in a production environment.

## Advice for Installation

In a test environment, the standard setup of your distribution will do, but if you are planning to set up Scalix in a production environment, you should consider the following:

- Set up a minimum of four partitions: swap, boot (/boot), root (/), and var (/var).

- Use a volume manager for the /var partition. LVM and EVMS are enterprise-level volume managers on Linux.

- Install a minimal system of your distribution. Each software package installed is a potential source of bugs, performance loss, and complexity. Disable all services that you do not need and install only the software needed.

# Checklist for Accessing the Graphical Installation

There are several reasons why you may not be able to access the graphical installer:

- You are accessing the Scalix server over a connection that is not capable of forwarding your X-display, for example an SSH-session without X support.

- Your connection to the Scalix server has a limited bandwidth, and you do not want to use the graphical interfaces.

- You have configured a server with a minimalistic software environment. This makes sense, even though many modern distributions or software packages may collide with this setup. The less software you have installed on your system, the less bugs and security holes may be present, it's just a matter of statistics.

- You are working on a client that cannot display remote graphical sessions from Linux systems, like a typical Windows system. The SSH-client PuTTY (http://www.chiark.greenend.org.uk/~sgtatham/putty/download.html) is a great tool for Windows users who need to access SSH-servers, and its configuration supports many functions. However, if you examine its configuration window, you will notice that this suite does not offer graphical sessions.

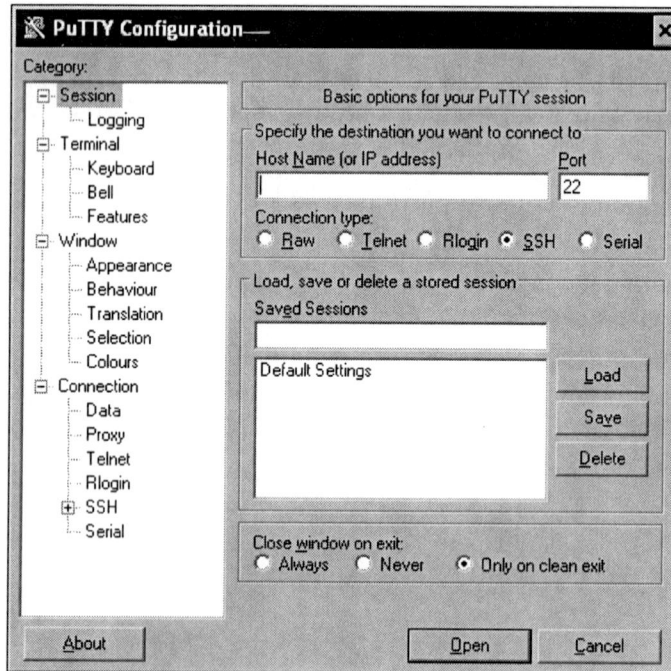

But, as always, there are some workarounds. Of course, the simplest solution for all Linux clients is to use the X option for the SSH-session as described in the previous chapter. The text-based installation is right for you, if your bandwidth or your security considerations do not allow a graphical installation. PuTTY may prove the right SSH-client for the Windows user.

# Graphical Installation on Windows Using NoMachine

If you are running Windows and nevertheless want to access graphical installation, you will have to install terminal server software on both server and client. Although there are solutions like Cygwin for Windows, the better mixture of speed, security, and interoperability is currently offered by NoMachine. This software offers a combination of SSH-connectivity, proxying, caching, and compression. A Linux machine with NX installed is a full-featured terminal server for Windows and Linux clients. With its efficient zlib compression algorithms, two concurrent Linux desktop sessions over a single 64kbit-ISDN line are possible. Thus, NX can also solve bandwidth problems for a variety of clients. And in setups where security issues are a concern, NoMachine can help by using SSH and its secure RSA/DSA encryption layer.

NoMachine's NX is based on the open-source libraries provided and can be used freely for two users and two concurrent sessions. The enterprise version of the software offers unlimited users, clustering, and more. If you prefer the open-source version FreeNX, go to `http://freenx.berlios.de`. One of the benefits of NoMachine's NX is a simple installation and easy-to-use Windows GUI. The following instructions will show how to install and setup a simple graphical session on a Linux server with NoMachine.

1. Got to NoMachine's website ( `http://www.nomachine.com`) and download the packages for your client operating system. If you are using a rpm-based system, download and install nxnode, nxserver, and nxclient.
2. Copy the three packages to your server.
3. Install the rpms on the server with `rpm -ivh package-name`.
4. Install the client package (rpm, deb, .exe) on your client.

```
scalix:~ # rpm -ivh *rpm
Preparing...                    ###################################
                                ###### [100%]
   1:nxclient                   ###################################
                                ###### [ 33%]
   2:nxnode                     ###################################
                                ###### [ 67%]
```

```
NX> 700 Starting: install node operation at: So Apr 29 15:05:45 2007.
NX> 700 Autodetected system 'suse'.
NX> 700 Install log is '/usr/NX/var/log/install'.
NX> 700 Creating configuration in /usr/NX/etc/node.cfg.
NX> 700 Inspecting local CUPS environment.
NX> 700 Generating CUPS entries in: /usr/NX/etc/node.cfg.
NX> 700 Installation of version: 2.1.0-22 completed.
NX> 700 Bye.

   3:nxserver                     ######################################
## [100%]
NX> 700 Installing: server at: So Apr 29 15:05:49 2007.
NX> 700 Autodetected system: suse.
NX> 700 Install log is: /usr/NX/var/log/install.
NX> 700 Creating configuration file: /usr/NX/etc/server.cfg.
NX> 723 Cannot start NX statistics:
NX> 709 NX statistics are disabled for this server.
NX> 700 Version '2.1.0-22' installation completed.
NX> 700 Showing file '/usr/NX/share/documents/server/install-notices':
(...)
NX> 700 Bye.
scalix:~ #
```

# Setting Up Your First NoMachine Session

After installation of the .exe file on your Windows machine, the client will ask if you want to set up a first session and start the NoMachine Connection Wizard. For later configuration, this program can be found in your main menu on both Windows and most Linux distributions.

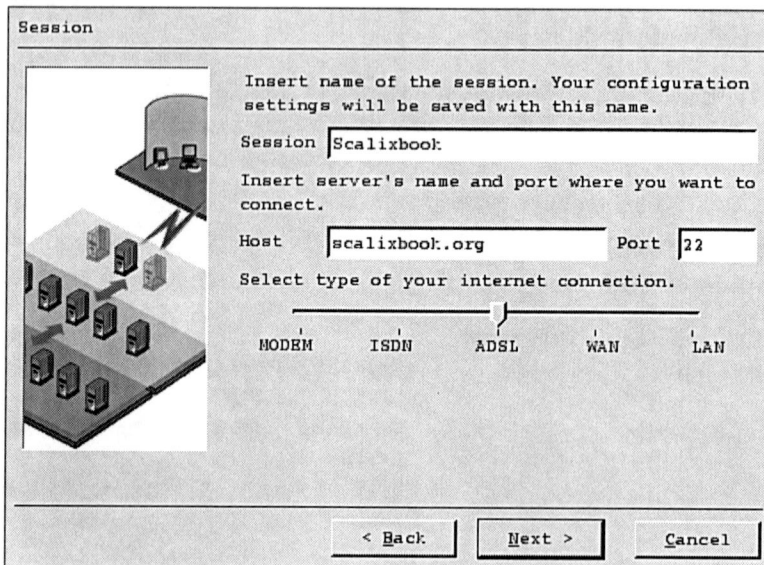

For initial configuration, you will need to enter a name for the connection and a host to which to connect to. It's as easy as that: just type name or IP of your server in the field **Host**, and click on **Next**.

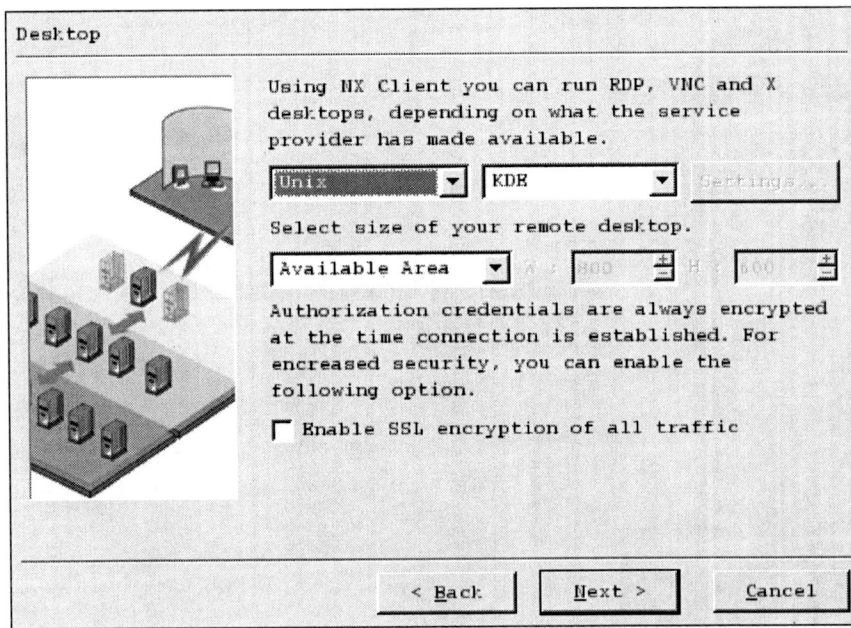

In the second dialog, select the Desktop (**KDE** or **GNOME**) or a single program that you want to be started (**Custom**) from the dropdown menu **Desktop**. If you choose to run a custom program in seamless mode, enter the full path in the dialog available via the **Settings** button. A last dialog will ask you if you want to have a shortcut for this connection on your desktop, which may be a convenient way to start your NoMachine session.

The following screenshot shows the seamless integration of Linux desktop applications in a client session. You may note that this works even across operating systems. If you select **Custom** in the NX client, instead of **KDE** or **GNOME**, you will receive a single window containing the chosen program from which you can start other program windows.

The example below shows a Windows desktop with Konsole, the KDE terminal application. At this command line, the user has started a X-Window enabled SSH-Session to the Scalix server, and after that the graphical installer of Scalix, which is presented on the Windows Desktop in another seamless Window, just like a local application.

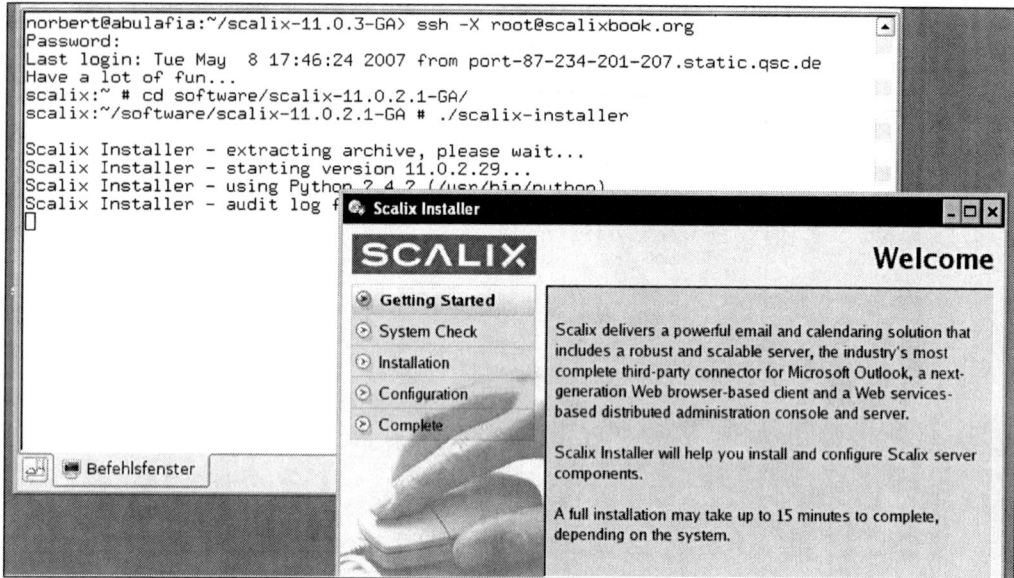

# Text-Based Installation

If you chose not to use the graphical installation of Scalix, the text-only installation will be the best solution. It follows the same steps like the graphical installation wizard. If the Scalix installer cannot detect a graphical environment, the text-based installation will be started automatically.

In a nutshell: Open an SSH-connection to the server. If you are using a Windows operating system, you should now download the SSH-client PuTTY from `http://www.chiark.greenend.org.uk/~sgtatham/putty/download.html`.

Download and extract the Scalix software with `wget` and `tar`. Change to the download directory and enter `./scalix-installer`. The following example shows the output of this command in an SSH-session without X support:

```
mfeilner@tuvok:~$ ssh root@192.168.1.175
Last login: Tue Mar 27 00:22:48 2007 from tuvok.linux-magazin.de
Have a lot of fun...
scalix:~ # cd scalix-11.0.2.1-GA/
scalix:~/scalix-11.0.2.1-GA # ./scalix-installer

Scalix Installer - extracting archive, please wait...
Scalix Installer - starting version 11.0.2.29...
Scalix Installer - using Python 2.4.2 (/usr/bin/python).
Scalix Installer - audit log file is /var/log/scalix-installer-
20070327.log

=== Welcome to the Scalix Installer ===

(...)


=== License Agreement ===
          SCALIX COMMUNITY EDITION LICENSE AGREEMENT
(...)
```

You are prompted to read and accept the Scalix license. Read it carefully and hit *Enter* to proceed to the following page. Once you are through, accept the license by typing yes.

```
-> I have read and accept the above license agreement (yes/no) [no]
yes
Please choose an action from the list:
[1] Install all Scalix components (typical)
[2] Install one or more Scalix components (custom)
-> Please enter your choice [1]:
```

Enter 1 to install all Scalix components and confirm that you want to install.

```
-> Do you want to continue installing the packages? (yes/no) [yes]
```

Scalix then performs a system check and reports its warnings:

```
(...)
Performing system check...
* Environment check... OK
* Filesystem check... OK
* Network check... OK
* Dependency check... WARNING
* Running services check... OK

System check report:
  Environment check passed.
  Filesystem check passed.
```

```
   Network check passed.
   Dependency check warning -- The following packages will be installed
next to resolve conflicts:
                        libical
   Running services check passed.

-> There were warnings during the system checks, are you sure you want
to continue with installation? (yes/no/check again) [no]
(...)
```

In this case, your system has passed the Scalix system check with only one warning: The Software package libical that is part of the Scalix tarball will be installed additionally. We are lucky, there is no need for any measures to be taken. Enter **yes** to accept the suggestion from Scalix. In Chapter 3, there are typical examples for troubleshooting typical software issues like missing packages. Press *Enter* to begin the installation.

After a short while, you are prompted to enter the domain name and select the mail address format that the Scalix server is supposed to use.

```
(...)
Please wait while Scalix components are installed...
(
=== Server Configuration ===

-> Enter the name of the primary mailnode on this server [scalix]:
scalix
-> Domain name []: scalixbook.org

=== Default Address Format ===

Display name format:
[1] Firstname Lastname
    (e.g. "James Kirk")
(...)
[4] Lastname, Firstname Middleinitial.
    (e.g. "Kirk, James T.")
-> Please enter your choice [1]: 1

Internet address format:
[1] Use display name format
    (e.g. "james.kirk@scalixbook.org")
(...)
[10] firstinitialmiddleinitiallastinitial
    (e.g. "jtk@scalixbook.org")
-> Please enter your choice [1]: 1
```

The listing shows the correct selections for the test domain scalixbook.org and the email address format markus.feilner@scalixbook.org. As the last step, we have to enter the Admin user account and password. What follows are exactly the same steps that are provided by the graphical installation:

```
(...)
The Admin user account is used to manage the Scalix Server using the
Management Console.  Enter an admin username and password:
-> Username [sxadmin]:
-> Enter password:
-> Confirm password:
-> Unique Email Address [sxadmin-scalix@scalixbook.org]:
Configuring Server...
(...)
-> Enter the location of your license key file or enter "None" to run
the server without a license []:.
No license key entered, continuing without one
=== Java Runtime Configuration ===
JRE version 1.5.0_06-fcs already installed, skipping.
=== Secure Communication ===
Please enter a password that the Scalix Management Services will
use to authenticate with the Scalix Server. If you plan to install
multiple Scalix Servers, please keep this password in a safe place.
You MUST use the same password during installation of additional
servers.
-> Enter password:
-> Confirm password:
=== PostgreSQL Configuration ===
-> Enter database password:
-> Confirm password:
Configuring PostgreSQL...
Configuring Web applications...
(...)
Restarting Scalix DB...
Starting Tomcat...
Installation finished.
Scalix Installer - cleaning up...
Scalix Installer - done.
scalix:~/scalix-11.0.2.1-GA #
```

After entering the credentials for Admin user, secure communication of services and database connection, the installer sets up the system, finishes installing, and starts required services. Now, it's time to fire up your local browser and go to the URL of your Admin console, in the example it is: http://scalixbook.org/sac. Test the server by logging in with the credentials of the Admin user, you can also test access to the webmail client by its URL http://servername/webmail.

# Uninstalling, Updating, and Reconfiguring Scalix

The Scalix installer offers a graphical dialog for several administrative tasks around installation. If you have a Scalix server installed, starting the Scalix installer will prompt you with the following dialog of the Wizard Mode:

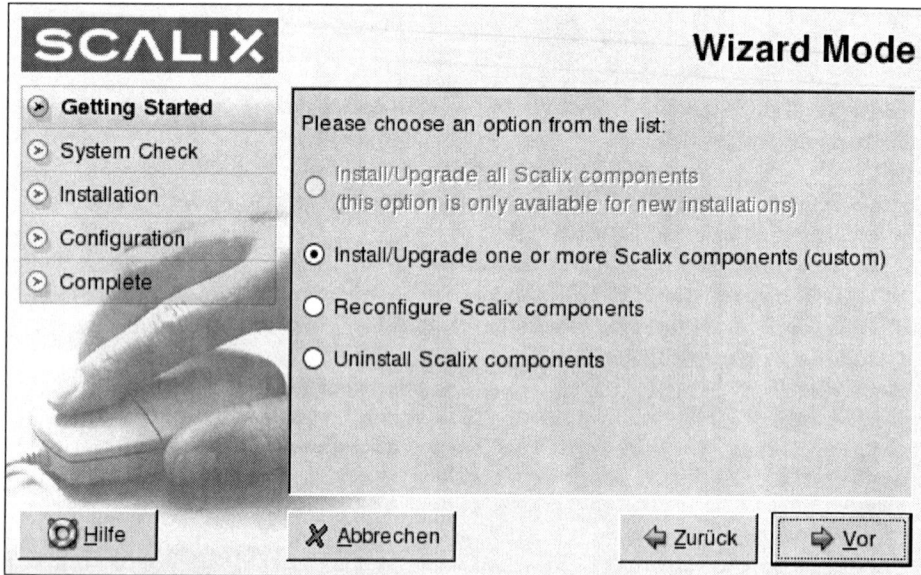

The button **Upgrade all Scalix Components** will be gray, unless you do a complete new installation. In all other cases, you can choose from upgrading, reconfiguration, and uninstalling Scalix.

## Uninstalling Scalix

Uninstalling Scalix is simple. Just select the **Uninstall Scalix Components** button and click on the **Forward** button You are prompted with a Window with a long list of services that you want to uninstall from your server. For a complete uninstall, select all components and click **Forward** again.

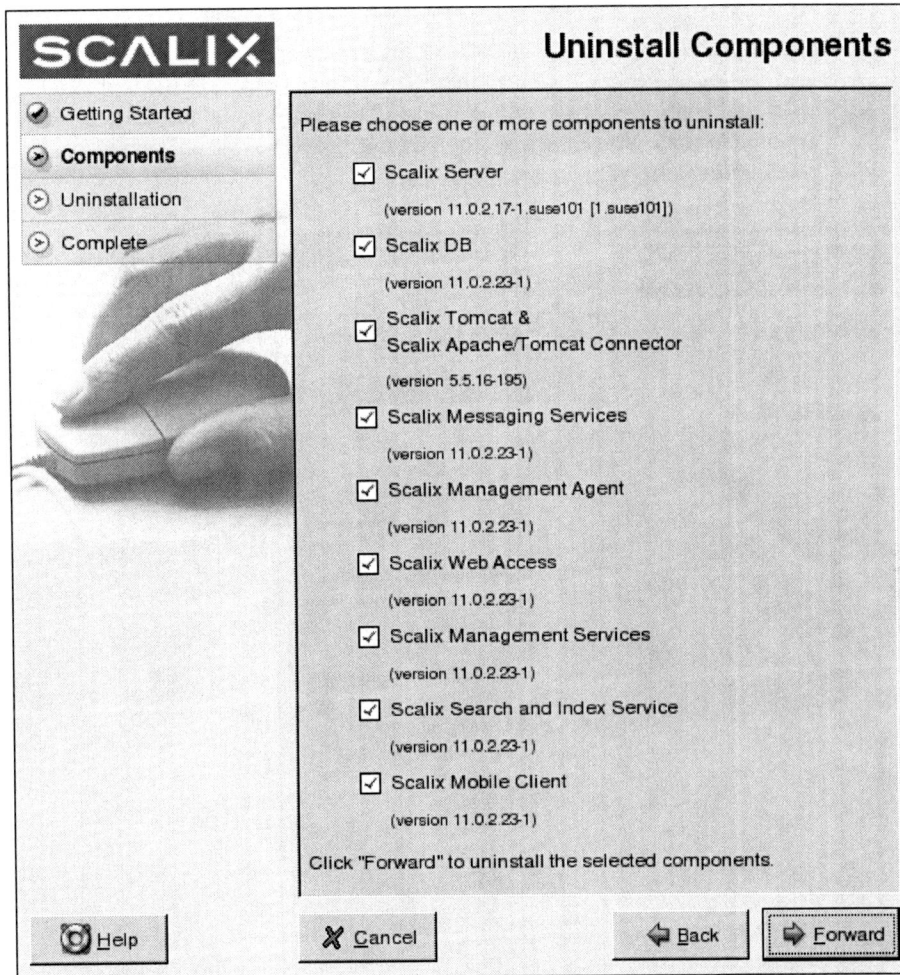

Three message boxes are presented: First, confirm that you want to uninstall the software. Then, Scalix will ask you whether the cache data and the user indexes should be removed with the software. In most cases, you may click **yes**. Cache and index data can be rebuilt by the system automatically, if you later decide to install Scalix again on this machine.

> On a large server, this recreation can take several days and come at a noticable performance penalty. And, if you wish to delete the message store, answering yes here will remove all Scalix users, email, and associated data. You may lose all your data here, so be cautious on productive systems!

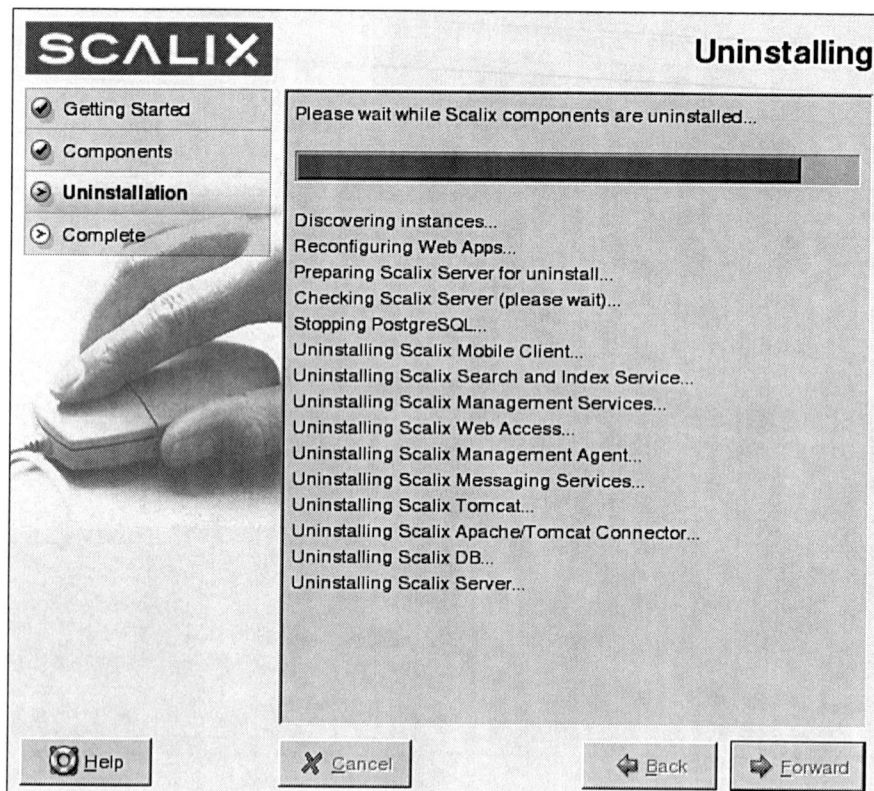

Scalix is uninstalling and prompts with a message box once it has finished.

# Updating and Reconfiguring

Updating and Reconfiguration are as simple as that. For an update, choose **Upgrade one or more Scalix components (custom)** from the list.

After a system check, Scalix asks for the directory containing the software you want to install. If you have started the installer of the new version, the right directory will be selected. If not, click on **Browse** and select the source directory where you have unpacked the Scalix software. Click on **Forward** to proceed. The Scalix wizard presents a list of components that can be updated, including the versions that are involved.

The following screenshot shows an update from Scalix 11.0.2.17.1 to 11.0.3.31.

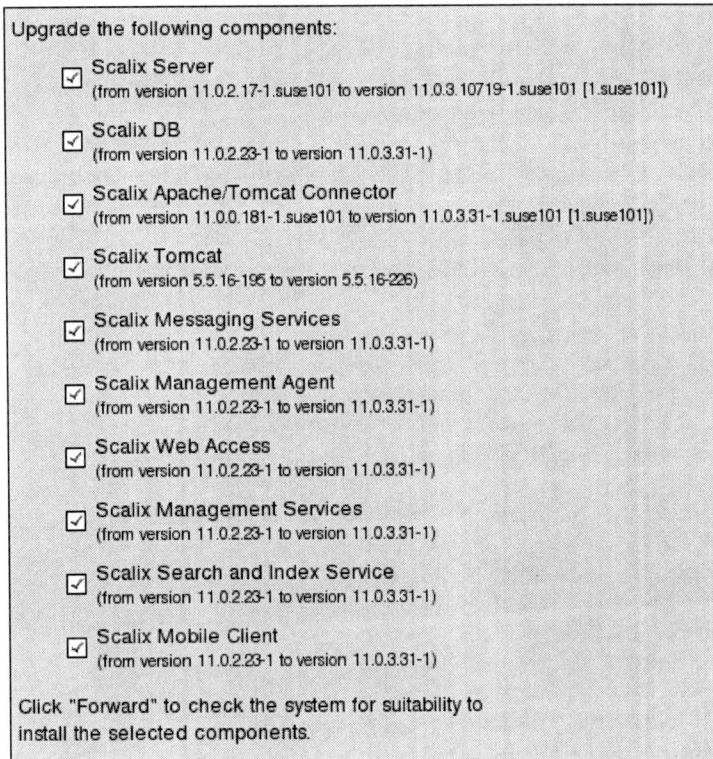

```
Upgrade the following components:

  ☑ Scalix Server
     (from version 11.0.2.17-1.suse101 to version 11.0.3.10719-1.suse101 [1.suse101])

  ☑ Scalix DB
     (from version 11.0.2.23-1 to version 11.0.3.31-1)

  ☑ Scalix Apache/Tomcat Connector
     (from version 11.0.0.181-1.suse101 to version 11.0.3.31-1.suse101 [1.suse101])

  ☑ Scalix Tomcat
     (from version 5.5.16-195 to version 5.5.16-226)

  ☑ Scalix Messaging Services
     (from version 11.0.2.23-1 to version 11.0.3.31-1)

  ☑ Scalix Management Agent
     (from version 11.0.2.23-1 to version 11.0.3.31-1)

  ☑ Scalix Web Access
     (from version 11.0.2.23-1 to version 11.0.3.31-1)

  ☑ Scalix Management Services
     (from version 11.0.2.23-1 to version 11.0.3.31-1)

  ☑ Scalix Search and Index Service
     (from version 11.0.2.23-1 to version 11.0.3.31-1)

  ☑ Scalix Mobile Client
     (from version 11.0.2.23-1 to version 11.0.3.31-1)

Click "Forward" to check the system for suitability to
install the selected components.
```

Normally, all check boxes are checked, and you can click on **Forward** again. The Scalix installer does the system environment check that we know from initial installation and presents the results. If your Scalix system was running up to then, there will be no error here. Click on **Forward** again to start the update.

At this point, Scalix is stopping services, upgrading packages, and restarting the Scalix server software. After that, a series of dialogs gives you the opportunity to reconfigure your services. The configuration dialogs are identical to the ones presented during installation and reconfiguration.

The Scalix software checks for host and domain names, users, services, and locales. In addition, you can enter specific configuration options like changing the LDAP port or adding hosts to the lists of allowed hosts for database access. After you have completed confirming your existing configuration, your Scalix server is immediately available in the new version.

Of course, the upgrade or reconfiguration can also be done with the text-based installation procedure:

```
scalix:~/software/scalix-11.0.3-GA # ./scalix-installer
Scalix Installer - extracting archive, please wait...
Scalix Installer - starting version 11.0.3.31...
Scalix Installer - using Python 2.4.2 (/usr/bin/python).
Scalix Installer - audit log file is /var/log/scalix-installer-
20070429.log
=== Welcome to the Scalix Installer ===
-> I have read and accept the above license agreement (yes/no) [no]
yes
Please choose an action from the list:
[1] Install/Upgrade one or more Scalix components (custom)
[2] Reconfigure Scalix components
[3] Uninstall Scalix components
-> Please enter your choice: 2
(...)
Please choose one or more components to configure:
[1] Scalix DB
    (version 11.0.3.31-1)
[2] Scalix Tomcat
    (version 5.5.16-226)
[3] Scalix Messaging Services
    (version 11.0.3.31-1)
[4] Scalix Management Agent
    (version 11.0.3.31-1)
(...)
```

# Advanced Installations—Multi-Server Setup

The typical Scalix server installation consists of only one server performing all the tasks of the groupware. However, Scalix consists of several components that can easily be split over several servers, at least if you own an EE or SBE license.

## Distributing Scalix Services on Multiple Hosts

Choosing **Custom Installation** during the first dialogs of the Scalix installer offers an advanced installation process, where single services can be selected that are supposed to be installed on this particular host. But to get this multi-server scenario working, some advanced configuration has to be done that is not covered by the Scalix installer. For example: authentication between the servers should be done by Kerberos. Thus, all Scalix servers need a working Kerberos setup, including suitable keytab files, synchronized local time on the servers, suitable network configuration, and more. If you need more information on that, have a look in the Scalix Setup and Configuration Guide.

But Scalix multi-server setup also offers scenarios where all servers are full-featured Scalix servers:

## Failover Cluster

In this setup, two or more Scalix servers guarantee permanent email and calendaring access, even in case one of the servers hangs, e.g. because of hardware failures. Scalix offers clustering software with which the administrator installs two or more machines with full installation and identical setups. One of the servers is defined as "Master", the other one as "Slave". If a Slave detects a problem on the Master, it takes over the Master's services, ensuring services to clients while the Master is down.

## Load Balancing Cluster

If you have many users and you are not sure if one Scalix server may manage the load of the incoming connections, then a load balanced cluster setup for multiple Scalix servers will be your first choice. In the easiest setup, round-robin DNS ensures that a client always seems to connect to the same server, while in reality there are several physical machines serving. Each of these share the same installation and configuration of Scalix, and synchronize their directories. In this setup, there are two, three or more identical servers, permanently updating the directory contents while answering queries from users. Adding servers is an easy, three-step process: Install an identical system, configure directory synchronization, and adjust your DNS entry. This is scalability.

## Synchronizing Remote Scalix Servers

If an organization has several branches in different locations, each of the branches may have a Scalix server. The two Scalix servers' directories are synchronized, so that an employee logging into Scalix at location A receives identical information like when logging in at location B. For such a synchronization, only little bandwidth is needed compared to the amount of data that has to be transferred when several users log in to a remote server

There are more handy scenarios that are supported by Scalix. One of them may be the usage of multiple Web-frontends of Scalix Web Access to a single Scalix server. This setup might help to handle the load caused by JAVA and Tomcat. The only limit for administrators is their creativity, and the Scalix license they own.

# Troubleshooting Installation

The Scalix installation wizard is a powerful and reliable tool. If your installation fails, uninstall Scalix and do a fresh reinstall. In almost any case, the installer will give you detailed and concise information on the reason why it failed to install. Nevertheless, the following list of questions may be helpful when you run into problems:

- Does your server have a static IP?

- Is your network setup working?

- What about DNS? Can your server resolve its own name and IP?

- Is there a firewall on your system blocking services?

- Are any other mail or directory services running?

- Is Apache or Tomcat running or (mis)configured? Does this installation conflict with the Scalix services?

- Check the files responsible for network configuration and name resolution like /etc/hosts, /etc/networks ...!

- Is your software management working properly? Check your ZENworks, YaST Online Update, Red Hat Network configuration and adjust the automatic update settings. If you are unsure, disable all services that might automatically change your software.

- Are there any tools, services or programs running that might automatically change your configuration?

# Summary

In this chapter, we have learned how to use the Scalix graphical installation from a Microsoft Windows client with the help of the Linux terminal server software NoMachine NX. Then, this chapter dealt with the text-based installation, upgrading, uninstalling, and reconfiguring Scalix server software. The chapter closed with multi-server setup, troubleshooting, and basic hints for professional installations.

# 5
## First Steps with Scalix Admin Console and Scalix Web Access

This chapter deals with the Scalix Administration Console (SAC). This web interface is the central point of administration for the Scalix server. User, group, and resource management are done here as well as controlling services and settings. In this chapter, we will take a short tour through the interface, add a first user, and have a closer look at the configuration options available for him/her. Towards the end, we will test the account by logging into the web client, and sending (and receiving) emails.

## SAC at a Glance

Point your Browser to the URL of your Scalix server, following this syntax: `http://<servername>/sac`. A pop-up window with the Administration Console Login is opened. If you are using Firefox or another browser with pop-up suppression, perhaps the configuration will need some corrections. Allow the Scalix server to open popups. In Firefox, you can easily configure this by clicking in the yellow bar on top of the displayed page. Other browsers may require editing the preferences. Otherwise, Scalix will provide a web page for you with a link, which opens the Admin Console in the same browser window.

# Logging In

On Scalix 11, the Scalix Administration Login looks like this:

Enter the Administrator's name in the field **Login ID**, exactly as configured during installation. Activate the reminder that you are connected via http and not through https by clicking on option field **Not using a secure https connection**. Once we have configured https for Scalix, the login dialog will not provide this option anymore. However, enabling https is not that easy, and therefore not standard in Scalix, except for the installations on Red Hat Enterprise. We will deal with this topic later in the chapter on Security.

Click on the button **Login** to start the Administration console.

# A First Look Around

The Scalix Administration Console is a Web application provided by a Tomcat application server. The only requirement for it is a modern browser supporting JavaScript. Firefox and Internet Explorer do fine, Konqueror may work soon. The Admin Console window is split in three parts:

- A menu with icons called Toolbar
- A list view on the lower left named Contents Pane and
- The main window on the right, called Display Pane

The icons in the menu bar let you choose the administration task you want to accomplish, the content pane lists the possible entries that can be edited, and the options and parameters of a selected entry are presented in the display pane.

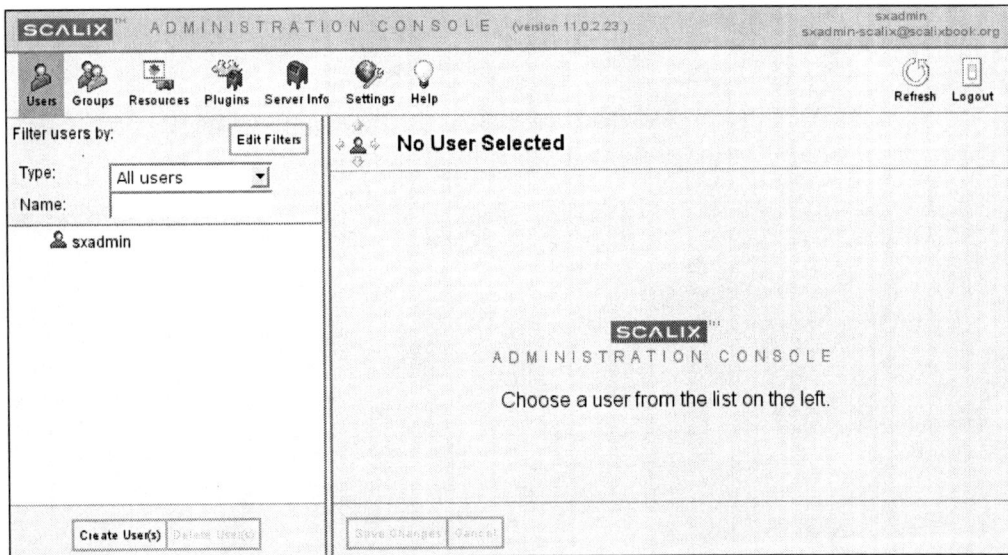

By clicking on one of the icons on the Toolbar, you can access the different sections of the Scalix Administration Console. The first three sections are about users, groups, and resources, and will be used in daily administration for adding, deleting or modifying these objects. The section **Plugins** offers a management GUI for your own or third-party Scalix plug-ins. The **Server Info** icon leads to a concise list of running services, where the administrator can set the log level of these services and browse through the services' log files. The **Settings Icon** allows you to set preferences for the server and new users. A concise online help is available, and the icons **Refresh** and **Logout** complete the menu bar's icons.

# Navigating in the Admin Console

A nice gadget in SAC is the little icon on the top left of the main window. Surrounded by four arrows, this icon displays the icon of the current section and enables the administrator to navigate in a quick and easy manner through the administration console.

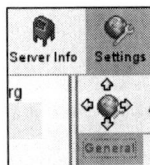

Clicking the up or down arrows will select and activate the next entry upwards or downwards in the list view to the left, and the left/right arrows navigate you back and forth in a browser-like fashion.

# Users, Groups, Resources...

Now click on the **Users** icon in order to switch to the user management dialog. Click on the entry of the only user present at this time, **sxadmin**.

For every user, there are six tabs where the user information is stored. The tab **General** holds the most important information: Username, Display Name, and Email address. This information is all that is necessary to add an user and use the new account. The other tabs contain contact information, group memberships, and administrative delegations. The mailbox quota, that is the amount of storage that the user's account may sum up to, is configured in the Mail dialog. On the Advanced tab, the administrator can add a role to the user, decide whether this user is a Standard or a Premium User, and give him a different authentication ID.

# Changing Passwords

There are other features in the Admin Console that you will be using frequently once you are master of some Scalix users. One of them is probably the button **Change Password** on the lower right corner leading directly to the password dialog. This button is present in every user's configuration dialog.

Enter new password: 

Confirm new password: 

☐ User must change password on first login

Change Password    Cancel

# Filtering the List

In a large environment, the list view can be very long, and it may be tricky to find a user, group or resource in time. Thus, Scalix offers filters that can be combined and configured to reduce the displayed objects to a manageable amount. In the standard setup, a drop-down menu allows you to select the displayed user type, with special features like **Logged in Users**. Specifying a part of the username in the Name field will automatically display only the usernames in the list fitting to this mask.

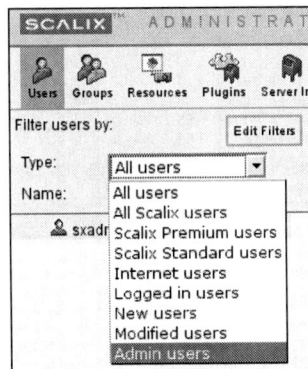

SCALIX™ ADMINISTRAT

Users  Groups  Resources  Plugins  Server In

Filter users by:                    Edit Filters

Type:    All users  ▼

Name:    All users
         All Scalix users
   sxadr Scalix Premium users
         Scalix Standard users
         Internet users
         Logged in users
         New users
         Modified users
         Admin users

The **Edit** button filter on the top right edge of the list pane is an especially useful helper in large environments. Normally, Scalix only returns the first 100 entries, but this can be configured. Here, the administrator may define extended filter criteria to avoid long listings ,for example, of users or groups. Click on it to receive the following dialog:

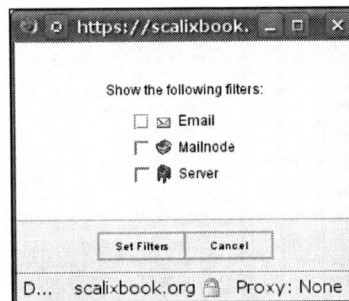

◎ ◎ https://scalixbook. _ □ ✕

Show the following filters:

☐ ✉ Email

☐ ◈ Mailnode

☐ 🖳 Server

Set Filters    Cancel

D...  scalixbook.org 🔒 Proxy: None

Because a typical Scalix environment may consist of several thousand users, the Admin Console can manage a scenario consisting of multiple Scalix servers and mailnodes. Each arrow that you set in this tiny dialog adds a drop-down menu or entry field to the list of available filters in the list view. This convenient feature enables the administrator to search and find a user much faster than in any other groupware solution I know.

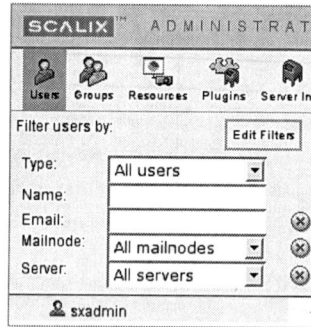

# Adding a User

Let's add a first user now. Click on the **Users** icon in the menu bar, and then on the **Create User(s)** button in the lower half of the list view. Again, a pop-up window appears. It is called **Create New User** and offers several fields where the administrator can enter the user data. All that is needed for a new user is a name, an email address, and a password. The email address is generated automatically from the user name and the domain name, so all we need to enter here is our name and a password:

Nevertheless, the adminisrator can choose several interesting settings here. One of them is selecting the user type. Whereas a Scalix Premium user has full access to the groupware (including MS Outlook), the Standard user will only have groupware in the Scalix webclient. An Internet mail user is barely an entry in the global address book for an email account for SMTP, POP, and IMAP.

Four options in the lower half can be either checked or unchecked. Locking new users or forcing them to change passwords on first login are features that may be useful for security aware administrators. If you do not want the new user to access the Scalix Web client SWA (Scalix Web Access), then deselect this arrow.

Like some other groupware servers, Scalix supports delegating email features to a colleague while the user is on holiday. Identifying the sender in a delegate's outgoing mail may be tricky, and thus there is a feature enabling special headers in the email that contains information on the sender. If you check the setting **Add Sender header to delegate's outgoing messages,** any mail sent from this user on behalf of someone else will contain a header identifying him.

Click on the **Next** button to proceed. The dialog window contact information holds eighteen fields where you can enter administrative user data like telephone number, department or address.

**Create New User**

**Contact Information**
Enter in personal information that can be published in the address book.

☑ Display in address book.

| | | | |
|---|---|---|---|
| Company: | | Work Phone: | |
| Department: | | Work Phone 2: | |
| Office: | | Home Phone: | |
| Title: | | Home Phone 2: | |
| Street: | | Mobile Phone: | |
| City: | | Fax: | |
| State/Province: | | Pager: | |
| Zip/Postal Code: | | Notes: | |
| Country: | United States | | |
| Language: | English (American) | | |

< Back    Next >    Finish    Save and Create Another User    Cancel

If the option **Display in address book** is checked, the data entered here will be displayed in the Scalix address book and is thus available to other users. Click on the **Next** button again.

```
Create New User

Group Membership
Select the groups that the user belongs to.
Filter groups by: Type: [All groups      ▼] Name: [                    ]

  ☐  Group Name
  ☐  👥 ScalixAdmins
  ☐  👥 ScalixGroupAdmins
  ☐  👥 ScalixUserAdmins
  ☐  👥 ScalixUserAttributesAdmins
```

In the last dialog, during creation of a user, the administrator may choose the groups that the new user is a member of. After installation, there are only four groups available with different functions. The members of these groups have special administrative rights, which our standard user does not need.

Click on the button **Finish** to complete the process of adding a new user to the Scalix system. By the way, you can click this button at any time. Once you have entered a user name and a password, then you do not need to enter any address data.

The Scalix administrator can access all user data at any time later via the Scalix Admin Console. All dialogs are present, identically, in the user management. An admin is allowed to edit user name and user data, and there are some small but useful features.

# Playing with Filters

This might be a good time to play with the filters: In the field **Name** in the list view, enter one or more letters that are different from the one your user's name starts with. The user will then disappear from the list. In the example above, if I type ", the user **sxadmin** will vanish from the list, and after having typed **Mart**, my list is empty.

Do you notice the little crown on the head of the new user? Scalix Premium Users can be identified by this cap and a green shirt. Standard Users like the admin account **sxadmin** are dressed in blue.

The Scalix user management offers some more features worth mentioning. If you click on the **Add Address** button, additional email addresses for this user account are added. You can add addresses and collect the email on one particular account. Simply select real name, user part, and domain part of the email address. The drop-down menu shows that Scalix is capable of administrating multiple domains on one server.

In the dialogs **Member of** and **Manager of**, this user can be assigned as a member or manager of Scalix groups. Click on the **Advanced** tab to edit the user's login name.

In Standard setup, Scalix uses the full email address as login name for all access to the Scalix system. This makes perfect sense for most users, because they only have to remember the email address and password. However, being lazy, I prefer a handy, short login name like "mfeilner" in addition to the email address markus.feilner@scalixbook.org. Especially, since the Scalix login is case sensitive.

Enter the login name for this user in the field **Authentication ID**. There are three other interesting options on this page:

- Under some circumstances, for example if a user has met the maximum amount of failed logins, his account will be locked. This is marked in the Scalix Admin Console by an arrow in the check box **is locked**. Un-checking this checkbox may be a regular administrative task for users with a bad memory, but sometimes if you want to lock out a user, this is the right place to do so.

- With Smart Cache, a copy of the mailbox is stored on the user's client. Smart Cache can be enabled or disabled globally or on a per-user base. Enabling the Smart Cache is a task that may take some time for large mail boxes, but it is worth it. However, if you decide to let some users have other caching settings than the server default, please note that this cannot be reversed anywhere other than from the command line.

- Indexing speeds up most of Scalix groupware actions. The index contains meta information on mail, contacts, and appointments helpful for searches. However, such an index needs to be built before it can be used. The Scalix Indexing Service (SIS) builds this index automatically. This dialog allows the administrator to deactivate the Indexing Service for a single user. The **Recreate SIS index** button helps if you receive error messages about a corrupt index.

# Testing the New Account—Logging into SWA

Immediately after clicking on the button "**Save**" in SAC, the user can log in to the web client (or connect through Outlook) using his short ID. The URL of the webmailer is simply `http://<servername>/webmail`, in our example setup, it is `http://scalixbook.org/webmail`.

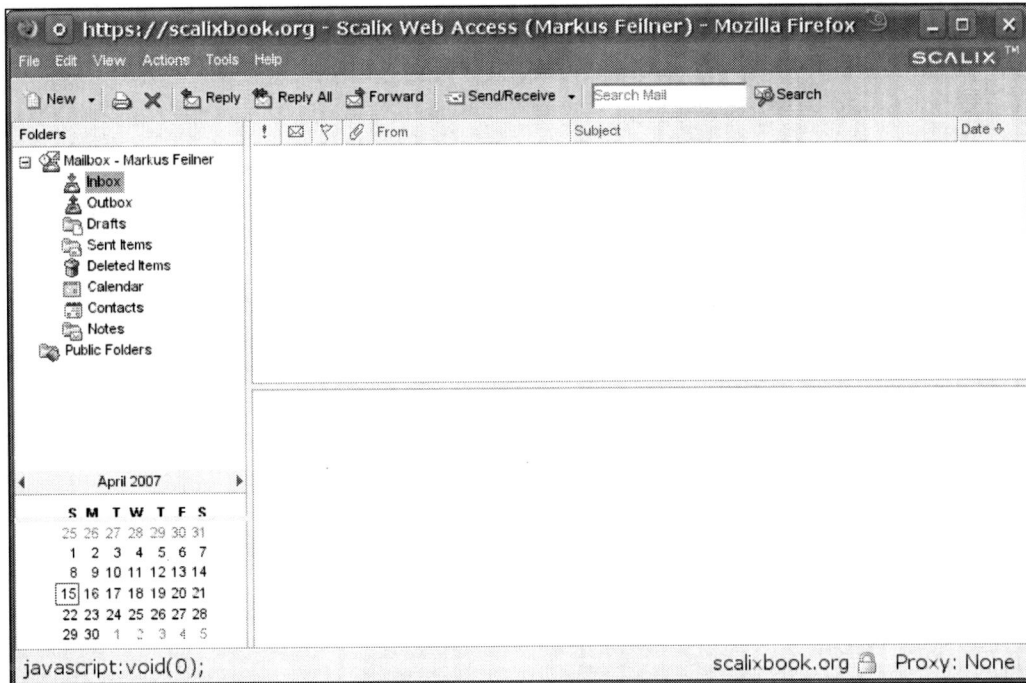

The Scalix Web Access (SWA) is a full-featured standard Webclient. It supports drag'n'drop actions in Ajax-style and has a front end that is very similar to Outlook, which makes it easy for newbies. Again, a menubar is accompagnied by a list view and a main window. Furthermore, a calendar view at the bottom rounds up this groupware client. The proprietary versions of SBE and EE, contain some features that are very helpful to Admins of larger companies. Perhaps the most valuable option is the **Recovery** folder that every user has by default. This folder contains all deleted emails for the last week. This may significantly reduce the amount of calls from your users.

# Sending the First Email

Our server is configured, the user account has a mail address, and the user is logged in. All that is left to do is checking if the user can send and receive emails. Click on the **New** button to start editing your first email. A pop-up window with the title "New Message" will appear. As you can see, the editor window is kept as close to the Outlook look and feel. By the way, both HTML and clear text email are supported.

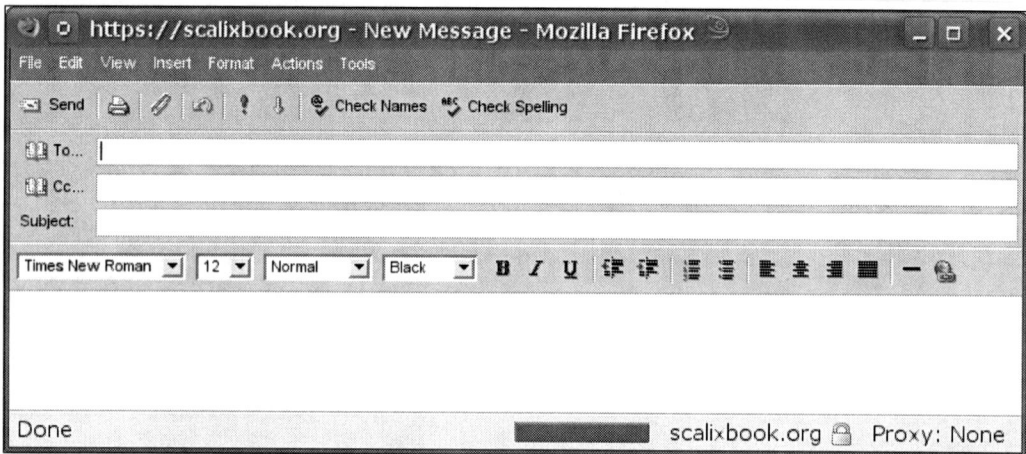

In the first step, local delivery is checked: Enter your own email address in the **To:** field, some text in the subject and the body of the mail and click on the button **Send**. Don't hesitate to click on the Button **Send/Recieve** in SWA. The mail is being delivered locally, so it should be in the Inbox instantaneously. Unread messages are displayed in bold characters.

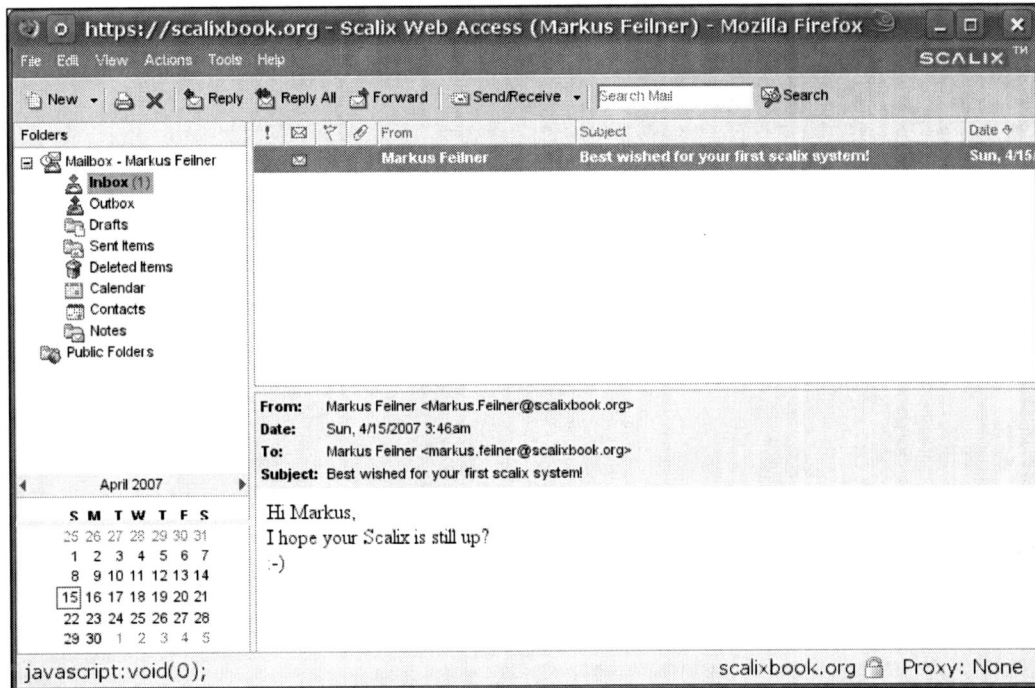

Second step, test the email functionality from and to the outside world. Send an email from either of the configured mail addresses to an external recipient and confirm the success. Answer to the emails and check your Inbox. In most cases, Scalix simply works after installation.

# Summary

In this chapter, we learned how to start and use the Scalix Administation Console. We added a user, looked at advanced filter and search criteria, and changed some advanced settings for this user. After that we logged in as the new user and tested the Scalix server by sending a local email.

# 6
# Administration and Configuration

In this chapter, you will learn how to deploy Scalix Connect for Microsoft Outlook, to your Windows clients. After that, the integration of the supported Scalix groupware client Evolution and other IMAP mail clients is shown.

## Deploying Clients

Because Scalix and its predecessors have always been developed with a special focus on the Microsoft Outlook user, the proprietary Windows mail client is definitely the second standard way to access the Scalix server. To make it work with Scalix, we need to install a connector software from Scalix.

## Installing Scalix Connect for Outlook

The first step is the download. The Scalix Outlook connector can be found on the Scalix website, and it is included in the commercial Scalix bundle. Click on the link **Community** and proceed to the Scalix Download Area. In the lower half of the screen, in the section **Binary Client Packages** there is a link called **Scalix Connect for Outlook**, which leads to the Connector file called `scalix-`*version*`-GA-outlook-connector.zip`. For example in Scalix 11, this file is called `scalix-11.x.x-GA-outlook-connector.zip` and needs unzipping with a packager like WinZip or UnZip.

Once unpacked, the file offers a directory structure with a file called `setup.exe` in the subdirectory : `scalix-11.x.x-GA/software/scalix_connect_outlook/11.x.x.x-xxxx`. Change to this directory and double-click on this file.

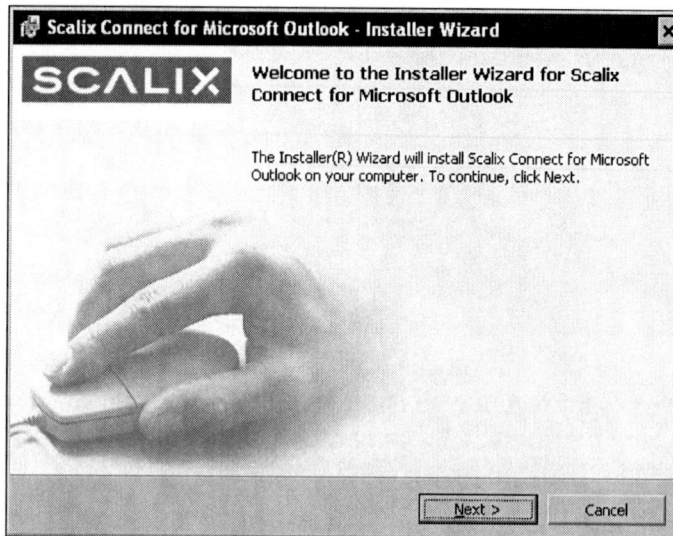

The Scalix Connect Installation Wizard has started. You should have Administrator rights for this step, but almost no interaction from your part is necessary. The wizard simply installs its libraries on your system and gives the standard confirmation once it has finished.

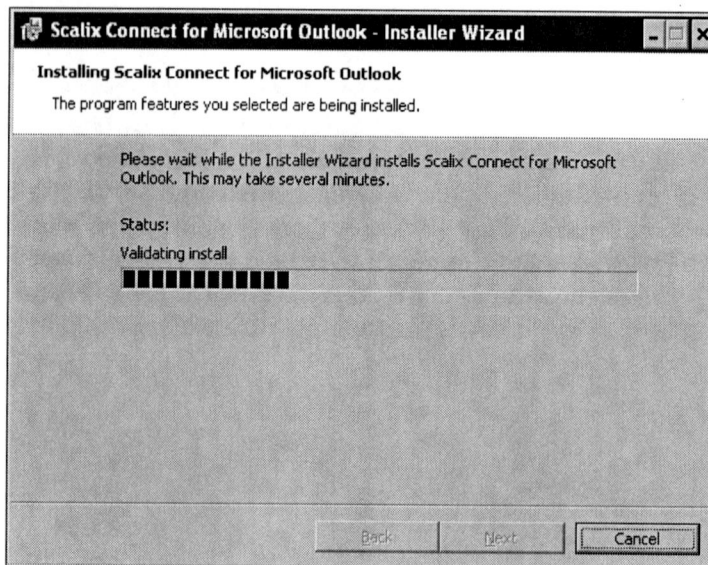

There are no known problems and only few reports on problems with the installation wizard. If Murphy's law should be at your side though, the Scalix forums are the right place to ask for help. A very common mistake here seems to be that users forget to switch Outlook to Groupware mode, especially if it has been used with POP before.

# Installing Outlook as a Client

After the wizard has completed, we can set up our email client, Outlook. As the first step, we will walk through Outlook 2000. Basically, there may be three kinds of Outlook 2000 clients: Ones already set up with a groupware server like Exchange, clients with a non-groupware setup, and totally new accounts. Because all procedures meet at one point—the selection of the groupware server to use—we have to split up the first steps in three parallel tracks:

## A New Account

On a new user account, open MS Outlook for the first time. Outlook's startup wizard gives its welcome greeting. Click on **Next** and select **Corporate/Exchange** mode in the following dialog. Right now, you have told Outlook to use a groupware server for its data.

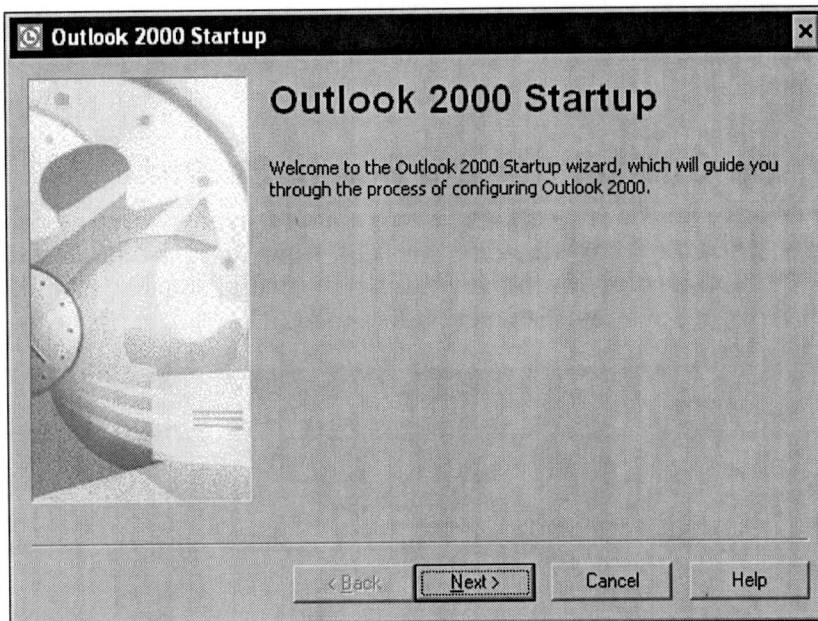

Click on the **Next** button and proceed with entering your personal data until Outlook asks you, which groupware server (**information service**) it is supposed to use.

# Changing an Existing Account

If you already have configured an email account in MS Outlook, all you have to do now is add a new profile to your Outlook setup. In this case, you can skip the first three steps of the following description. However, if you have been running Outlook in a non-groupware environment before, you may have to switch to **Corporate** mode by following these steps:

- Select **Tools** from Outlook's menu and click on **Options**. If there is no **Options** entry, expand the menu by clicking on the double arrow.
- Change to the tab **Mail Delivery** click on **Reconfigure Mail Support**.
- Select **Corporate or Workgroup** from the list and click on **Next** and **Yes** to confirm the new mode.
- Add a new profile (see below).

# Adding an Outlook Profile

Start the Windows Control Panel and select the **Mail** icon, which will take you directly to the setup of a new profile, unless you already have an existing one. If there is a profile on your machine, you will be presented a list to choose from if you click on the **Show Profiles** button. In both scenarios, you will find a button called **Add** in the following dialog that takes you directly to the window shown in the following screenshot, where Outlook asks for the type of "information service" it is supposed to use.

# Setting Up Outlook for the Scalix Server

No matter whether you have configured a new account, added a profile or changed an existing account, the following procedure is the same from now on. The standard version of MS Outlook supports Exchange, Internet email, Lotus Notes, and if the Scalix connector plug-in is installed, our Scalix server:

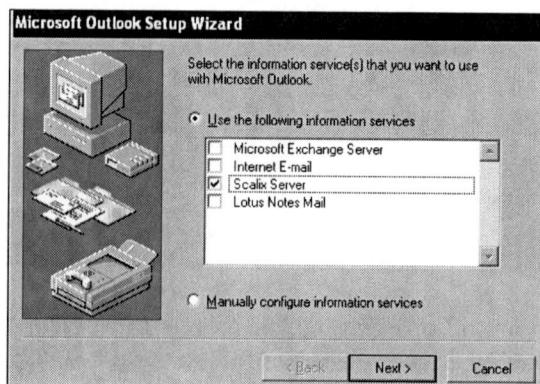

Activate the entry **Scalix Server** in the list of information services and click
on **Next** again. Now,you are asked to enter your login data in the following
dialog. Enter your Scalix login name and password here. *Don't* click on
**Next** here, but on the button **Advanced**.

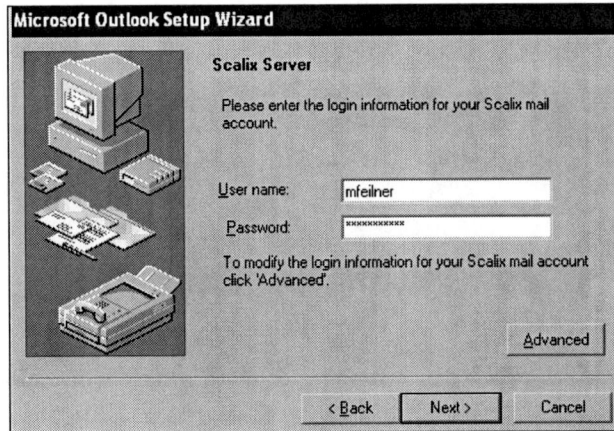

The user setup's advanced dialog is also pretty simple, all that is needed here is the
location of the Scalix server you want to use. In our example, the server is called
scalixbook.org:

Activate the entry **Save Password** if you don't want to be asked for credentials every
time you fetch mail or log into Scalix with your Outlook client. Click on **OK** to proceed.

# SmartCache

MS Outlook uses Scalix's SmartCache technology to store mail and groupware data locally on your hard drive. In the next step of the client installation, you can choose the directory where the cached data should be stored. Enter the directory or browse to your directory tree with the **Browse** button. After selecting the directory, click on **OK** to continue.

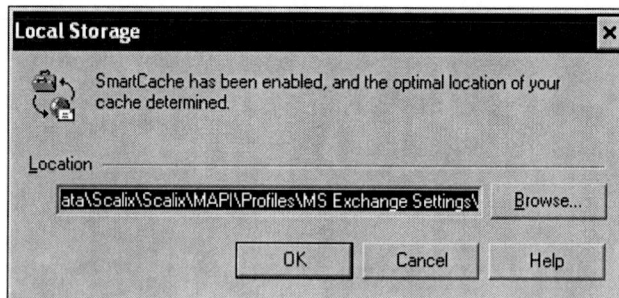

Once you have made it to this point, your Scalix account is available for Outlook. You receive congratulations from Scalix again. Click on the **Next** button to finish your client's setup.

Please note the following two options **Use SmartCache** and **Optimize for mobile Use**. The first option is always a good choice, because Scalix's SmartCache technology will speed up Outlook's mail and groupware functions only if it is checked, but maybe you have a network setup or file server environment where you do not want to use local storage. The same applies to **Optimize for mobile use**. If your system is a desktop system with continuous network connection to the Scalix server, leave this option unchecked. If you are running a laptop or if you are using a dial-up connection, activate this option to get a better performance.

Click on the **Next** button again, accept another round of friendly congratulations and click on the **Finish** button to exit configuration and start Outlook, if the installer does not do that automatically.

# Starting Outlook 2000

If you have set up a new account, or previously used a different mail program, Outlook will ask you if you want to make it the default **Manager for Mail, News and Contacts**:

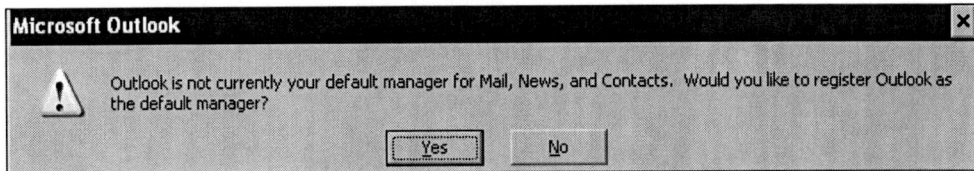

Obviously, if you are setting up a Scalix client, **Yes** is the best choice here. Outlook starts and the following screenshot shows the Microsoft program as a client for our server. You can see, there is no obvious difference to the standard (Exchange) look and feel.

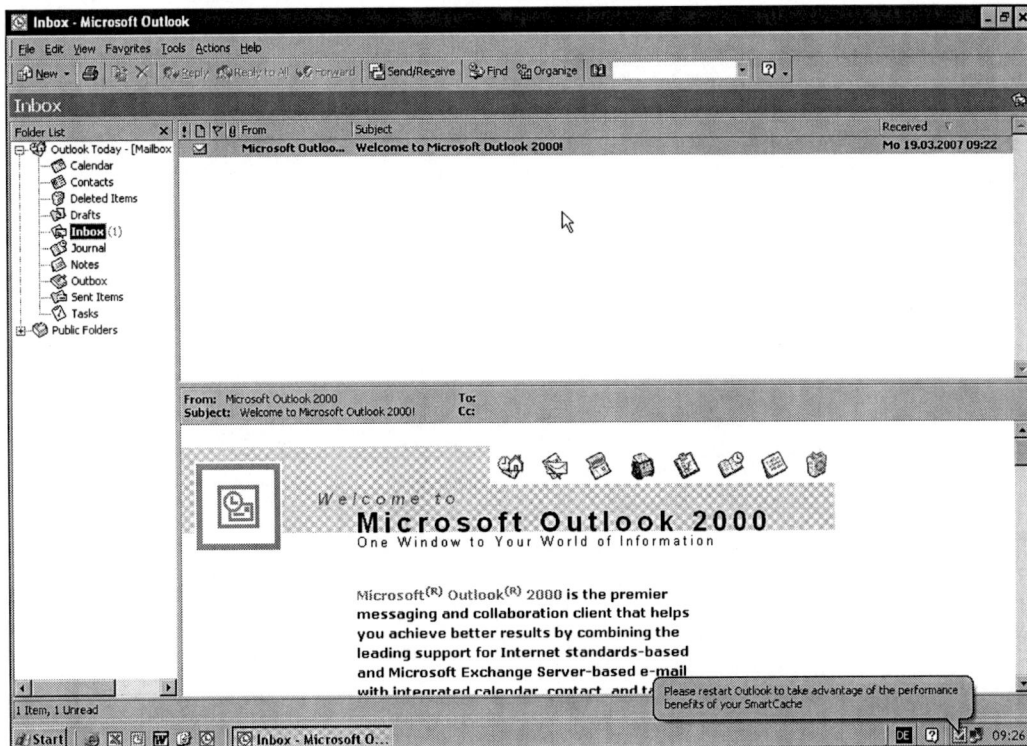

# The SmartCache Icon and Context Menu

There is a new icon in Window's system tray that pops up, saying **Please restart Outlook to take advantage of ... SmartCache**. Nothing serious has happened, the Scalix SmartCache needs to be initialized, and therefore a restart of Outlook is necessary. Shut down Outlook and start it again. After that, right-click on the new icon in the system tray and take a look at the context menu:

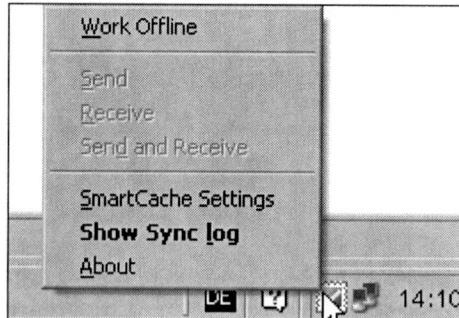

This context menu offers three interesting entries: Here you can tell SmartCache that your local Outlook should work offline now. You have full control over the SmartCache settings and examine the Synchronisation Log if you notice failures. Click on the entry **SmartCache Settings**:

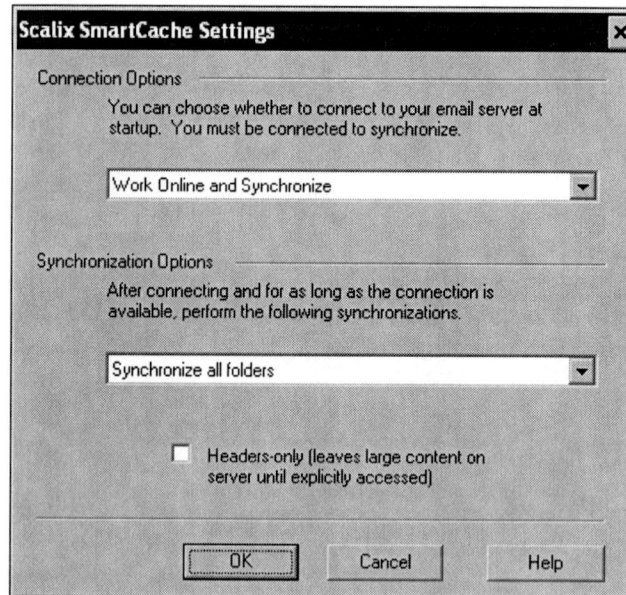

In this dialog, you (or the user you are preparing the account for) can tell SmartCache about the mode it should enter after startup, and specify details of the synchronization. This is another place where the setup for notebooks can be fine-tuned differently, compared to those of desktop PCs. If you run into trouble, check the file synclog.txt, which is displayed in Notepad when you select the entry **Show Synclog** from the menu. The level of detail of this logfile should be sufficient to solve most problems, or provide concise information to the Scalix people in the forum or at the support.

```
synclog.txt - Notepad
File  Edit  Format  View  Help
14:05:51   ========================= Scalix Cache Manager Log =========================
14:05:51   =============== Scalix Cache Manager Log ===============
14:05:51   Synchronization started 16.04.2007 14:05:51 for scalix
14:05:51   ========================================================

14:05:51   Connecting to Scalix server...
14:05:51   Connected

14:06:05   ========================================================
14:06:05   Starting Synchronization: FullSync: Hierarchy remote->local
14:06:05   ========================================================
14:06:05   Initializing
14:06:05     Connecting to cache
14:06:05     Succeeded
14:06:05     Connecting to Scalix server
14:06:05     Succeeded
14:06:06     Update Inet Gateway Address In Local Server
14:06:06     Succeeded
14:06:06     Update local/remote time
14:06:06   Synchronizing the following folder(s):
14:06:06     Mailbox - ngraf
14:06:06   Synchronizing folder hierarchy
14:06:06   Searching for changes on the Scalix server
14:06:06     Total transfer size is 1,087 bytes
14:06:06     Retrieving change definitions (size is 1,087 bytes)
14:06:06     Applying changes to cache folders
14:06:06   Searching for conflict candidates
14:06:06     No changes found
14:06:07   Summary Report:
14:06:07     The synchronization took 1.592 seconds
14:06:07     1 changes were applied to the cache, consisting of:
14:06:07       0    addition(s)
14:06:07       1    modification(s)
14:06:07       0    move(s)
14:06:07       0    deletion(s)
14:06:07     No changes were applied to the Scalix server
14:06:07     Messages submitted: 0
14:06:07     Conflicts: 0
14:06:07     Warnings: 0
14:06:07   Synchronization completed successfully
14:06:07   Initializing
14:06:07   Synchronizing the following folder(s):
14:06:07     Net Folder Inbox
14:06:07   Searching for conflict candidates
14:06:07     No changes found
14:06:07   Searching for changes on the Scalix server
14:06:08     Total transfer size is 800 bytes
14:06:08     Retrieving change definitions (size is 800 bytes)
14:06:08     Applying changes to cache folders
14:06:09   Summary Report:
14:06:09     The synchronization took 1.092 seconds
```

# Outlook 2003

If you are running Outlook 2003, the procedures are quite similar to the ones described above. However, there are some differences. Like we did before, switch to the Control Panel and double-click on **Mail**. Depending on your setup, you may be offered a list of existing profiles or get redirected directly to the **New Profile** dialog. If not, select **Prompt for a profile to be used** and click **Add**. Now, your system should be showing the following window:

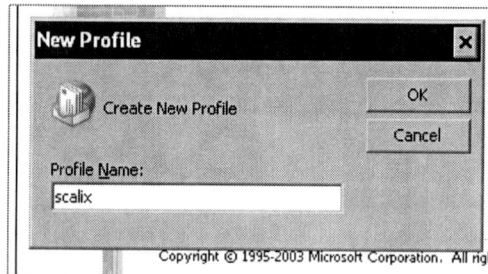

Enter a name for your profile, (we chose scalix, feel free to choose any name you like) and click on **OK**. Outlook's E-Mail Account Wizard will take you to the screen where you configure your new profile. Select **Add a new e-mail account** and click on **Next**.

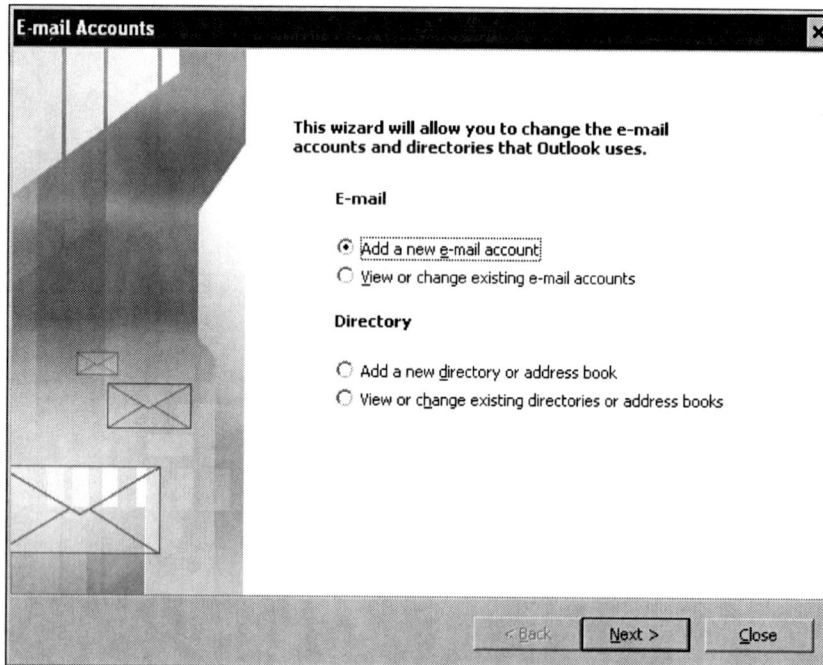

As you may have noticed, the dialog window where the user selects the groupware server he wants to use has changed. The former listing of Outlook 2000 has become a bulleted list of options, where Scalix — like the Lotus Notes plug-in — is hidden in another dialog. Select **Additional Server Types** and click on **Next** to reach the non-Microsoft groupware servers.

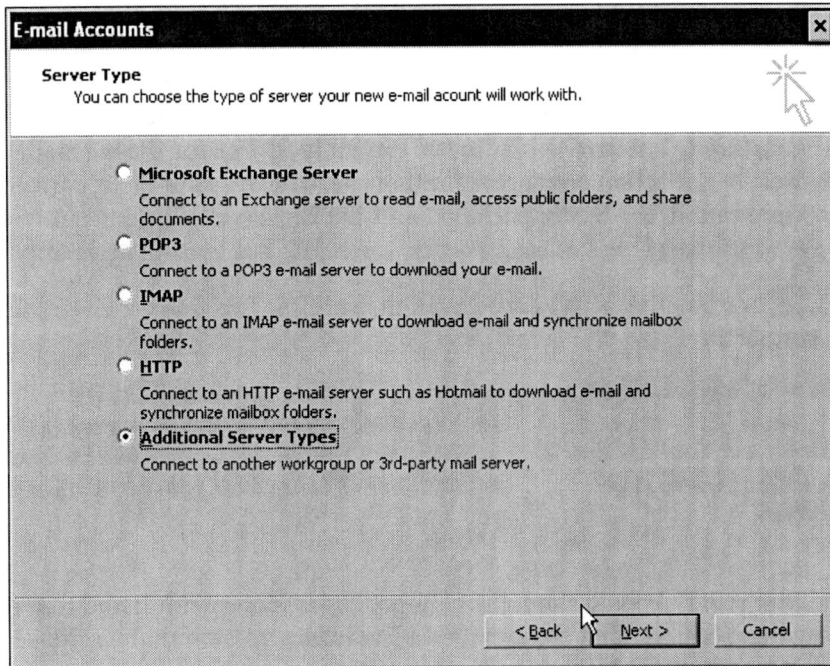

The next dialog contains a list of available groupware servers similar to that of the old Outlook version. Select **Scalix Server** and click on the button **Next**. Outlook now prompts you for your name and password on the Scalix server. Like before, the **Advanced** button is hiding the dialog where the URL of the Scalix server has to be entered.

What follows is very similar to the Outlook 2000 setup: Select a SmartCache location and check that the option **Use SmartCache** is checked in this dialog window. If you want to setup a mobile device like a laptop, check the entry **Optimize for mobile use**.

That's all, you receive congratulations and can proceed to start Outlook 2003 with your new Scalix account. Like before, the Scalix SmartCache icon in the system tray gives you control over synchronization and online or offline mode of your Scalix client.

# Installing the Scalix Evolution Connector

The only open source desktop client that is supported by Scalix is Evolution. Even though the GNOME program has a rich set of functions and is definitely the favorite Linux mailer of most groupware vendors, it suffers from huge problems concerning stabilitity. Even though the GNOME people are working hard to fix Evolution, there has not yet been a version of the program that could be used on a corporate desktop. Nevertheless, there is strong support for Evolution: Novell provides a Groupwise connector plug-in, there is a MS Exchange connector, and therefore many people believe that the strong support from the industry will one day push Evolution to enterprise readiness. Probably, it was for those reasons that Scalix provides an Evolution connector for their groupware suite. This connector is a standard component of the Scalix package, and the RPM containing it can be found in /scalix-version-GA/software/scalix_connect_evolution after unpacking.

On openSUSE or any other RPM-based system, a simple "rpm -ivh *package*" will install the connector:

```
scalix:~ # rpm -ivh evolution-scalix-11.0.1.22-ev26.i386.rpm
Preparing...               #####################################
## [100%]
   1:evolution-scalix      #####################################
## [100%]
scalix:~ #
```

Please note that you will need the following packages along with it and that there are very few distributions that come with an Evolution version that works—Fedora users who dare to compile Evolution from sources may have the best chances.

- Evolution-data-server
- Evolution -data-server-Devel
- Evolution -Devel
- Evolution -Webcal
- GNOME-common
- Evolution
- And probably many other GNOME-related packages, if you do not have GNOME installed

Once installed, you can fire up Evolution. On SUSE, the menu entry is hidden under **Internet | E-Mail | Evolution E-Mail** in the main menu. After first start, Evolution returns you to its setup wizard where the Scalix installer should be in the list of available groupware servers.

If you already had Evolution running, add a new account and select the Scalix server entry from the list of available servers. The Evolution Setup Assistant requires a user name and an address:

Click on the **Forward** button and select the Scalix server from the list of available groupware servers. This item is only available if you have successfully installed the Evolution-Scalix plug-in above. Enter your server's data and click on **OK**. If you are lucky, Evolution will start and present to you all the data the Scalix account contains.

# Kmail/Kontact as IMAP Client

According to Scalix's license policy, you are free to use as many IMAP-accounts as you like. The number of Internet users is not limited, but the functionality is: there is no groupware, only SMTP and IMAP services can be used. But there are some interesting features for other clients. For example, Kontact, the KDE groupware program is able to integrate LDAP directories with read and write support. Furthermore, it can store all of its groupware data in standard IMAP. If you are planning to use the KDE groupware client as the only groupware program, this may offer some possibilities.

The mail client component of the Kontact groupware suite is called Kmail. It is installed with every standard KDE environment. In order to integrate it with Scalix IMAP services, you have to configure a new IMAP or cached IMAP account for it. Select **Settings | Configure Kmail** from Kmail's or Kontact's menu. Click on **Accounts** and make sure that you are presented the **Receiving** tab . Now, click on the **Add** button. Depending on your preferences, select IMAP or cached IMAP. There is no SmartCache support for any other mail program but Outlook, so caching is done completely on your PC by the KDE program. In most cases, disconnected IMAP will be the best choice, since there is always a cached storage of your account on your local disk.

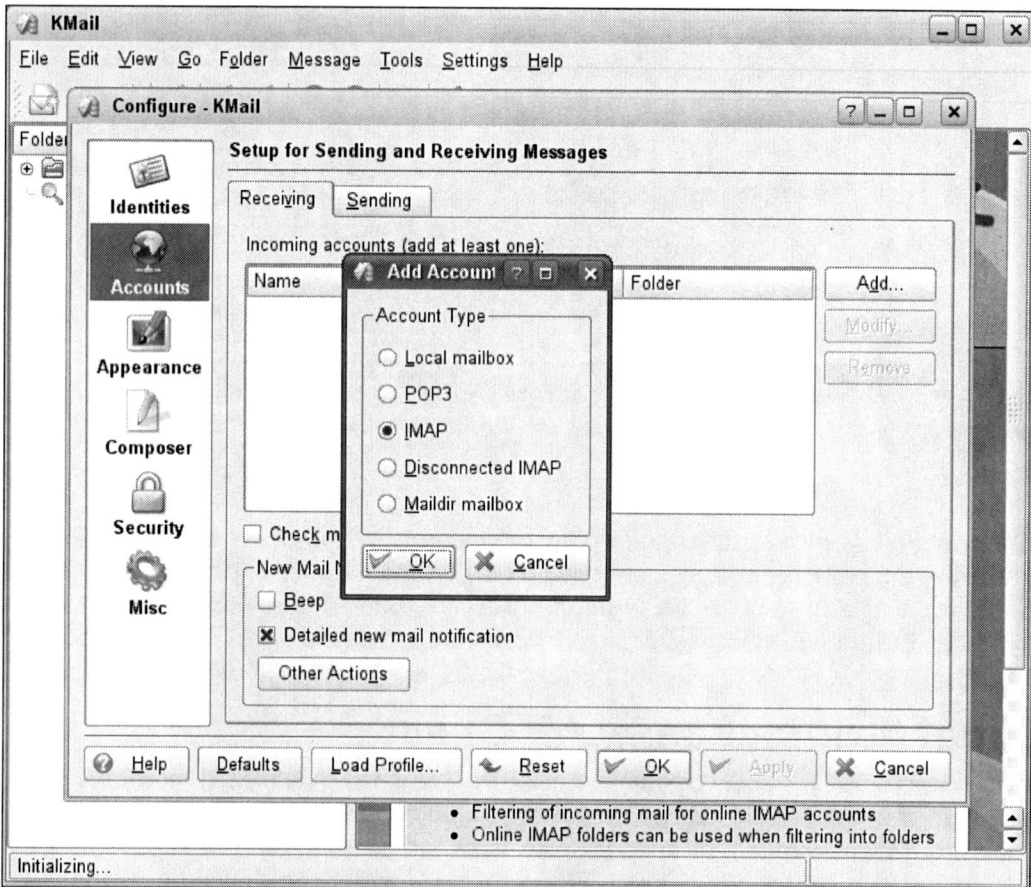

Select **Disconnected IMAP** or **IMAP** and click on **Ok**. Fill out the following forms with the IMAP data of your account on your Scalix server. If you want to send mail via the Scalix server, enter the SMTP data in Kmail's **Sending** tab.

# Kontact as Groupware Client with a Scalix Server

A very recent development shows the chances the KDE groupware client Kontact might have in the future. Some years ago, a friendly fork took place in the development, and a Kontact version specially optimized for the Kolab groupware started to gain ground. Later, this version was dubbed "KDE-PIM-Enterprise" and many other groupware connectors were integrated.

Enhanced stability, better performance, and slight differences in design and features made the enterprise version a success, and beginning with KDE 3.5.9, the two branches shall be merged again, and future versions will have the advantages of both branches.

One of the most interesting features of KDE-PIM-Enterprise may be the Scalix connector and the configuration utilities delivered with it. Unfortunately, only openSUSE 10.3 currently provides the KDE-PIM_Enterprise packages. All other users are waiting for a stable release and have to compile the source code. And, to get the sources, you have to download them from the online repository:

```
mfeilner:~/Temp/test/svn$ svn co svn://anonsvn.kde.org/home/kde/
branches/kdepim/enterprise/kdepim kdepim_enterprise
A    kdepim_enterprise/akregator
A    kdepim_enterprise/akregator/HACKING
A    kdepim_enterprise/akregator/AUTHORS
A    kdepim_enterprise/akregator/TODO
A    kdepim_enterprise/akregator/INSTALL
A    kdepim_enterprise/akregator/ChangeLog
(...)
A    kdepim_enterprise/kresources/exchange/resourceexchange.cpp
A    kdepim_enterprise/kresources/scalix
A    kdepim_enterprise/kresources/scalix/kabc
A    kdepim_enterprise/kresources/scalix/kabc/contact.h
A    kdepim_enterprise/kresources/scalix/kabc/resourcescalix.h
A    kdepim_enterprise/kresources/scalix/kabc/Makefile.am
A    kdepim_enterprise/kresources/scalix/kabc/resourcescalix_plugin.
cpp
A    kdepim_enterprise/kresources/scalix/kabc/scalix.desktop
(...)
```

Next, change into the newly created directory `kdepim_enterprise`, configure and compile the sources, for example, with `configure`, `make`, `make install`. If that does not work, you will have to read the documentation or perhaps wait until a stable version of the connector comes for your distribution.

After a successful installation, type `scalixwizard` at a command line under KDE.
The Scalix Configuration Wizard is started:

You should take this warning seriously, if you do not want to lose data. Click on **Run
Wizard Now** once you have stopped all KDE mail and groupware programs. In the
following window, type your Scalix server's data:

The Scalix Configuration Wizard enables the user to also set filtering rules, and shows the changes made. Once you are ready, click on **OK**, which will immediately cause Kontact to start the initial synchronization with the server:

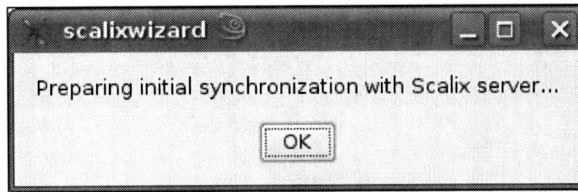

Don't worry, if this window disappears after you click on **OK**. Kontact is already started and is busily downloading mail, addresses, and calendar data from your server. The following is a screenshot from SUSE 10.3, which was the first distribution to deliver the enterprise branch of Kontact as default.

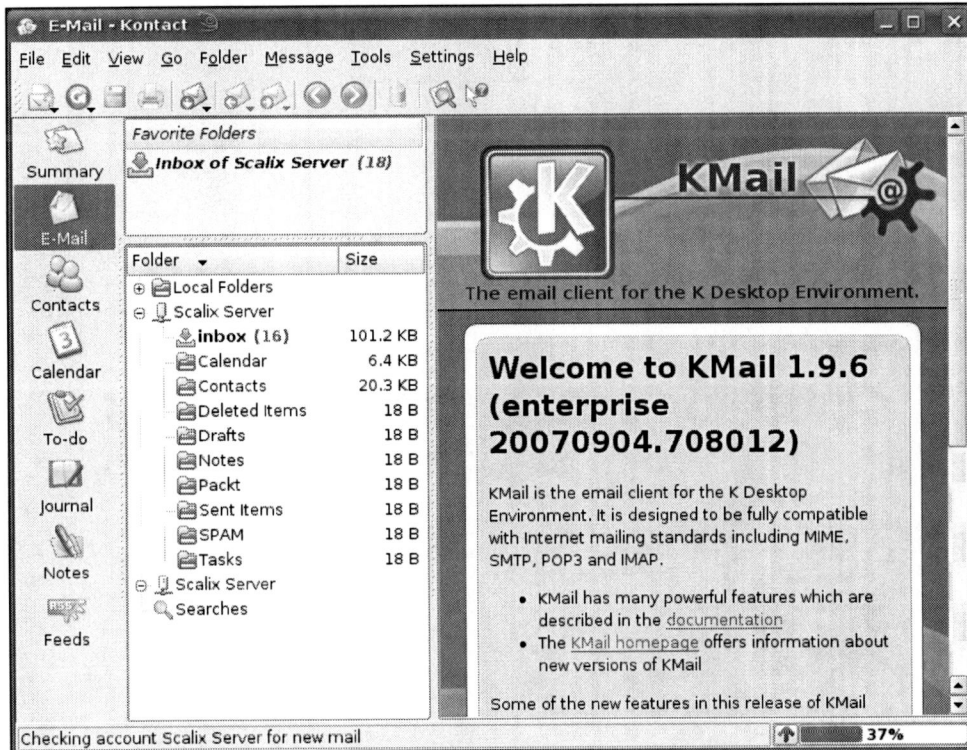

But the setup wizard is not the only feature in the KDE-PIM-Enterprise branch that comes with the Scalix connector. There is also a user-space tool called **scalixadmin**, which offers management for other accounts, delegations, out-of-office-replies and password change for the Scalix user.

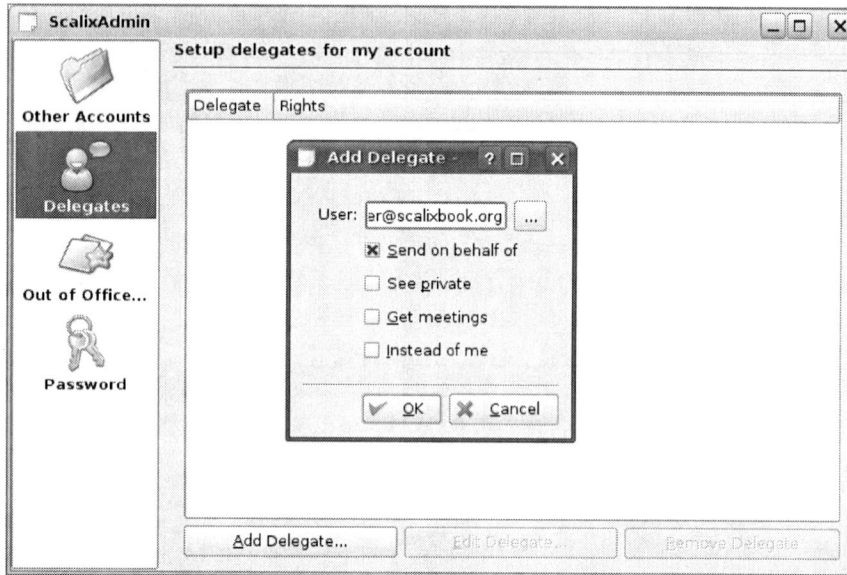

With the icon **Other Accounts**, the user controls visibility of other users' accounts in his client, the Add **Delegate**- dialog lets him decide who would represent him during his holiday.

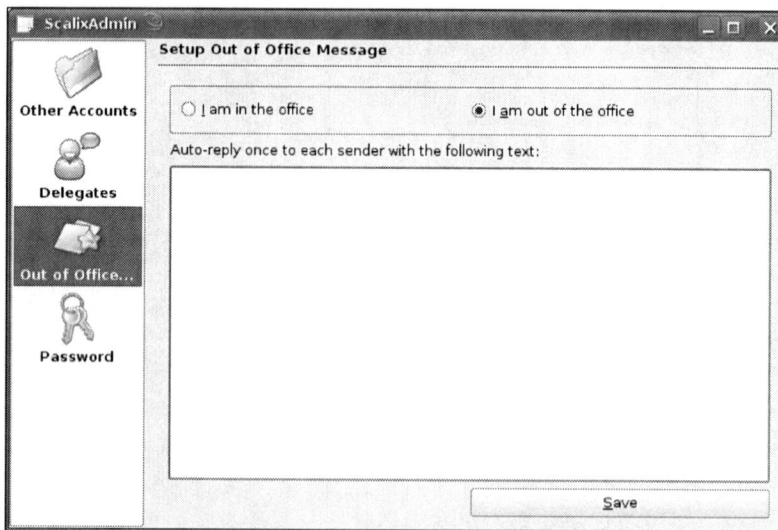

And if an out-of-office message is to be setup, the KDE user can simply enter it in this dialog. Finally, the password icon allows changing the login data without login into Scalix web acess anymore.

# Scalix Email with Thunderbird

A similar procedure applies to Thunderbird. Either you add a new account or you let the Account Wizard do this for you. Select **E-Mail Account** and enter your Scalix server's SMTP and IMAP data. Unlike Kontact/Kmail, Thunderbird has a concept of Online/Offline mode where you have to select single folders for offline use. The mailer from the Mozilla project then creates the local cache on-the-fly. And Thunderbird's address book tool can also read contacts from LDAP-directories.

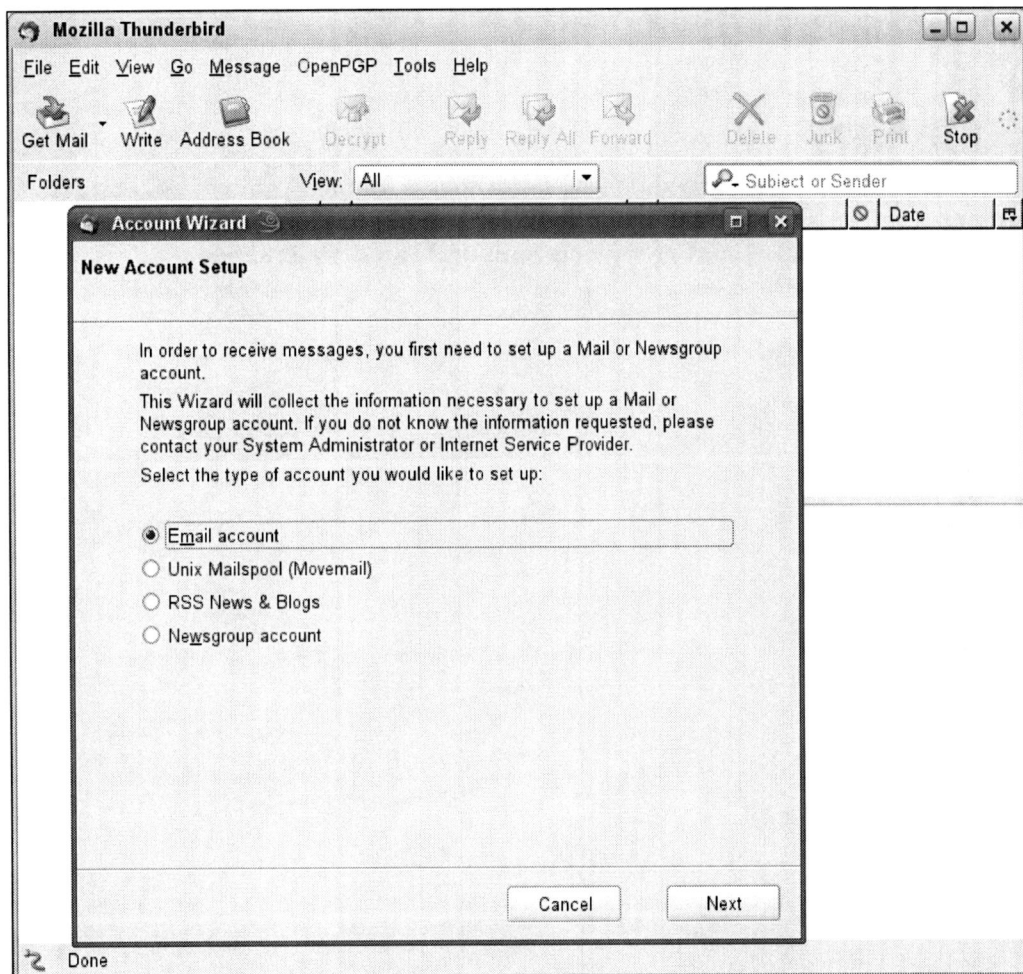

Beginning with Scalix 11.3, the developers have integrated a Caldav server, which allows Thunderbird's calendaring plug-in, Sunbird, to access the calendar data stored on the server. However, the client has only limited calendaring features and it may still take a while until Thunderbird can be used as a full-featured groupware client in companies. However, with the Caldav server, it is possible for the first time for Mac users to connect to a Scalix groupware server using ical.

For Evolution, Kontact/Kmail, and Thunderbird, there is very good online help and documentation, and all three programs have proven to be reliable IMAP clients. I leave it up to you to decide which one is the best for you. And, for the future, there is even more hope: First, among the KDE developers, there are some busily working on a free Scalix connector, including full groupware support. Second Scalix is planning to implement full Caldav support. This open Calendaring protocol is spoken by a wide variety of clients, including Apple's ical, Kontact, Thunderbird's calendaring tool Sunbird, and others.

# Summary

In this chapter, we have learned how to setup clients for our Scalix server. Besides Outlook 2000, we have also set up Outlook 2003 and Evolution. Kontact served as classical IMAP client without groupware support for the Scalix server.

# 7
# Common Options and Documentation

Beyond the scope of the Scalix Administration Console, there are a lot of places and programs with which the administrator can configure the Scalix server. To cover every aspect in detail would go beyond the scope of this book, but the following part of this chapter shows the most important configuration files and commands.

If you want to change parameters in these files, you should know exactly what you are doing. Although the Scalix configuration files are excellently documented, and the Scalix Administration guide gives a far more detailed overview of all options described here, you should nevertheless be very cautious.

Scalix is very strict concerning the exact syntax of each variable's parameters. Blanks, newlines, and other special characters are possible dangers for your server's configuration, and you may spend a lot of time recovering, searching the failure.

And last but not least, your changes are very likely to vanish the next time you are updating the software on your server.

# Global Configuration Files and Directories

There are some locations on a Scalix server where the administrator can set or override standard Scalix behavior. These settings are configured in the following files:

| File | Content |
| --- | --- |
| `/var/opt/scalix/sx/s/sys/general.cfg` | General configuration options for all Scalix users |
| `/var/opt/scalix/sx/s/sys/client.cfg/*` | Configuration for single hosts, the filename must be the hostname of the host that the configuration is meant for. |
| `/var/opt/scalix/sx/s/sys/user.cfg/*` | Configuration options for single users. The name of the file is the name of the user. |
| `/var/opt/scalix/sx/s/sys/route.cfg/*` | Configuration files for single routes. |
| `/var/opt/scalix/sx/s/sys/lang.cfg/*` | Configuration files for single languages. |

The first file is used for the general configuration of the server, and the directories below contain information for single hosts, clients, users, routes, and languages. The name of the configuration file is then used by Scalix to identify the host or client to which the configuration has to be applied for.

All configuration parameters in these files follow the same syntax: A parameter name is followed by an "=" and the value of the parameter. Please note that if you have or wish to use blank spaces or underscores in these parameters, you have to quote its value:

```
PARAMETER = " my_new_parameter with a blank space"
```

## Scalix—Outlook: mapi.cfg

For Windows users, there is a file called `mapi.cfg` that holds the client-side configuration of the Outlook client including:

- Auto-Upgrade
- Startup
- Addressing
- Directories
- Name Attributes

# Options and Parameters

Due to its age and the great amount of installations in big environments, Scalix has received a lot of contribution from developers regarding configuration. The list of valid options for the server configuration sums up to some 90 pages in the official Scalix documentation; the concise and always up-to-date list of valid parameters can be found online in the Scalix Knowledge base. The following part of this chapter shows some options, it is far from complete and can only show an excerpt of Scalix abundant set of options. In over 90 percent of all installations, you will not need to touch this. In fact, you should feel rather alarmed, whenever your Scalix server requires the usage of these commands.

The valid options are grouped in an alphabetical order:

- Archiver
- Audit Log
- Auto Actions
- Client Directory Access Server
- Daemon
- Directory, Directory Relay Server, Synchronization
- IMAP Clients
- Internet Addressing
- Mail Gateway
- Item Structure Server
- Local Delivery Services
- LDAP Server
- Non-Delivery Notification
- Offline Folder Synchronization
- omscan Options
- POP Server Options
- Public Folder Server
- Queue Management
- Search Server
- Service Router
- UAL Client Interface
- Virus Protection
- Xport Process

and miscellaneous options that obviously did not fit in any of the categories.

# General Options

Archiving, Directory Services, and more are specified with the options of the first section:

| Archiver, Auto Actions, and Directory Services | |
|---|---|
| Parameter | Function |
| ARCHIVE=TRUE | All messages will be archived to ~/scalix/archive, or to a different path specified here. An archiving server can be used, when you enter a third-party SMTP server here. |
| AUD_LOG_UX_NAME=TRUE | Users are identified with their Linux user names in the Scalix Audit Log. |
| AA_DEFAULT_LOGGING_ ON=TRUE | Starts logging on Scalix' Auto Actions. |
| AA_GLOBAL_LOGGING_ OFF=TRUE | Overrides all other logging directives and shuts down logging of Auto Actions. |
| AA_MAXCFG_LOG_ SIZE=1000000 | Sets the maximum size of a user's automatic action log file to 1 000 000 Byte. |
| DADM_DAEMON_TIME_TO_ EXIT=50s | As a standard, Scalix waits 30 seconds for a server daemon to exit. After that time, the daemon will receive a SIGKILL from Scalix. |
| DRS_HOST_RETRY_ TIMEOUT=time | How much time should Scalix wait if a remote Directory Server fails to answer, before trying again? |
| DRS_MAX_ CHILDREN=number | Specifies the number of processes that the Directory Relay Server can process at once. If you change this, remember that a directory server may have a limited number of binds. |

# IMAP and Addressing Options

The options in the IMAP client section define the behavior of the Scalix IMAP server:

| IMAP Client Options | |
|---|---|
| IMAP_AUTOMATIC_ MDN=FALSE | Do not send Automatic Message Delivery Notifications (MDN). |
| IMAP_FOLDER_PREFIX= | Define the string that precedes all public folders, so that users can easily distinguish them from normal folders. |
| IMAP_BB_FOLDER_ SEPARATOR= | Define the separator used for public folders. |
| IMAP_FOLDER_SEPARATOR= | Define the separator used for users' folders. |
| IMAP_CAPABILITIES= | Define the IMAP capabilities of the Scalix server. Valid options are: IMAP4, IMAP3rev1, CHILDREN, IDLE, LITERAL+,NAMESPACE. |

## IMAP Client Options

| | |
|---|---|
| IMAP_CONNECTION LIMIT=0 | The maximum number of concurrent IMAP connections. Not limited in a standard setup. |
| IMAP_CONNRATE_LIMIT= | The maximum number of concurrent IMAP connections the server accepts per second. |
| IMAP_IDLE_TIMEOUT= | Timeout before an open, unused IMAP connection is closed by Scalix. |
| IMAP_LOGLEVEL=number | Turns Scalix IMAP logging on or off. A value of 0 turns logging off, a value of 8 enables detailed IMAP protocol logging for debugging purposes. |
| IMAP_LOGFILE=file | Location and name of the IMAP log file that Scalix is supposed to use. Allows some macros like %p for the PID of the IMAP server process, %h for the client's host name, and %u for the client's user ID. |
| IMAP_MAILSTORE_ HOST=hostname | Specifies an external IMAP server to be used as the Scalix IMAP server. |
| IMAP_SEARCH_TIMEOUT=0 | After this amount of seconds, Scalix will abandon an IMAP search. |

The next set of options deal with how Scalix is supposed to handle emails traveling through the system:

## Internet Addressing Options

| | |
|---|---|
| INET_AUTOGEN_IA_ON_MODIFY, INET_DISPLAY_IA_ COMMENTS, | Internet Address Options: define the behavior of the Scalix server concerning messages, content, addresses, and attachments. |
| INET_INLINE_MAX_FILE_SIZE | |
| INET_... (...) | |

## Internet Mail Gateway Options

| | |
|---|---|
| BRW_MIME... | Options concerning handling of MIME attachments. |
| BRW_NAME_MAPPING=FALSE | The name of the sender will be mapped to the value set in the INTERNET-ADDR attribute in the Scalix directory, if this option is set to TRUE. |
| UX_NAME_MAPPING_ATTRIB= | Specify a different directory attribute for BRW_NAME_ MAPPING. |
| UX_NAME_MAPPING_DIR= | Use a different directory for mapping the sender or recipients' email addresses. If this is not set, Scalix's x.400 directory is used. |
| UX_NAME_MAPPING_DIR_ PASSWORD= | Specify a password for the directory to be used for emaill address mapping. |

# Item Structure Server, Local Delivery, and More

## Item Structure Server

| | |
|---|---|
| ISL_DISABLE_LOGGING=TRUE | Disables logging of the Item Structure Server. |
| ISL_LOG_IF_OFF=TRUE | Enables logging of the ISS even when the IS Server is turned off. Logs directly to the log files, saving performance. |

## Local Delivery Service Options

| | |
|---|---|
| LD_AUTOREPLY_CHECK_ON=TRUE | After a user has started auto-reply, a file with a list of addresses is created in /var/opt/scalix/user/. This list contains recipients that have received e.g. out-of-office replies (OOORs). Setting TRUE here makes Scalix check this list and helps to avoid sending OOORs more than once to a recipient. |
| LD_AUTOREPLY_EXPIRY_TIME=*days* | How many days should pass before a recipient receives a second Out-Of-Office-Replay? The address will be removed from the list. |
| LD_MAX_NEST_LEVEL=*depth* | How many levels of nested messages are allowed in one message? |

## Non-Delivery Options

| | |
|---|---|
| NDN_EM_SERIOUS_ONLY=TRUE | Only serious error messages for nondelivery failures are sent to the error manager. |

## Notification Server

| | |
|---|---|
| NS_INITIAL_MEM=*bytes* | How much memory should the Notification Server use at startup? |

## Offline Folder Synchronization

| | |
|---|---|
| OFS_ENABLED=FALSE | Activates Offline Folder Synchronization on the Server. TRUE can be overridden by setting FALSE in a user-specific config file. |
| OFS_LOG_AGE_LIMIT=*days* | Sets the limit of days for storing offline sync change logs. |
| OFS_LOG_SIZE_LIMIT=*kilobyte* | Sets the size limit for offline sync change logs. |
| OF_WORK_FILE_DIR=*path* | Where to store temporary files during synchronization. |

# POP, Public Folders, Queue

| **Pop Server Options** | |
|---|---|
| POP3_MAILSTORE_HOST=*hostname* | Use this external server as Scalix Message Store. |
| POP3_MAX_THREADS=*number* | Maximum amount of threads a single pop process will use. |
| **Public Folder Options** | |
| BBS_LOCAL_SYNC=FALSE | No synchronization with public folders on the local machine is allowed. |
| BBS_... | Several options defining Scalix's Public Folder Management. |
| **Queue Options** | |
| QM_DONT_READ_MSG_AT_STARTUP=FALSE | If set to TRUE, the Queue Manager will not try to read and send messages left in the message queue. This is useful for example if there are old, corrupt messages that made the queue manager stop its service. New messages will be transferred normally. |
| QM_FAILURE_DELAY_SEC=*seconds* | How many seconds should pass between two retries of the queue manager in case of a failure? |
| QM_MAX_FAILURES=*number* | How many times should the queue manager try to send a mail before giving up? |
| Q_TIME_OUT=*seconds* | After this amount of time, the Scalix queue manager will time out. Standard is 30 seconds. |
| **Search Server Options** | |
| SE_DEFAULT_DELAY=*seconds* | Within this span of seconds, no new search will be performed. Standard is 300 seconds. |
| SE_MAX_CHILDREN=*number* | How many child processes will the search service create as a maximum? |
| SE_MAX_OVERDUE_TIME=*seconds* | After how much time should a background search become priority over one-off searches? |

# Service Router and UAL Client Options

The Service Router Options make a large part of the options. They all start with SR_ , while the UAL Client Options start with UA. These two blocks of options cover the main part of the server side option set.

| Service Router Options | |
|---|---|
| SR_LD_BYPASS_ LSERVER=TRUE | Bypass local delivery and hand over the mail directly to the local Scalix server daemon like public folder server, error manager, request server, print server or directory sync server. |
| SR_MAX_HOP_COUNT=*number* | Defines the number of hops (normally one for each server) a mail can make before Scalix considers it as caught in a mail loop. |
| SR_MAX_NEST_LEVEL=*number* | Specifies the maximum level of nested messages within one mail. |
| SR_ROUTE_X400_TOOMX400_ *n=route_match* | Reroute messages from the X400 queue to the OMX400 queue for recipients whose addresses match the pattern. Whereas the OMX400 is used for internal mail traffic, the X400 queue is used for external, non-Scalix systems. "n" can be of 1 to 8 and thus allows eight policies for this option, the long list of allowed targets for route_match can be found in Scalix's documentation. |
| SR_USEX500_DIR=TRUE  SR_USEX500_DIR=*dirname* | Use the x500 Directory to resolve DDNs. Add a directory named dirname to add an external directory server. |
| **UAL Client Options** | |
| UAKD_CONNRATE_LIMIT | Maximum number of client connections allowed per second. |
| UAKD_LISTEN_Q_SIZE | Number of TCP/IP socket connections that are allowed to the UAL server. |
| UAKD_NICE_VALUE | Priority of the UAL server. Values between -20 and 20 are accepted, where -20 is highest priority. Default is -10. |
| UAKD_SERVER_PUSH_ NOTIFS=TRUE | Activates the Push Mechanism where clients receive notifications automatically. Deactivating this option will increase performance, but cause problems with Outlook and other IMAP clients. A lot of network traffic will result, as clients will start polling for results. |
| UAL_ALLOW_DISABLED_ CLIENTS=FALSE  UAL_DISABLED_CLIENTS=*list* | Allow only IMAP clients that are not on list, if set to FALSE. |

## Service Router Options

| | |
|---|---|
| UAL_BB_ACL_ DEFAULT=*permissions* | Standard permissions for public folders, specified in a comma separated list of S (see), R (read),A (attach) ,D (delete), C (config). Standard is S, R, A. |
| UAL_DIR_LIST_SORT_ORDER | Specifies the sort order of Directory attributes. |
| UAL_DIR_LIST_SORT_PROG | Specifies the sort program used for sorting of directory entries for UAL clients. Standard is /usr/bin/sort -f. |
| UAL_DISABLE_BB=FALSE | Disables public folder access. |
| UAL_DISABLE_NESTED_ BBS=TRUE | No UAL client is allowed to create public folders under top-level public folders. |
| UAL_DISALLOW_AUTO_ PASSWORD | Forbid client access if the client has received his password from a configuration file. |
| UAL_DISALLOW_NON_USER_ PASSWORD | Forbid client access if the client has not received his password interactively from a user. |
| UAL_DL_SIZE_LIMIT=*kilobyte* | Sets the maximum size of distribution lists. |
| UAL_DO_LONG_INET_CHECK | Have Scalix do the POP and IMAP services check for Internet addresses. Checks are specified in the files /var/opt/scalix/sx/s/sys/unixin.rules and unixmap.in. |
| UAL_IDLE_TIMEOUT UAL_IDLE_SHUTDELAY UAL_SERIAL_IDLE_ SHUTDELAY UAL_LOCAL_IDLE_ SHUTDELAY UAL_DEAD_TIMEOUT UAL_LOCAL_DEAD_TIMEOUT | Local and Remote Timeouts and additional buffers (SHUTDELAY) for client connections. |
| UAL_ISO7... | Some options around ISO7 conversion to ISO8859/1. |
| UAL_KILL_REMOTE_SIGNON2 | Allow Scalix to kill a current session if a user signs in again. |
| UAL_LIST_CACHE_ SIZE=*number_of_message_prts* | Maximum amount of message parts held in memory by an UAL process. Standard is 4 (header and three body parts). This feature reduces I/O on the server. |
| UAL_LOCAL_IGNORE_ PASSWORD | No password is required for logging in. Works only for local clients and Linux logins. |
| UAL_MAX_SIGNON_PER_ USER | Maximum number of simultaneous sessions from a single user. The default is 17. |

## Service Router Options

| | |
|---|---|
| UAL_MSTORE_SIZE_<br>LIMIT=*kilobyte* | Maximum size of the message store. |
| UAL_NO_WB_EMPTY | Don't clear Waste Paper Basket on signing off. |
| UAL_WB_SIZE_LIMIT=*kilobyte* | Maximum size of the Waste Basket. |
| UAL_PASSWORD_AGED= | What effect should an expired password have? Allowed values are IGNORE (no action is taken), WARN (the user is warned), ERROR (signon fails). |
| UAL_PWD_WARNING_<br>DAYS=*days* | Users are warned for days before their passwords are invalid. |
| UAL_POP3_HOSTNAME<br>UAL_POP3_LANGUAGE<br>UAL_POP3_TIMEOUT | Specify hostname, language, and timeout for messages received via POP. |
| UAL_POP3_TRACE | Define the location of the log file for POP3 connections. |
| UAL_PRINT_SERVER_ONLY | If set to TRUE, all printing goes through the Scalix Print server. |
| UAL_SINGLE_TEMP_DIR | The location of the directory with the temporary files of users. Should have read/write/execute access and SUID bits set (chmod 771 path), an owner of Scalix and the group called office. |
| UAL_SIZE_ERR_TO_USER<br>UAL_SIZE_ERR_TO_ENU<br>UAL_SIZE_MSG_TO_USER<br>UAL_SIZE_ON_RECEIPT<br>UAL_SIZE_ON_SEND<br>UAL_SIZE_WARNING_<br>BOUNDS<br>UAL_SIZE_WARNING_LIMITS | Actions that have to be taken when a certain limit is exceeded. Whenever a limit is configured, one of these options have to be adjusted to have an action performed. |

Please note that whenever you set a user limit in any of these options, you will need to control or add an action if this limit is exceeded. Otherwise, no action will be taken and the limit is worthless.

# Virus Protection

| **Virus Protection** | |
| --- | --- |
| SR_VS_DO_VIRUS_SCAN=FALSE | Set this to TRUE to activate Virus Scanning. |
| SR_VS_IGNORE_ITEM_TYPES=*filetype* | Don't scan. |
| SR_VS_TEST_SCAN_SL=*path* | The location of the virus test library. |
| SR_VS_SCAN_TYPE=Test Scan / Generic | With "Test Scan", Scalix uses the Test library specified in SR_VS_TEST_SCAN_SL, with generic, the library specified in /var/opt/scalix/sys/omvscan.cfg is used. |

# Configuring Scalix Components

The various Scalix components have their configuration files. We will skip the configuration of Apache and Tomcat to the next chapter (security), where we set up Scalix with Https and concentrate on the following Scalix components:

- Web Access
- Admin Server
- Scalix Res Agent
- Web Access Mobile
- SIS Search and Indexing Server
- Messaging and API Platform

All of the following configuration files reside under /var/opt/scalix/instance/. For our example domain scalixbook.org, the *instance* will be *sx*.This parameter is chosen by Scalix from the first and last letter of your machine's hostname. In our example, the hostname is Scalix, thus the config file for Scalix web access resides in /var/opt/scalix/sx/webmail/swa.properties. Below are some example configurations from one of our test servers generated during the manual installation of Scalix. During this process, the administrator has to change some parameters manually. In normal installation mode, the Scalix Installer will do this for you.

| Service | Configuration file | Example configuration |
|---|---|---|
| Web Access | .../webmail/swa. properties | swa.email.domain=scalixbook.org<br>swa.email.imapServer=scalixbook.org<br>swa.email.smtpServer=scalixbook.org<br>swa.settings.rulesWizardURL=<br>http://scalixbook.org/Scalix/rw<br>swa.ldap.1.server=scalixbook.org<br>swa.ldap.1.port=389<br>swa.ldap.2.server=scalixbook.org<br>swa.ldap.2.port=389<br>platform.url=http://scalixbook.<br>org/api<br>swa.platform.enabled=true<br>swa.soap.soapRequestTimeout=60 |
| Admin Server | .../caa/scalix.res/ config/ubermanager. properties | ubermanager.query.<br>server=scalixbook.org<br>ubermanager.kerberos.mode=false<br>ubermanager.kerberos.principalName=<br>ubermanager.kerberos.kdc=<br>ubermanager.kerberos.realm=<br>ubermanager.console.<br>externalAuth=false<br>ubermanager.console.allowExternalAu<br>thChoice=false<br>ubermanager.console.maxListSize=100<br>ubermanager.console.<br>localDomains=scalixbook.org<br>ubermanager.console.authDomains=<br>ubermanager.console.modifyExternalS<br>yncedAuthId=false<br>ubermanager.query.server.port=389<br>ubermanager.configured=true<br>ubermanager.version=11.0.2 |
| Scalix RES Admin Agent | .../res/config/res. properties | res.kerberos.mode=<br>res.kerberos.kdc=<br>res.kerberos.realm=<br>res.kerberos.allowedclients=uberman<br>ager/scalixbook.org<br>res.ubermanager.host=scalixbook.org<br>res.tomcat.tcp.port=80<br>res.configured=true<br>res.version=11.0.2 |

| Service | Configuration file | Example configuration |
|---------|-------------------|----------------------|
| Scalix Messaging API Plattform | `.../platform/ platform.properties` | `imap.host=scalixbook.org` <br> `smtp.host=scalixbook.org` <br> `ldap.port=389` <br> `hibernate.connection.url = jdbc: postgresql://scalixbook.org:5733/ scalix` <br> `hibernate.connection.password = secret` |
| Web Access Mobile | `../mobile/mobile. properties` | `platform.url=http://scalixbook.org/ api` <br> `(...)` |
| SIS Scalix Search and Indexing Service | `.../sis/sis. properties` | `index.language=English` <br> `index.client.whitelist=192.168.1.1` <br> `search.client.whitelist=192.168.1.1` |

# Administration Commands

The second part of this chapter is all about Scalix commands. The mail server comes with an abundant list of administration commands. Scalix 11 has 254 commands in its path that provide administrative functions. The HP OpenMail heritage can be found here: all of these commands start with "om". Later, Scalix Inc. added quite a number of programs to that list, most of them start with "sx". The following pages contain a selection of commands with explanation, options, and examples:

# Start/Stop Scalix

| Program | Options | Function | Example |
|---------|---------|----------|---------|
| omon | **-s services**: start a list of services, if no services are specified, all will be started. | Starts one or more services/daemons. | Start every installed service: <br><br> omon -s |
|  | **-a daemons**: start a list of daemons. If no daemons are specified, all will be started. |  |  |
|  | **-w**: waits for the daemons to start or fail. |  |  |
|  | **-f file**: A file containing a list of services to start (one service per line). |  |  |

| Program | Options | Function | Example |
|---------|---------|----------|---------|
| omoff | **-d delay**: delay in minutes to wait until stopping services/daemons.<br><br>**-q**: be less verbose (quiet).<br><br>**-w**: wait for all services/daemons to stop.<br><br>**-s service**: list of services.<br><br>**-a daemon**: list of daemons.<br><br>-f **file**: file containing a list of services/daemons separated by a new line. | Stop one (or more) services/daemons. This will not affect daemons that are configured to run continuously. Have a look at omshut (below) to completely shutdown Scalix with all services and daemons. | Wait 30 minutes before stopping every running (Scalix) service on the system:<br><br>omoff -d 30 -s |
| omrc | **--noservices**: do not start any service.<br><br>**--nodaemons**: do not start any daemon.<br><br>**--quiet**: no non-essential output. | Start Scalix | omrc --quiet |
| omshut | **-t time-out**: wait time-out minutes for processes to terminate.<br><br>**--quiet**: be less verbose. | Completely stop Scalix (every running service and daemons) | Shutdown Scalix immediate:<br><br>omshut |

# Status and Other Information

| Program | Options | Function | Example |
|---------|---------|----------|---------|
| omstat | -s: show status on all installed services<br><br>-a: show status on all installed daemons.<br><br>-u *service*: print signed on users on the specified service.<br><br>-q *queue*: show messages in scalix queue. For a list of allowed queues have a look at **man 5 scalix-server**<br><br>-d: show the messages in the deferred message queue.<br><br>-m *msg_ref*: displays additional information about a message listed by `omstat -q` or `omstat -d`.. | Display the System status | List status of all installed services:<br><br>omstat -a |

| Program | Options | Function | Example |
|---------|---------|----------|---------|
| omshowlog | **-e** : show all entries in the event log.<br>**-f** *from-date*: show entries made from or after *from-date*.<br>**-F** *from-time*: show entries made at or after *from-time*.<br>**-t** *to-date*: show entries made on or before *to-date*.<br>**-T** *to-time*: show entries made at or before *to-time*.<br>**-p** *min*: show entries made during the previous *min* minutes.<br>**-d** *dir*: define an other directory with log files.<br>**-l** *level*: only show entries with log level *level* or higher.<br>**-n** *name[/mailnode]*: show entries related to the user *name* at *mailnode*.<br>**-s** *service*: only show entries made by *service*.<br>**-i** *pid*: show entries made by the process with process ID *pid*.<br>**-P**: show process ID for every shown entry. | Show the Event Log | Show messages from April 12th 2007 till now:<br><br>omshowlog -f 04.12.2007 |
| ommon | **-m** *mount-point* : mount point containing the Scalix message store.<br>**-q** *queue-limit*: show only queues with *queue-limit* or more messages in queue.<br>**-u** *mail-addr*: email output of omon to *mail-addr*. | Monitoring Scalix operations | Send output of ommon to private mail address:<br><br>ommon -u foo@ bar.org |
| omenquire | **-s** : output to system shell instead of generating a log file.<br>**-f** *file* : use *file* as log file.<br>**-o** : overwrite an existing log file, create otherwise.<br>**basic** : output basic system status.<br>**other** : output general system status.<br>**desk** : HP Desk Gateway status.<br>**x.400** : x.400 status.<br>**unix** : Internet gateway status.<br>**sms** : sms gateway status.<br>**all** : all of the above status information.<br>use "-" for above options to invert function (e.g. **-sms** means "do not report sms gateway status") | Display status information about the Scalix System and the underlying Operation System. | omenquire -s all |

# User Management

| Program | Options | Function | Example |
|---------|---------|----------|---------|
| omaddu | **-l** *language*: set the language a remote client should use. | Add user to mailnode | Create user fooadmin on mailnode scalixbook. org  with administration rights and the Authentication-ID 2323: |
| | **-p** *password*: defines user password. | | |
| | **--lock-password**: lock password after creating. | | |
| | **-e**: password is expired. This will force the user to change the default password, provided by you the first time he signs on. | | omaddu -n fooadmin/ scalixbook.org -c admin 2323 |
| | **-x**: do not add user to the system default directory. | | |
| | **--class** *full* | *limited*: define the user class for this user. | | |
| | **--swa** *Y* | *N*: user will be able to access SWA (or not). | | |
| | **--sender** *Y* | *N*: setting this option to N will suppress a sender header on outgoing mails. | | |
| | **-n** *name/mailnode[/internet-address]*: personal name and mailnode for the user. | | |
| | **-u** *login*: corresponding Unix/Linux login name (User account). | | |
| | **-a** *alias*: defines an alternative personal name. | | |
| | **-c** *admin* | *mboxadmin*: add special capabilities to the user account. | | |
| | **Authentication-ID**: a system wide unique ID for the user. Authentication-ID is **not** case sensitive. Will be created automatically if not provided. | | |

| Program | Options | Function | Example |
|---------|---------|----------|---------|
| omdelu | **-n** *name/[mailnode]*: personal name (and mailnode) of the user. This must be a unique identifier on the system. | Delete a user. | Delete user with authentication-id 2323: |
| | **-f** *file*: a file containing a list of name/mailnode pairs (one in each line). | | omdelu 2323 |
| | **-U** *Unix-ID*: the UID or Login name of the user. | | |
| | **Authentication-ID**: the user's Authentication-ID | | |
| omshowu | **-m** *mailnode*: show all users on mail node. | Show details on user account(s) | Display all locked user accounts: |
| | **-n** *authentication-id*: show user information for user with the exact authentication-id provided. | | omshowu -l |
| | **-n** *name[/mailnode]*: show user information for user name/ mailnode. | | |
| | **-U** *Unix Login*: show information on the user with the specified UID or Unix login name. | | |
| | **-r** *Y | N*: list all users with open (Y) or closed (N) mailboxes. | | |
| | **-a**: list users with admin capabilities. | | |
| | **-l**:list locked user accounts. | | |
| | **-e**: list users with expired passwords. | | |

# Installation and Configuration

| Program | Options | Function | Example |
|---------|---------|----------|---------|
| omcptree | **-p**: preview mode<br>**-v**: verbose output<br>*source*: source directory<br>*target*: destination directory | Copy Directory hierarchy tree | |
| ommakeom | **-h** *hostname* : use *hostname* as hostname instead of default value.<br>**-d** *directory* : the directory where the Scalix instance should be created.<br>**-n \| --noautostart** : do not start this instance automatically at system startup.<br>*name*: name of the instance. | Create a Scalix instance | Create an instance named scalixbook:<br><br>ommakeom scalixbook |
| omdelom | **-f**: be quiet.<br>**-a**: delete all Scalix instances.<br>*name*: delete Scalix instance with the specified name. | Delete a Scalix instance | Delete the Scalix instance named scalixbook and ignore error messages:<br><br>omdelom -f scalixbook |
| ompatchom | **-a**: update all instances.<br>*name*: update a specific instance. | Update a Scalix instance. | Update all instances:<br><br>ompatchom -a |
| omcheck | **-i**: check every component for correct file permissions and ownerships.<br>**-s**: output shell-script to correct file permissions to stdout.<br>**-d**: check (with -i) or fix (with -s) ownership and permissions of user data files. | Check ownership and file permissions on Scalix files | Check all components installed on the system:<br><br>omcheck -i |
| omvers | **-f file**: specify a script, binary or message catalog to list detailed version information.<br>**-v**: only show version number. | Version information on Scalix binaries, scripts, and message catalogs. | Print version of omvers:<br><br>omvers -f /opt/scalix/bin/omvers |

# Tuning

| Program | Options | Function | Example |
|---|---|---|---|
| omdiropt | **-a** *tag*: Directory is sorted on *tag* (e.g. Surname). Omshowatt will display a list of valid (language dependent) attributes.<br>**-d** *directory*: optimize *directory*.<br>**-t** *type*: directory type—either **(p)**ersonal or **(s)**hared.<br>**-p** *password*: the password needed to access the directory (if set).<br>**-u**: regenerate all probe attributes. | Optimize a Directory | Optimize personal directory CONTACTS for efficient search on the X.400 surname attribute (S):<br>omdiropt -a S -d CONTACTS -t p |
| omdoptall | *tag*: The (language dependent) attribute *tag*, the directory is sorted by. | Optimize all directories | Optimize all directories sorted by the X.400 Common Name (CN):<br>omdoptall CN |

# Services

| Program | Options | Function | Example |
|---|---|---|---|
| omldapadd | **-b**: any value starting with '/' are treated as binary values.<br>**-c**: do not stop operations on errors.<br>**-r**: replace existing values<br>**-n**: performe a test run. This will not edit any entry.<br>**-v**: verbose mode<br>**-k**: use kerberos authentication<br>**-K**: same as -k, but only performs the first step of authentication.<br>**-d** *level*: set LDAP debugging level to *level*.<br>**-f** *file*: read entries from file (instead of stdin).<br>**-D** *binddn*: bind to X.500. Directory as *binddn* (LDAP DN).<br>**-w** *passwd*: use *passwd* for simple authentication.<br>**-h** *hostname*: the hostname that the LDAP server is running on.<br>**-p** *port*: (TCP-)port where the LDAP servers is listening for connections.<br>**-V** *version*: LDAP version (2 or 3) to be used to connect to LDAP server.<br>**-e** *encoding*: set character encoding for non-LDIF data (including command line).<br>**-L** *ldformat*: set character encoding for LDIF-data. | Add LDAP entries | Read entries in /tmp/ entries.ldif and store them in your ldap-server:<br><br>omldapadd /tmp/entries. ldif |

| Program | Options | Function | Example |
|---------|---------|----------|---------|
| omldapdelete | **-n**: perform a test run. | Delete LDAP entries | Directly delete entry in LDAP using kerberos authentication: |
| | **-v**: be verbose. | | |
| | **-k**: use kerberos authentication. | | |
| | **-K**: only perform first step of kerberos auth. | | |
| | **-c**: continue operation even on errors. | | omldapdelete -k "cn=Markus Feilner, o=Scalix" |
| | **-d level**: set LDAP debuging level. | | |
| | **-f file**: read file and perform an ldapsearch on each line. | | |
| | **-D binddn**: bind to the X.500 Directory as binddn. | | |
| | **-w passwd**: use passwd for simple authentication. | | |
| | **-h host**: the hostname of the machine the LDAP server is running on. | | |
| | **-p port**: TCP-port where the LDAP server is listening for new connections. | | |
| | **-V version**: specify LDAP version (2 or 3). | | |
| | **-e encoding**: set character encoding for non-LDIF data. | | |
| omldapsearch | **-n**: perform a test run. | Perform an LDAP search | Search for entry with the CommonName "Markus Feilner": |
| | **-u**: output user friendly form of DN. | | |
| | **-v**: be verbose. | | |
| | **-k**: use kerberos authentication. | | |
| | **-K**: same as -k, but only performs first step of authentication. | | omldapsearch "cn=Markus Feilner" |
| | **-t**: write retrieved attributes to temporarily created files (useful for non-ASCII attributes like photos). | | |
| | **-A**: only retrieve attributes without values. | | |
| | **-L ldformat**: display results in LDIF format. | | |
| | **-R**: do not follow referrals. | | |
| | -F seperator : specify a field separator (default is "="). | | |
| | **-S attribute**: sort entries by attribute. | | |
| | **-d level**: set the LDAP debugging level. | | |
| | **-f file**: read file and perform a search on each line. | | |
| | **-D binddn**: bind to the X.500 directory as binddn. | | |

| Program | Options | Function | Example |
|---------|---------|----------|---------|
| | **-w passwd**: use passwd for simple authentication. | | |
| | **-h hostname**: the hostname the LDAP server is running. | | |
| | **-p port**: the TCP port the LDAP server is listening for incoming connections. | | |
| | **-b searchbase**: start search beginning from searchbase. | | |
| | **-s scope**: specify a search scope (base, one or sub). | | |
| | **-a deref**: specify alias dereferencing (never, always, search or find). | | |
| | **-l timelimit**: maximum number of seconds to wait for a search. | | |
| | **-z sizelimit**: maximum number of entries to retrieve from a search. | | |
| | **-V version**: specify LDAP version (2 or 3) the server is using. | | |
| | **-e encoding**: set character encoding for non-LDIF data. | | |
| omdelete | **-u** *name[/mailnode]*: The personal name (and mailnode if necessary) of the Scalix user. | Delete a message | Delete second message for the user Markus Feilner using the password DefAceD: |
| | **-p** *passwd*: the user's password (if set). | | |
| | **-m**: message number is an absolute reference (instead of temporary). | | |
| | **-q**: quiet mode. | | omdelete -u "Markus Feilner" -p DefAceD 2 |
| | *message-number*: The number of the message to be deleted. | | |
| omlist | **-u name[/mailnode]**: The personal name (and mailnode if necessary) of the Scalix user. | List messages | Display all unread messages for user Markus Feilner: |
| | **-p passwd**: the user's password (if set). | | |
| | **-k character-set**: the character-set configured for his terminal. | | |
| | **-m**: display absolute reference number. | | omlist -u "Markus Feilner" -p DefAceD -n |
| | **-n**: list only messages that have not been read yet. | | |
| | **-o format**: set the output format. See man page for details. | | |
| | **-q**: quiet mode. | | |

| Program | Options | Function | Example |
|---------|---------|----------|---------|
| omread | **-u** *name[/mailnode]*: the personal name (and mailnode) of the Scalix user. | Read a message | Read second message of user Markus Feilner: |
| | **-p** *passwd*: the user's password. | | |
| | **-i**: interactive mode. | | omread -u "Markus Feilner" -p DefAceD 2 |
| | **-m**: specify message number as an absolute reference number. | | |
| | **-k** *character-set*: the character set configured for the user's terminal. | | |
| | **-q**: quiet mode. | | |
| | **-w** *width*: the column at which message text is truncated. | | |
| | **-x** *indent*: a text, preceding every line of text displayed in the message. | | |
| | *message-number*: the number of the message to be shown. | | |
| omsend | **-u** *name[/mailnode]*: the personal name (and mailnode) of the Scalix user. | Send a message | Markus sends a message to Norbert containing the text in /tmp/message: |
| | **-p** *passwd*: the user's password. | | |
| | **-s** *subject*: the subject of the message. | | |
| | **-t** *to*: the recipients address of the message. | | omsend -u "Markus Feilner" -p DefAceD -s Testmail -t "Norbert Graf" -a /tmp/message |
| | **-f** *from*: the senders address. | | |
| | **-c** *cc*: the address of a copy recipient. | | |
| | **-b** *bcc*: the address of a blind copy recipient. | | |
| | **-l** *list*: a text file containing one or more recipients (one name per line). | | |
| | **-a** *file*: the name of an ASCII-File to be attached to the message. | | |
| | **-r** *file*: the name of a binary file to be attached to the message. | | |
| | **-z** *filetype file*: the numerical file code as listed in ~/nls/*LANGUAGE*/filetype and the filename of a binary file to be attached. | | |
| | **-ad**: request a delivery acknowledgment. | | |
| | **-ar**: request a read acknowledgment. | | |
| | **-ap**: request a reply acknowledgment. | | |
| | **-mp**: mark message as private. | | |
| | **-mu**: mark message as urgent. | | |
| | **-d** *delay*: defer message delivery for the specified time (in seconds). | | |
| | **-k** *character-set*: specify the character set for the user's terminal. | | |
| | **-q**: quiet mode. | | |

| Program | Options | Function | Example |
|---|---|---|---|
| omaddmn | **-m** *mailnode*: name of the mailnode to be added.<br><br>**-R** *file*: a file to which an omaddrt command is appended (e.g. To update the routing table).<br><br>**-D** *domain*: the internet domain corresponding to this mailnode.<br><br>**-N** *name* \| *ia-map*: a simple rule or script that generates the name part of the mailnode or the complete Internet address.<br><br>**-Q**: do not create a domain or Internet address or address mapping information for this mailnode. | Add a mailnode | Add a mailnode named scalixbook to the local system:<br><br>omaddmn -m scalixbook |
| omdelmn | **-m** *mailnode*: the name of the mailnode to be deleted.<br><br>**-f** *file*: a file containing a list of mailnodes to be deleted (one name per line).<br><br>**-R** *file*: a file to which an omdelrt command is appended for each deleted mailnode. | Delete a mailnode | Delete mailnode named scalixbook:<br><br>omdelmn -m scalixbook |
| omshowmn | **-m** *mailnode*: display detailed information on the named mailnode.<br><br>**-D**: include domain and name mapping information.<br><br>**-f**: do not truncate fields. | List mailnodes | Show details about the mailnode scalixbook including domain/name mappings:<br><br>omshowmn -m scalixbook -D |

# Summary

In this chapter, we learnt about the location of various Scalix configuration files and the options therein. The main part of these pages dealt with an excerpt of the abundance of configuration parameters, followed by a long list of administrative commands of the Scalix server, including examples. If you need this information in more detail, please see the official Scalix documentation.

# 8
# Monitoring Scalix

This chapter deals with standard Scalix monitoring tools and the integration of Scalix in your centralized Nagios monitoring. After some details on Scalix administration programs like omstat or omlimit, this chapter shows how Outlook clients can be monitored. In the end, some of our Nagios scripts and configuration files serve to add another host to an existing Nagios configuration.

## Standard Monitoring Commands

Some of the commands that we learned in the last chapter should be run on a regular basis. In an interactive mode, the administrator gets an overview over his Scalix server's health status. The first command that is useful is omstat -s, which returns the state of the Scalix services. A typical output of a Scalix server, feeling fine, looks like this:

```
scalix:~ # omstat -s
Service Router             Started       29.04.07        0
Local Delivery             Started       29.04.07        0
Internet Mail Gateway      Started       29.04.07        0
Local Client Interface     Enabled       29.04.07        0
Remote Client Interface    Enabled       29.04.07        0
Test Server                Started       29.04.07        0
Request Server             Started       29.04.07        0
Print Server               Started       29.04.07        0
Bulletin Board Server      Started       29.04.07        0
Background Search Service  Started       29.04.07        0
CDA Server                 Started       29.04.07        0
POP3 interface             Started       29.04.07        0
Omscan Server              Started       29.04.07        0
Archiver                   Started       29.04.07        0
scalix:~ #
```

There are 10 possible states that the service might be in:

- Started: The service is running.
- Starting: The service is just initializing.
- Stopping: The service is about to be shut down.
- Stopped: The service is down.
- Enabled: Service is ready and awaiting work.
- Enabling: The service was enabled and is preparing.
- Disabling: The service is not yet completely shut down.
- Disabled: The service is down.
- Aborted: The service has suffered from a failure and therefore was forced to shut down.
- Part Aborted: The service has partly failed and therefore a part of it has been forced to shut down.

Omstat can also check daemons when envoked with the -a option:

```
scalix:~ # omstat -a
PC Monitor                  Started        NON-STOP        0
Directory Relay Server      Started        29.04.07
Notification Server         Started        29.04.07        0
Shared memory daemon        Started        NON-STOP
Notification Monitor        Started        NON-STOP
Session Monitor             Started        NON-STOP
Indexer                     Started        NON-STOP
Stats Daemon                Started        NON-STOP
Container Access Monitor    Started        NON-STOP
Item Structure Server       Stopped
Database Monitor            Started        29.04.07
Licence Monitor Daemon      Started        NON-STOP
LDAP Daemon                 Started        29.04.07
Queue Manager               Started        NON-STOP
Item Delete Daemon          Started        NON-STOP
IMAP Server Daemon          Started        29.04.07
SMTP Relay                  Started        29.04.07
Mime Browser Controller     Started        29.04.07
Event Server                Started        29.04.07
scalix:~ #
```

If you receive an output like the one above, everything should be fine. For daemons, there are six possible states they can be found in:

- Starting and Started
- Stopping and Stopped
- Aborted and Part Aborted

Whereas the first six can be interpreted analog to the daemons' status, the last column of the output of the command omstat -a shows an entry called NON-STOP. While a date in this column signalizes when the daemon (or service) has been restarted for the last time, a NON-STOP means: This daemon can not be restarted with omon and omoff, it is running continuously, and can only be restarted by a system restart or omrc and omshut. In case of failures, keep an eye for services or daemons that have the flag Aborted or Part aborted.

With omstat -q *mailqueue*, you have control over the Scalix message queues. For example, omstat -q SMERR lists messages rejected by the system, and omstat -q error will show more generalized error messages. But the normal output of this command should be:

```
scalix:~ # omstat -q SMERR
omstat : There are no messages on the queue
scalix: ~#
```

A omstat -u service shows you all users currently logged in through the specified service. The following services are possible:

- Local Client Interface "lci"
- Remote Client Interfaces "rci"
- Imap Service "imap"

A typical test server setup may look like this:

```
scalix:~/scalix-nagios/scalix # omstat -u rci
Markus Feilner / scalix/CN=Markus Feilner  60536        R        5205
22:22:35
scalix:~/scalix-nagios/scalix # omstat -u lci
omstat : There are no active users for this subsystem
scalix:~/scalix-nagios/scalix # omstat -u imap
Markus Feilner / scalix/CN=Markus Feilner  60536        I        5204
22:22:35
scalix:~/scalix-nagios/scalix #
```

One user is logged in, he is using the remote client interface rci and IMAP. This is the typical output if you are connected with the web client. The option -c controls the output format of omstat in this context.

The command omshowlvl -l will always give you a list of services available.

# Log Files and Logging

On our system scalixbook.org, the Scalix log files can be found in the path /var/opt/scalix/sx/s/logs/:

```
scalix:/ # cd /var/opt/scalix/sx/s/logs/
scalix:/var/opt/scalix/sx/s/logs # ls -l
insgesamt 356
-rw-rw----  1 scalix scalix      0 2007-04-02 20:39        audit
-rw-rw-rw-  1 scalix scalix      0 2007-04-02 20:39        daemon.stderr
-rw-rw----  1 scalix scalix    336 2007-04-15 13:51        fatal
-rw-rw-rw-  1 scalix scalix      0 2007-04-02 20:39        ftlvis.log
-rw-rw-r--  1 scalix scalix      0 2007-04-02 20:39        lock_fatal
-rw-rw----  1 scalix scalix      0 2007-04-02 20:39        lock_log
-rw-rw----  1 scalix scalix 355225 2007-05-23 17:09        log.0
-rw-rw----  1 scalix scalix      0 2007-04-02 20:39        log.1
-rw-rw----  1 scalix scalix      0 2007-04-02 20:39        log.2
scalix:/var/opt/scalix/sx/s/logs #
```

There are 5 relevant files in this directory:

- audit: This file holds auditing and statistical information.
- daemon.stderr: The Standard error log from the Scalix daemons.
- fatal: Serious errors and failures.
- ftlvis.log and ftlvis.fatal: Database errors.

The Scalix monitoring command ommon will read these files, organize the data, and send this report as an email to the administrator. Because ommon deletes the files after its run, these files may be very small or empty.

Another monitoring task that Scalix suggests, is to run omscan -a -f -x or omscan -avfx on a weekly basis. omscan checks the Scalix message store for corruptions and fixes several problems, if there are any. If you don't want to lose recoverable email, it is a good idea to run omscan -a once. Furthermore, you receive a detailed statistical breakdown of the data stored on your server. On a Scalix 11 system, this may look like:

```
scalix:~ # omscan -a -f -x
omscan running on 28.05.07 at 19:45:43.
Host computer : scalix.scalixbook.org.
```

```
Fix mode requested.
Last omscan tool run on 01.03.07 at 02:34:13; duration 1 minute(s).
Previous server cycle run on 21.05.07 at 20:41:05; duration 1
minute(s).
Current server cycle not started; service reset or delayed.

Extra check option requested.
Passive scan option requested.
Scanning file/dir links .... done.
CAUTION: Scanning of message store has started.
         Mounted file/dir links must be maintained during the scan.
         VxFS file system must not be reorganized - see omscan(1M).
Checking/Scanning data domain ........... done.
Checking data orphans .... done.
Checking data orphan files .... done.
Checking/Scanning bulletin board area .... done.
Checking/Scanning user trays .... done.
Checking/Scanning message lists .... done.
Scanning name directories .... done.
Scanning temp domain .... done.
Checking/Scanning message queues .... done.
Disk usage ....
USER NAME               IN   OUT   PDG   FCAB   DLST    WB   TOTAL (KB)

Bulletin Board area      -    -     -     -      -      -      3
sxadmin /scalix/CN=sxadmin   10    1    1     1      1      0     14
sxqueryadmin /scalix/CN=sxquer   1   1   1   1      1      0      5
Markus Feilner /scalix/CN=Mark   2157   1   125   19     1      5   2188
Norbert Graf /scalix/CN=Norber  .7401   1   153   27     1      1   7584
Arne Baeumler /scalix/CN=Arne   3441   1   153   27     1      1   3634
scalix:~ #
```

Beginning with Scalix 11.3, this output may have changed.

Apart from these tools, there is a Scalix event log where all Scalix services can log data. As a circular log, it works in a FIFO style and can be configured with the omconflvl command. For example,

```
omconflvl "Internet Mail Gateway" 3
```

will configure the Scalix Internet mail gateway to log only errors and serious errors. The range goes from 1 (serious errors) to 9 (reports, warnings, errors, and serious errors are logged.) For debugging purposes, there are log levels called 11-21. The program omshowlvl shows the current log level of your system:

```
scalix:~ # omshowlvl
Service Router                                         7
Local Delivery                                         7
Internet Mail Gateway                                  7
```

```
Sendmail Interface                              7
Test Server                                     7
Administration                                  7
Converters                                      7
Browser                                         7
Request Server                                  7
Print Server                                    7
Directory Synchronization                       7
Bulletin Board Server                           7
Background Search Service                       7
Dump Server                                     7
CDA Server                                      7
POP3 interface                                  7
Omscan Server                                   7
Archiver                                        7
scalix:~ #
```

You can have a look at the Event Log with the command `omshowlog`.

# Scalix Applications

Every Scalix application provides its own log file: the log files for the Admin Console can be found in `/var/opt/scalix/sx/tomcat/logs/scalix-caa.log`; the log file of the Remote Execution Service is at `/var/opt/scalix/sx/tomcat/logs/scalix-res.log`. Depending on your instance name, this may vary, but the locate utility can help.

```
scalix:~ # locate caa.log
/var/opt/scalix/sx/tomcat/logs/scalix-caa.log
scalix:~ # locate res.log
/var/opt/scalix/sx/tomcat/logs/scalix-res.log
scalix:~ # locate log4j
/opt/scalix/web/template/caa/config/log4j.properties
/opt/scalix/web/template/res/config/log4j.properties
```

The log level of these services can be set in the `log4j.properties` files. On our system scalixbook.org, this file is quite self-explanatory and looks like this:

```
# switch on or off level and log destinations here
log4j.rootLogger=INFO
log4j.logger.com.scalix.caa.util.CAALogger=INFO, file
# stdout (Tomcat uses catalina.out)
log4j.appender.stdout=org.apache.log4j.ConsoleAppender
log4j.appender.stdout.layout=org.apache.log4j.PatternLayout
log4j.appender.stdout.layout.ConversionPattern=%5p [%t] (%F:%L) - %m%n
# file (normal file)
log4j.appender.file=org.apache.log4j.FileAppender
log4j.appender.file.File=${catalina.base}/logs/scalix-caa.log
```

```
log4j.appender.file.layout=org.apache.log4j.PatternLayout
log4j.appender.file.layout.ConversionPattern=%d %5p [%C{1}.%M:%L] %m%n
# rfile (rolling file)
log4j.appender.rfile=org.apache.log4j.RollingFileAppender
log4j.appender.rfile.File=${catalina.base}/logs/scalix-caa.log
log4j.appender.rfile.MaxFileSize=100KB
log4j.appender.rfile.MaxBackupIndex=1
log4j.appender.rfile.layout=org.apache.log4j.PatternLayout
log4j.appender.rfile.layout.ConversionPattern=%d %5p [%C{1}.%M:%L]
%m%n
```

As you can see in the second paragraph, the Scalix Tomcat server uses its own log file: `catalina.out`. On our system, this can be found at `/var/opt/scalix/sx/tomcat/logs/catalina.out`. If there is another `catalina.out` on your Scalix server in `/opt/scalix-tomcat/logs/catalina.out`, it has no significance in Scalix.

# Checking the Limits

We have learned that the command `omlimit` can be used to limit resources for users. But this tool is also very handy for monitoring purposes. With:

```
scalix:/etc/mail # omlimit -u "Markus Feilner" -r

  Name : Name :
  Message Store Size Limit        : 0Kb
  Intray Size Limit               : 0Kb
  Filing Cabinet Size Limit       : 0Kb
  WasteBasket Size Limit          : 0Kb
  Pending Tray Size Limit         : 0Kb
  Distribution List Area Limit    : 0Kb

  scalix:/etc/mail #
```

The administrator receives detailed information on the percentage of space that the user Markus Feilner has "consumed". The percentage is relative to the limit set with `omlimit`. There are several useful features offered by `omlimit`: For example, the command `scalix:/etc/mail # omlimit -g -x 90` lists all users that are using at least 90 % of their allocated size limits and who might be close to problems. How about a little script informing you before they call?

# The Error Manager

One of the Scalix users is configured as the "Error Manager". Ok, this is how all administrators feel, and consequently the standard setup declares the administrative account as error manager. A program called `omshowenu` lists the name of the currently configured error manager who will receive error messages per email:

```
scalix:/etc/mail # omshowenu
sxadmin /scalix/CN=sxadmin
scalix:/etc/mail #
```

With the program `omconfenu`, you can define a different error manager:

```
scalix:/etc/mail # omconfenu -n "Markus Feilner"
omconfenu : Error Notification user correctly configured
scalix:/etc/mail # omshowenu
Markus Feilner /scalix/CN=Markus Feilner
scalix:/etc/mail #
```

From now on, Markus Feilner will receive all mails with error messages from this system. This may be a good advice, because you do not have to log in as administrator in order to look for system error mails.

Besides these tools, there is a very powerful script called ommaint that can be downloaded from `http://downloads.scalix.com/ark/ommaint`, and then added to your local cron configuration. From then on, your administrator will receive status reports on a regular basis.

# Monitoring Scalix with Nagios

The most widespread open source monitoring program is called Nagios (`http://www.nagios.org`). It comes with all major distributions and has a very simple installation. But because Nagios is a very powerful and complex system with many options and opportunities, this chapter cannot deal with the Nagios setup and configuration. But if you happen to have a Nagios server around, there is a collection of scripts available that easily integrate your Scalix server(s) with your Nagios monitoring.

If you have not done so, install Nagios from (30) and set it up correctly. Like the software itself, the Nagios documentation (http://www.nagios.org/docs) is very extensive: The current manual for Nagios 3.0 spans over 323 pages. Furthermore, there are excellent books in the market.

# Download and Installation

Download the archive of the Nagios scripts from: (http://downloads.scalix.com/ark/scalix-nagios.tar.gz) and unpack them to a local directory. The tar.gz file contains three directories: scalix-nagios/scalix/etc, scalix-nagios/scalix/libexec, and scalix-nagios/scalix/nrpe:

```
scalix:~ # wget -c http://downloads.scalix.com/ark/scalix-nagios.tar.
gz
--22:09:09--  http://downloads.scalix.com/ark/scalix-nagios.tar.gz
           => `scalix-nagios.tar.gz'
Resolving Hostname »downloads.scalix.com«.... 216.240.133.162
Connection with downloads.scalix.com|216.240.133.162|:80... connected.
HTTP Request sent, waiting for response... 200 OK
Length: 10.720 (10K) [application/x-gzip]

100%[====================================================================
===============================>] 10.720          30.50K/s

22:09:10 (30.39 KB/s) - »scalix-nagios.tar.gz« saved [10720/10720]
scalix:~ # tar -xzf scalix-nagios.tar.gz
scalix:~ # cd scalix-nagios/
scalix:~/scalix-nagios # ls -l
total 4
drwxr-xr-x 5 10006 2000 4096 2004-11-19 20:14 scalix
scalix:~/scalix-nagios # cd scalix/
scalix:~/scalix-nagios/scalix # ls -l
total 12
drwxr-xr-x 2 10006 2000 4096 2004-12-30 23:27 etc
drwxr-xr-x 2 10006 2000 4096 2004-12-30 21:30 libexec
drwxr-xr-x 2 10006 2000 4096 2004-12-30 23:27 nrpe
scalix:~/scalix-nagios/scalix #
```

Create a directory /etc/nagios/scalix, change its ownership to the user nagios and copy all files from scalix-nagios/scalix/etc into it:

```
scalix:~/scalix-nagios/scalix # mkdir /etc/nagios/scalix
scalix:~/scalix-nagios/scalix # chown nagios /etc/nagios/scalix/
scalix:~/scalix-nagios/scalix # cp etc/* /etc/nagios/scalix/
scalix:~/scalix-nagios/scalix #
```

Copy the content of the directory `libexec/` to `/usr/lib/nagios/plugins/`. This is the place where Nagios plug-ins are stored.

If you want to monitor a remote Scalix host, copy the NRPE files to this machine. NRPE stands for the Nagios Remote Plugin Executor and makes a Nagios client report to the server. For this Nagios, NRPE and the Nagios-Scalix plug-ins have to be installed.

# Editing the Nagios Configuration

Now that the plug-ins are in place, we have to edit the Nagios configuration, so that Nagios can use it. We will do this in a three-step process. After we have adjusted the host definitions, we have to manually change every service that is supposed to be checked by Nagios. Finally, we have to tell Nagios about the contact persons and groups it should contact in case of failures.

The Scalix-Nagios plug-in comes with some templates. In the directory, `scalix/etc` of the archive, we find the following files (and now also in `/etc/nagios/scalix`):

```
scalix:~/scalix-nagios/scalix/etc # ls -l
total 68
-rw-r--r-- 1 10006 2000 40650 2004-12-30 21:30 services.cfg
-rw-r--r-- 1 10006 2000  2572 2004-12-30 23:13 hosts.cfg
-rw-r--r-- 1 10006 2000   669 2004-12-30 21:30 hostgroups.cfg
-rw-r--r-- 1 10006 2000   932 2004-12-30 23:10 contacts.cfg
-rw-r--r-- 1 10006 2000   683 2004-12-30 21:30 contactgroups.cfg
-rw-r--r-- 1 10006 2000   689 2004-12-30 21:30 escalations.cfg
-rw-r--r-- 1 10006 2000  4331 2004-12-30 23:09 checkcommands.cfg
scalix:~/scalix-nagios/scalix/etc #
```

These files serve for the following tasks:

| File | Function |
| --- | --- |
| `services.cfg` | Scalix Services to be monitored. |
| `hosts.cfg` | Scalix Server(s) to be monitored. |
| `hostgroups.cfg` | Hosts can be grouped for simpler administration. |
| `contacts.cfg` | The Persons who are to be contacted if an error occurs. |
| `contactgroups.cfg` | Contacts can also be grouped for simpler administration. |
| `escalations.cfg` | Optional measures that can be taken. |
| `checkcommands.cfg` | Here the commands for Nagios are defined. |

Add all of these files to your central Nagios configuration file by adding the lines:

```
cfg_file=/etc/nagios/scalix/scalix/services.cfg
cfg_file=/etc/nagios/scalix/scalix/hosts.cfg
cfg_file=/etc/nagios/scalix/scalix/hostgroups.cfg
cfg_file=/etc/nagios/scalix/scalix/contacts.cfg
cfg_file=/etc/nagios/scalix/scalix/contactgroups.cfg
cfg_file=/etc/nagios/scalix/scalix/escalations.cfg
cfg_file=/etc/nagios/scalix/scalix/checkcommands.cfg
```

to the file `/etc/nagios/nagios.cfg`.

## Customizing the Configuration

After this, we have to edit these configuration files so that they fit to our setup. First, we have to change the host configuration, so that Nagios knows where our Scalix server is to be found. Our `hosts.cfg` now looks like this:

```
# Generic host definition template
define host{
    name                generic-host     ; The name of this host template
    notifications_enabled       1    ; Host notifications are enabled
    event_handler_enabled       1    ; Host event handler is enabled
    flap_detection_enabled      1     ; Flap detection is enabled
    process_perf_data       1    ; Process performance data
    retain_status_information    1     ; Retain status information across
program restarts
    retain_nonstatus_information    1    ; Retain non-status information
across program restarts
    register        0    ; DONT REGISTER THIS DEFINITION - ITS NOT A
REAL HOST, JUST A TEMPLATE!
    }
# Scalix Server 1 host definition
define host{
    use     generic-host        ; Name of host template to use
    host_name    scalixbook.org
    alias        scalixbook.org
    address      192.168.0.23
    check_command       check-host-alive
    max_check_attempts    10
    notification_interval    120
    notification_period    24x7
    notification_options d,u,r
    }
```

Enter your host's IP, hostname, and alias in this file. The alias is the name of the host addressed in the other Nagios configuration files later on.

# Services and Commands—the Hard Work

Nagios Service definitions define which services on a client system Nagios is supposed to check. The Scalix-Nagios plug-in offers 51 tests. For most of them, it is fully sufficient to change the hostname of the Scalix server, but there are also some tests where you have to place log file locations in the right place. A correct service configuration looks like this:

```
( . . . )
# Service definition for remote RES
define service{
        use                             generic-service         ; Name
of service template to use
        host_name                       scalixbook.org
        service_description             Scalix RES
        is_volatile                     0
        check_period                    24x7
        max_check_attempts              3
        normal_check_interval           5
        retry_check_interval            1
        contact_groups                  Scalix-Admins
        notification_interval           120
        notification_period             24x7
        notification_options            w,u,c,r
        check_command                   check_res
        }
( . . . )
```

The Parameter host_name has been changed to the value defined in the host.cfg file. The check_command check_res is defined in the file checkcommands.cfg, it points to this entry:

```
# 'check_res' command definition
define command {
        command_name    check_res
        command_line    $USER1$/check_http -H $HOSTADDRESS$ -u /res/
RESDispatcher?query=monitor -p 8080
        }
```

Thus the command check_res will execute an check_http to scalixbook.org with the parameters specified. This is what has to be done now: Walk through the configuration file services.cfg and edit each specified service to your needs. If you are unsure, what the command specified does, have a look in checkcommands.cfg. It may also be a good idea to open the scripts specified with an editor, because very often there are a lot of comments inside.

# Contacts and Contact Groups

As the last aspect, we must have a look inside the `contacts.cfg` file:

```
define contact{
    contact_name          Scalix-Admin
    alias            Scalix Admin
    service_notification_period    24x7
    host_notification_period    24x7
    service_notification_options    w,u,c,r
    host_notification_options    d,u,r
    service_notification_commands    notify-by-email
    host_notification_commands    host-notify-by-email
    email            norbert.graf@nogait.de
    pager            norbert.graf@nogait.de
    }
```

This block of definitions declares the account data for the Scalix administrator, who is to be informed by Nagios in case of an error. Every block in this file represents a Nagios contact, and these contacts can be grouped together in contact groups, which are specified in `contactgroups.cfg`. Since our above service definition contained `contact_groups    Scalix-Admins` for notification, it is a good idea to enter the Scalix-Admin in this group's file.

Simply edit the file, so that it looks like this:

```
# Scalix Admins contact group definition
define contactgroup{
        contactgroup_name        Scalix-Admins
        alias                Scalix Administrators
        members                Scalix-Admin,admin
        }
```

Replace the `members` line with your data.

If you have several servers, you may want to use the `hostgroups.cfg` file to group them. From now on, you can make your changes only for this group of hosts, and all Scalix servers will have the updated monitoring. Escalation is defined in the file `escalations.cfg`.

# Nagios NRPE

If your Scalix server is not the Nagios server, you will need the NRPE plug-in on your Scalix machine. Depending on your setup, this file may need some changes. The following listing shows the working NRPE setup on our testserver scalixbook.org:

```
###################################################################
########
# Sample NRPE Config File
# Written by: Ethan Galstad (nagios@nagios.org)
(...)
server_port=5666
allowed_hosts=127.0.0.1,xx.xx.xx.xx
nrpe_user=nagios
nrpe_group=nogroup
dont_blame_nrpe=0
debug=1
command_timeout=60
command[check_users]=/usr/lib/nagios/plugins/check_users -w 5 -c 10
command[check_load]=/usr/lib/nagios/plugins/check_load -w 15,10,5 -c
30,25,20
command[check_disk1]=/usr/lib/nagios/plugins/check_disk -w 20 -c 10 -p
/dev/hda2
command[check_disk2]=/usr/lib/nagios/plugins/check_disk -w 20 -c 10 -p
/dev/hdc1
command[check_zombie_procs]=/usr/lib/nagios/plugins/check_procs -w 5
-c 10 -s Z
command[check_total_procs]=/usr/lib/nagios/plugins/check_procs -w 150
-c 200
command[check_swap]=/usr/lib/nagios/plugins/check_swap -w 95% -c 85%
command[check_mailstore]=/usr/lib/nagios/plugins/check_disk -w 20 -c
10 -p /dev/hda2
command[check_local_sxqueue]=sudo /usr/lib/nagios/plugins/check_
queues.py -c 100 -w 75 -q LOCAL
command[check_router_sxqueue]=sudo /usr/lib/nagios/plugins/check_
queues.py -c 100 -w 75 -q ROUTER
command[check_smtp_sxqueue]=sudo /usr/lib/nagios/plugins/check_queues.
py -c 100 -w 75 -q SMINTFC
command[check_error_sxqueue]=sudo /usr/lib/nagios/plugins/check_
queues.py -c 100 -w 75 -q ERROR
command[check_unix_sxqueue]=sudo /usr/lib/nagios/plugins/check_queues.
py -c 100 -w 75 -q UNIX
command[check_sxdaemons]=sudo /usr/lib/nagios/plugins/check_daemons.
py -d
command[check_sxservices]=sudo /usr/lib/nagios/plugins/check_daemons.
py -s
```

```
command[check_inodes]=/usr/lib/nagios/plugins/check_inode.py -c 80 -w
70 -f /dev/hda2
command[check_memory]=/usr/lib/nagios/plugins/check_memory.py -c 90%
-w 80%
command[check_log]=/usr/lib/nagios/plugins/check_log -F /var/opt/
scalix/s1/tomcat/logs/scalix-res.log -O /tmp/res.log.old -q FATAL
command[check_tcp_connections]=/usr/lib/nagios/plugins/check_inet_
connections.py -c 250 -w 200 -T tcp
```

Once you are finished, you receive a great reward: Nagios is automatically monitoring your Scalix server. Although this involves some work, it is worthwhile.

## Summary

In this chapter, we have learned about Scalix Tools that provide information on monitoring and status reports of the Scalix server. Apart from built-in tools, there is a Nagios plug-in for Scalix, offering full integration and alarming through the widespread monitoring tool. Configuring this plug-in takes place in a three-step process of editing the config files: First step, entering the hosts. Second step, configuration of services, and third step, configuring the contact persons and groups.

# 9
# Scalix and Security

The standard setup of the Scalix server may be OK for most installations, but if you are running Scalix on an Internet site or if your local server is available from the Internet, extended security measures have to be taken. In this chapter, we will deal with several recommendations that make your Scalix server safe—like minimizing the number of services running and listening. We will set up a firewall that allows Scalix users to connect. After that we will set up Stunnel to provide SSL-encrypted Scalix services. Then, we will use OpenVPN to protect the server. Last but not least, we will have a look at the services running and discuss advanced possibilities of securing the server.

## Basic Security and Firewalls

An administrator installing a Scalix server in a productive environment must make some considerations before setting up his system:

- Is the server accessible from the Internet?
- Is the server accessible to untrusted users?
- Who must access Scalix? Who must access administration?
- Who must be prevented from gaining access?
- Which services must be accessible from where?

Though this may sound theoretical, such thoughts should always play an important role when you are planning any productive server. In most cases, there are only three different setups for a groupware server:

- There are only local users in the company's network and the server is located in the company.
- There are local users and remote users connecting to the Scalix server located in the company.
- There are both local and remote users connecting to the Scalix server located on the Internet.

Most of the installations can be classified in one of these categories. If you are running a local site with a small network and only trusted users, this chapter may be of no interest for you. But most of the Scalix installations are in big networks, often accessible from the Internet. While the installation leaves a perfectly configured system that is stable, there are several possible precautions that should be taken when your Scalix server is accessible from the Internet: the access should be controlled by a firewall; connections should be encrypted; and users must be forced to use strong authentication mechanisms. As always, there are several ways to achieve this.

Before we start, here is a list of services that have to be available for Scalix users accessing the server remotely:

- SSH: TCP port 22, the standard remote administration for the admin.
  - SMTP: TCP port 25: Sending mail.
  - IMAP: TCP port 143: Retrieving mail with the IMAP protocol.
  - POP: TCP port 110: Retrieving mail with the POP protocol.
- HTTP: TCP port 80: Accessing the Web interface.
- Scalix UAL uses port 5287.
- And as of 11.3, secure UAL connects over 5767.

# Linux Firewall Terminology

Basically speaking, a firewall is a piece of software that controls Internet connections to and from a server. SUSE's Linux systems come with a built-in firewall named SUSEfirewall that can easily be configured with YaST. On Red Hat Linux systems, there is Bastille and firewall GUIs like Shorewall, which are a good choice for any Linux system. All common Linux firewalls are based on `iptables` or its predecessor `ipchains`. Its concept is pretty simple: the administrator defines a chain of rules that are worked through by the operating system one after another for every incoming or outgoing connection or package. So-called targets define what to do with packages matching the rule specified. Targets may be, for example, Accept, Reject, Drop or Log. Furthermore, there are policies that define the default behavior for connections where no rule matches. The Linux program `iptables` controls these rules. A little glance on this tool may help understanding how a Linux firewall works.

# iptables—the Standard Linux Firewall Tool

iptables (http://www.netfilter.org) is a simple command-line tool that controls the kernels' IP tables. In these tables, rules that define how network packets are treated on this system can be stored. As always, the simple commands offer the best solutions when they are combined with an abundance of options. There is a vast amount of options and extensions for iptables, so this short description is far from perfect and far from complete. However, I hope that it may help in some cases.

The iptables syntax is very simple:

```
iptables <rule command> <chain> <matching extensions><target>
```

A typical rule command is -A, which means "Add the following rule". Since iptables use different chains (by default, INPUT, FORWARD, OUTPUT), we must declare a chain where this rule is to be added to. The following table shows three examples:

| iptables Command | Function: |
| --- | --- |
| iptables -A INPUT <rule> | Adds a rule to the INPUT chain, which affects all incoming packets heading for the firewall itself. |
| iptables -A OUTPUT <rule> | Adds a rule to the FORWARD chain, which affects all packets that are supposed to be forwarded by the firewall. |
| iptables -A FORWARD <rule> | Adds a rule to the OUTPUT chain, which affects all outgoing packets originating from the firewall. |

Another typical command is -P that sets the default policy for a chain. This should always be set to DROP, because then all packets "arriving" in this chain are dropped if not specified explicitly by another rule. This is the only way to make sure that only the traffic allowed by us is handled and any unspecified traffic is dropped.

A typical example for this is:

```
scalixbook:~ # iptables -P FORWARD DROP
scalixbook:~ #
```

This would prevent your system from forwarding any traffic, unless specified otherwise, later on.

Then there are iptables' targets. A target can be either DROP, REJECT or ACCEPT (among others) and is invoked by the switch -j. Furthermore, so-called "matching extensions" are like a filter specifying exactly which packet is meant.

Thus a rule like `iptables -A INPUT <matching extension> -j DROP`
means: Drop every packet that is headed for my firewall and matches the
`<matching extension>`.

| Matching Extension | Meaning |
|---|---|
| `-i <interface>` | The incoming interface of the datagram |
| `-o <interface>` | The outgoing interface of the datagram |
| `-p <protocol>` | The IP protocol of the datagram |
| `--dport <destination port>` | The destination port of the datagram |
| `--sport <source port>` | The source port of the datagram |
| `-s <source IP>` | The source IP of the sender |
| `-d <destination IP>` | The destination IP of the recipient |

There are many other matching extensions, but these here should be sufficient to
understand the basics of `iptables`. Have a look at these lines:

```
#!/bin/bash

iptables -P INPUT DROP
iptables -P OUTPUT DROP
iptables -P FORWARD DROP

iptables -A INPUT -i eth0 -p tcp --dport 22 -j ACCEPT
iptables -A INPUT -i eth0 -p tcp --dport 25 -j ACCEPT
iptables -A INPUT -i eth0 -p tcp --dport 143 -j ACCEPT

iptables -A OUTPUT -o eth0 -p tcp --sport 22 -j ACCEPT
iptables -A OUTPUT -o eth0 -p tcp --dport 25 -j ACCEPT
iptables -A OUTPUT -o eth0 -p tcp --dport 143 -j ACCEPT

(...)
```

Do you already understand them? If you do, congratulations; if not, don't worry,
it's easy. These lines represent a shell script that can be used to start a very simple
firewall example. `iptables` is a command-line tool and therefore is simply called
from a script with parameters like the following:

| Command | Meaning |
|---|---|
| `iptables -P INPUT DROP` | Drop all incoming packets that are not specified by any other rule |
| `iptables -P OUTPUT DROP` | Drop all outgoing packets that are not specified by any other rule |
| `iptables -P FORWARD DROP` | Do not forward any packets that are not specified by any other rule |

| Command | Meaning |
|---|---|
| `iptables -A INPUT -i eth0 -p tcp --dport 22 -j ACCEPT` | Accept TCP connections for port 22 (SSH) coming in on network interface eth0 |
| `iptables -A INPUT -i eth0 -p tcp --dport 25 -j ACCEPT` | Accept TCP connections for port 25 (SMTP) coming in on network interface eth0 |
| `iptables -A INPUT -i eth0 -p tcp --dport 143 -j ACCEPT` | Accept TCP connections for port 143 (IMAP) coming in on network interface eth0 |
| `iptables -A OUTPUT -o eth0 -p tcp --sport 22 -j ACCEPT` | Accept outgoing TCP connections for port 22 going out on network interface eth0 |
| `iptables -A OUTPUT -o eth0 -p tcp --dport 25 -j ACCEPT` | Accept outgoing TCP connections for port 25 going out on network interface eth0 |
| `iptables -A OUTPUT -o eth0 -p tcp --dport 143 -j ACCEPT` | Accept outgoing TCP connections for port 143 going out on network interface eth0 |

In a nutshell:

- `eth0` is the external interface, where all traffic except SSH and Mail Services will be dropped.
- SSH Remote Administration is allowed via Port 22.
- SMTP Mail Services are allowed via Port 25.
- IMAP Mail Services via Port 143 are allowed.

The NIC `eth0` is the external interface, where all traffic except for TCP Ports 22 (SSH), 25 (SMTP), and 143 (IMAP) will be dropped. With this setup, clients could access the Scalix server for sending and retrieving mail. If you want to allow Web access, you will need to open TCP ports 80 (http), and 443 (https). Remember that for any service you want to allow, you have to add several `iptables` rules.

The above example is only rudimentary. There are lots of other options that may be necessary for your system. However, the abundance of functions offered by `iptables` goes far beyond the scope of this book. If you need more information, the manual page of `iptables` is the best place to look for help.

# The SUSEfirewall

On SUSE Linux, there is a very sophisticated firewall solution named SUSEfirewall2 (http://www.netfilter.org) with an administration GUI embedded in YaST. The big advantage of this system is that the administrator only needs to understand basic firewall concepts, and nevertheless is able to configure his system, at least, with a minimum security setup.

Start YaST on your SUSE Linux system and change to the **Firewall** module, which can be found in **Security and Users.** You can invoke this module by simply typing yast firewall at the command line:

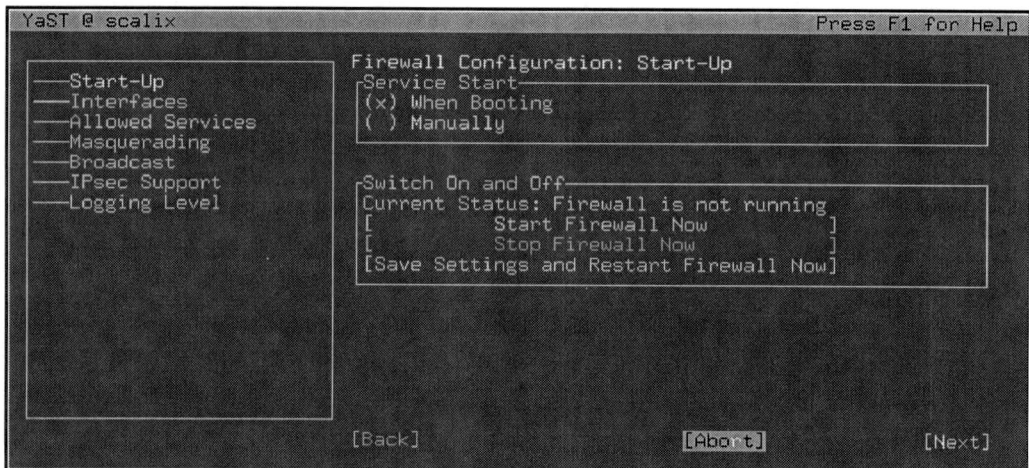

```
 YaST @ scalix                                              Press F1 for Help

                        Firewall Configuration: Start-Up
     ──Start-Up        ┌Service Start───────────────────────────────────────┐
     ──Interfaces      │(x) When Booting                                     │
     ──Allowed Services│( ) Manually                                         │
     ──Masquerading    │                                                     │
     ──Broadcast       └─────────────────────────────────────────────────────┘
     ──IPsec Support   ┌Switch On and Off───────────────────────────────────┐
     ──Logging Level   │Current Status: Firewall is not running             │
                       │[          Start Firewall Now          ]            │
                       │[          Stop Firewall Now           ]            │
                       │[Save Settings and Restart Firewall Now]            │
                       └─────────────────────────────────────────────────────┘




                        [Back]                  [Abort]              [Next]
```

The YaST firewall setup is very straightforward: In the left part of the window, we can select the dialogs to be set up for the interfaces, services, and some special features like logging, etc. The parameters and options for these features are entered in the right part of the window. The following list will give a step-by-step configuration:

Let the SUSEfirewall start on boot time. Activate the **When Booting** in **Service Start.**

- Change to the entry **Interfaces** in the left part of the window. Look up the MAC addresses of your network cards; double-click them in the interface list, and select the proper entry from the drop-down menu **Interface Zone.** Here, we must define our internal and external network devices. If there is only one, define this as the external interface.

- Click on the entry **Allowed Services** in the list on the left. Select **External Zone** in the drop-down menu, **Allowed Services for Selected Zone** and SSH from the drop-down menu, **Service to Allow.** Click on the **Add** button to confirm your changes. Now SSH access on the external interface is permitted.

```
 YaST @ scalix                                      Press F1 for Help

    Firewall Configuration: Allowed Services
    Allowed Services for Selected Zone
──Start-Up                                        v
──Interfaces          DHCP Client
──Allowed Services    DHCP Server
──Masquerading        DNS Server                        [   Add      ]
──Broadcast           HTTP Server                       [   Remove   ]
──IPsec Support       HTTPS Server
──Logging Level       IMAP Server
                      IMAPS Server
                      IPP Client
                      IPP Server
                      IPsec
                      LDAP Server
                      LDAPS Server
                      Mail Server
                      MySQL Remote Access
                      NFS Client
                      NFS Server
                      NIS Client
                      NIS Server
                      NTP Server
                      POP3 Server
                      POP3S Server
                      Portable Batch System (PBS)
                      Remote Access to Display Manager
                      Remote Administration
                      Remote File Alteration Monitor
                      Remote Synchronization
                      SLP Daemon
                      SSH
                      Samba Server            Zone     [ Advanced... ]
                      TFTP Server
                      iSCSI Target          ]                 [Next]
```

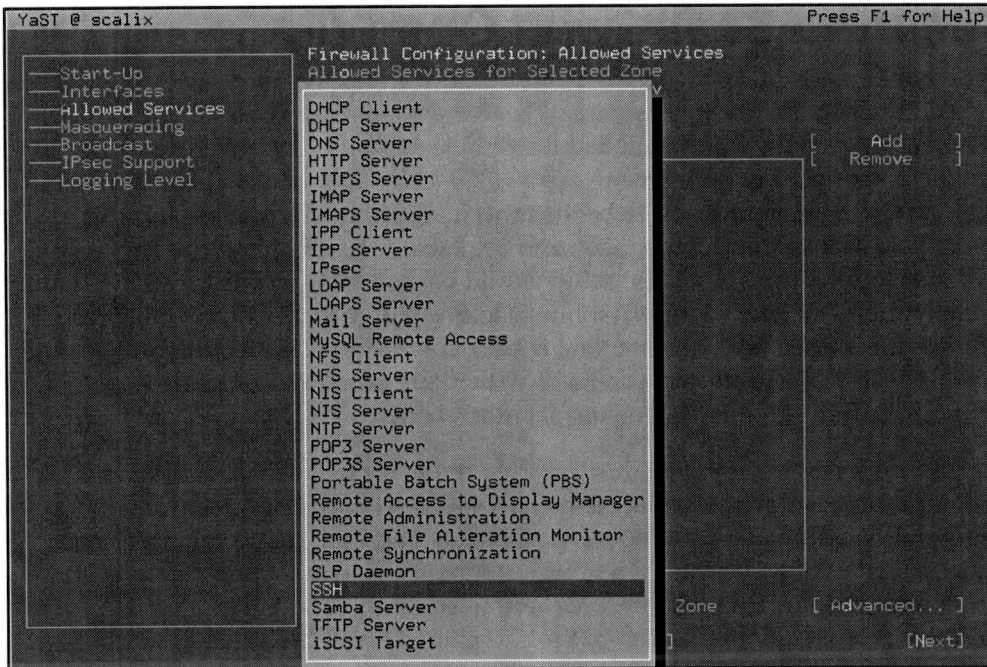

- Repeat this step for SMTP, IMAP, and HTTP to open mail and Web services for the Scalix users.

- Add any other services if you need to access them. For Outlook Clients Ports 5729/TCP and 5757/UDP will be needed. You can enter any port with YaST's **Advanced** firewall configuration dialog.

- Click on **OK** to close this window and on the button **Next** to finish SUSEfirewall setup. Check the settings displayed and click on **Accept** twice.

Now we have the SUSEfirewall configured to deny any access via the external interface except SSH, mail, and Web services. If you do not want to reboot and have your firewall start at once, type rcSuSefirewall start. You can control the ruleset with iptables -L: but don't be surprised the SUSEfirewall establishes quite a complex, and pretty safe firewall on your system.

For advanced configuration, there is a config file named /etc/sysconfig/ SuSEfirewall2 where you can enable logging, and define an external iptables script. Enter the name of the script in the variable FW_CUSTOMRULES. By default, this entry is in comments and points to the well-documented template script /etc/sysconfig/scripts/SuSEfirewall2-custom. It is a very good idea to read the two files /etc/sysconfig/SuSEfirewall2 and /etc/sysconfig/scripts/ SuSEfirewall2-custom, because the abundance of comments gives a thorough understanding of the concepts of the SUSEfirewall.

# Securing Scalix with OpenVPN

If you have external users who you want to allow access to your Scalix system, a Virtual Private Network software may be a convenient way to do so. With a VPN, all traffic between the local client and the remote system is encrypted once the "tunnel" is set up. Though there are many VPN technologies available, OpenVPN (http://openvpn.net) seems to be the most interesting one, because it is free, open source, safe, transparent, compatible, and available for every platform. And it's very easy to set it up. The easiest setup would be providing a configuration file and an encryption key (like a long passphrase) to every user that is supposed to have access to the VPN server. This method is perfect for a quick setup with only two or three users, but in a groupware scenario with many notebooks or home workers, certificate-based VPN-management suits much better.

The general scenario looks like this: A VPN server (we will use the Scalix server for that) accepts encrypted connections on a specified port. Encryption and configuration parameters are copied to all clients that shall connect. Furthermore, when a client establishes the VPN tunnel, a sophisticated authentication procedure is taking place. In our first example, the client would only send the key (a passphrase) and the server would grant access if the passphrase is valid. The better setup includes an encrypted handshake where the server and clients authenticate each other with x509 certificates. These are far longer than a passphrase, and because the authentication mechanism and encryption is much more complex, this method is also more secure. Furthermore, the administrator holds a list of valid certificates and is able to lock out single users or machines, for example if a laptop is stolen. Key Management software lets him create and delete certificates at a mouse click.

In this scenario, the administrator has to do a little work to connect a client to the Scalix server:

- Install OpenVPN on the server.
- Create a suitable configuration for the server.
- Generate server certificates.
- Create client certificates and configuration.
- Roll out OpenVPN, configuration, and certificates to the clients.

The first step is the easiest: Type `yast -i openvpn` or select OpenVPN from your installation source. This installs the OpenVPN software, documentation, and sample configuration files. A suitable server configuration file for use with certificates may look like this:

```
port 21
proto udp
dev tun
```

```
ca ca.crt
cert server.crt
key server.key  # This file should be kept secret
server 10.10.10.0 255.255.255.0
ifconfig-pool-persist ipp.txt
keepalive 10 120
comp-lzo
status /var/log/openvpn-status.log
log-append  /var/log/openvpn.log
verb 3
```

Place a file like this in /etc/openvpn/ and name it something like server.conf. Upon start, OpenVPN will look for .conf files in this directory and start the tunnels defined in these files. The following table gives an overview of the meaning of each of the configuration parameters specified above.

| OpenVPN parameter | Function |
| --- | --- |
| port 21 | OpenVPN connection will be setup over port 21. Make sure this is open in your firewall. We are using port 21 (FTP) because this is open per default in most outgoing firewalls. |
| proto tcp (or udp) | OpenVPN can use TCP or UDP connections. |
| dev tun<br>ca ca.crt<br>cert server.crt | The network device used will be called tun0 and uses the TUN driver. |
| key server.key | The locations of the certificates the server will use, relative to "/etc/openvpn/". |
| server 10.10.10.0 255.255.255.0 | This is the IP of the virtual subnet the tunnel partners are about to use. The VPN machine shall run as a VPN server. |
| ifconfig-pool-persist ipp.txt | The server assigns IPs to the clients. In this file it stores the IP, so that a client will mostly have the same IP. |
| keepalive 10 120 | Every 10 seconds the server checks if the tunnel is up. If it has not receieved an answer for 120 seconds, the server will try to reestablish the tunnel. |
| comp-lzo | OpenVPN uses sophisticated, adaptive LZO compression. |
| status /var/log/openvpn-status.log<br>log-append  /var/log/openvpn.log<br>verb 3 | Logs the status and the general protocol to the specified files. Log Level is defined with "verb", allowed range is from 0 (no logging) to 9 (very verbose) |

On the VPN client, a configuration like the following is required:

```
client
dev tun
proto tcp
remote scalixbook.org 21
resolv-retry infinite
ca ca.crt
cert mfeilner.crt
key mfeilner.key
comp-lzo
verb 3
```

| OpenVPN client parameters | Function |
| --- | --- |
| client | This machine is a VPN client that has to connect to the server. |
| dev tun | The network device used will be called tun0 and uses the TUN driver. |
| proto tcp | Use TCP connections. |
| remote scalixbook.org 21 | This parameter specifies the VPN server and Port to use. |
| resolv-retry infinite | The client will try endlessly to set up a connection, regardless DNS failures. |
| ca ca.crt | The file names of the certificate files. |
| cert mfeilner.crt | |
| key mfeilner.key | |
| comp-lzo | The client uses compression, too. |
| verb 3 | The client has a log level of 3. |

# Generating Certificates

In the next step, a set of certificates have to be created. We need:

- A certificate for the Certificate Authority. This authority is the common ground, on which all client and server certificates are built. It is stored in the file ca.crt and must be copied to every machine involved.

- A server certificate and key for each machine involved. On the server, this is called server.crt, whereas we used to call the client file by the name of the user or client machine (mfeilner.crt).

The files ending in .key are secrets and should be handled with great care, because here are the keys identifying your client. Creating these client certificates and keys is a two-step-process: first, a certificate is created ,which then needs to be signed by the CA. Don't worry: OpenVPN comes with several scripts that create these certificates for you. The toolbox is called "easy-rsa" and resides in the easy-rsa subdirectory of the OpenVPN installation.

I recommend reading the documentation to easy-rsa and following these steps:

- Edit the vars file, entering your company's parameters.
- Build the Certificate Authority file. Run build-ca to create it according to your company's data. With this file, you can create more client certificates for your VPN machines.
- Run build-key-server and build-key-client to generate certificates for your machines.

For each client, you should now have four files: a client configuration file client. conf, a CA certificate ca.crt, a client certificate client.crt and a client key file client.key. Rename the .conf configuration file to .ovpn if you are using a Windows client.

A very sophisticated tool to administrate your certificates for Linux users is tinyca (http://tinyca.sm-zone.net). If you're running Windows or a Mac, xca (http://xca.sourceforge.net) may be the program for you.

# VPN Client Access to the Server

All you have left to do now is: initial OpenVPN on the client, copy the configuration file and the certificates to the client's OpenVPN configuration directory, and start OpenVPN. For Windows and Mac, there is graphical software available, on Linux there are runlevel scripts called /etc/init.d/openvpn.

Once successfully started, OpenVPN adds a new network device on the machines involved, called tun0. In our example, the clients will have adresses in 10.10.10.0/32, whereas the server has 10.10.10.1. All mail services like IMAP, SMTP, and POP of the Scalix server are now available only to the VPN clients on the tunnel interface, with the IP 10.10.10.1.

Now, we can change the firewall configuration on the server, shutting down external access to SSH only, at the same time allowing access to all Scalix services from the VPN. We can do that with YaST, but it's faster to edit these two lines in `/etc/sysconfig/SuSEfirewall`:

```
(...)
FW_SERVICES_EXT_TCP="ssh"
(...)
FW_DEV_INT="tun0"
(...)
```

In our `iptables` example script above, you would need some lines that only allow SSH from outside and everything from the VPN:

```
#!/bin/bash

iptables -P INPUT DROP
iptables -P OUTPUT DROP
iptables -P FORWARD DROP

iptables -A INPUT -i eth0 -p tcp --dport 22 -j ACCEPT

iptables -A OUTPUT -o eth0 -p tcp --sport 22 -j ACCEPT

iptables -A INPUT -i tun0 -j ACCEPT
iptables -A OUTPUT -o tun0 -j ACCEPT

(...)
```

# Setting Up a Web Proxy

However, if you need the web administration console and the SWA, there is still a little work to be done. Unfortunately, the Tomcat connector listens by default only on the external interface, not on tun0. We could change that in the Scalix-Tomcat connector configuration and configure the Apache for the tunnel interface only, rewriting access with mod_proxy; but this would be lost after every Scalix update. It's easier to install a Web Proxy on the Scalix server. `yast -i squid` or `yum squid` installs the mighty Squid proxy (`http://www.squid-cache.org`). Only three settings in its configuration file `/etc/squid/squid.conf` need to be adapted:

Uncomment # `http_port 3128` to make the proxy available to your VPN, and add the two lines:

```
acl vpn src 10.10.10.0/255.255.255.0
(...)
http_access allow vpn
```

The latter one needs to be added at the very beginning of the `http_access` definitions. Make sure that you do not allow port 3128 for external connections in your firewall. Once you enter the proxy URL 10.10.10.1, port 3128 in your browsers connections tab, you will be able to access the Scalix web admin and webmail. Without the tunnel and the proxy, this is impossible. Pretty safe, isn't it?

# Stunnel

If you consider the setup of openVPN as oversized, there are some other solutions that may be more your taste. Because all Scalix versions before 11.3 unfortunately do not allow SSL/TLS encryption of its mail services, a workaround has to be found. Scalix encourages the use of the program Stunnel (`http://www.stunnel.org`) for redirection and encryption of mail connections. For example, a configuration like:

```
accept = 995
connect = 110
```

in its configuration would redirect SSL/TLS encrypted connections to port 993, (the standard POP3S port) to the unencrypted POP3 port 110. Thus, we can allow only connections to ports 993 (POP3S), 993 (IMAPS), and 465 (SMTPS) from our clients and internally redirect them to the local ports 110, 143, and 25. The firewall configuration could then be arranged to allow only the secure ports, while Scalix is running unencrypted. Don't close your SMTP port 25 in your firewall if your Scalix server might receive Internet mail by SMTP via its DNS entry.

Installing Stunnel is easy: `yast -i stunnel` or `yum stunnel` installs the software, and the configuration file in `/etc/stunnel/stunnel.conf` only needs these entries:

```
[pop3s]
accept = 995
connect = 110
[imaps]
accept = 993
connect = 143
[ssmtp]
accept = 465
connect = 25
(...)
cert = /etc/stunnel/stunnel.pem
```

The last line specifies the SSL certificate Stunnel is supposed to use for encryption. This file can be "built" with the OpenSSL tools in `/usr/share/ssl/certs`: Enter a simple `make stunnel` and follow the instructions. The "common name" entry in this certificate must be the full-qualified hostname of your server, if you don't want to run into any problems.

# Securing Scalix with https Redirection

Stunnel helps with SSL/TLS encryption of mail services. Enabling https web services is a little more tricky. Depending on the platform you are using, Scalix may or may not automatically use https. For example, on Red Hat Enterprise Linux, https seems to be the default. However, this is not the case with SUSE and other systems. Once you have your system up and running, it might be a very good idea to restrict access to both webmail and administration console to connections using the secure https protocol.

Please note that the following howto proved to be very tricky, and maybe it will not work at all on future releases or untested environments. Also, know-how of the Apache2 Web server (`http://httpd.apache.org`) and the Tomcat application server (`http://tomcat.apache.org`) configuration is needed. We have tested the following procedure on openSUSE 10.1, using various Scalix 11 versions. Unfortunately, because these changes are so deep in the Scalix-Tomcat and—Apache configuration, an upgrade of Scalix will almost certainly kill this setup. Nevertheless, the work we are going to do here gives you an insight in how the web server and Tomcat on a typical Scalix system work together, and how you can adjust and restrict access for your users. Needless to say, back up all files edited in the following process and don't try it on a productive system before you have had success on a test system and know what you are doing.

- Create a SSL Key for Tomcat with:

  ```
  /usr/java/jre1.5.0_06/bin/keytool -genkey -alias tomcat -keyalg RSA
  ```

- When asked, use `changeit` as a temporary password (this is specified in the Scalix-tomcat connector configuration).

- Edit `/var/opt/scalix/sx/tomcat/conf/server.xml`,, beginning with line 82 to the following:

  ```
  <!-- Define a non-SSL HTTP/1.1 Connector on port 8080 -->
  <!--
  <Connector port="8080" maxHttpHeaderSize="8192"
   maxThreads="150"
   minSpareThreads="25"
   maxSpareThreads="75"
   enableLookups="false"
   redirectPort="8443"
   acceptCount="100"
   connectionTimeout="20000"
   disableUploadTimeout="true"
   URIEncoding="UTF-8" />
  -->
  ```

```
<!-- Note : To disable connection timeouts, set connectionTimeout
  value to 0 -->
<!-- Note : To use gzip compression you could set the
  following properties :
 compression="on"
 compressionMinSize="2048"
 noCompressionUserAgents="gozilla, traviata"
 compressableMimeType="text/html,text/xml"
-->
<!-- Define a SSL HTTP/1.1 Connector on port 8443 -->
<Connector port="8443" maxHttpHeaderSize="8192"
 maxThreads="150"
 minSpareThreads="25"
 maxSpareThreads="75"
 enableLookups="false"
 disableUploadTimeout="true"
 acceptCount="100"
 scheme="https"
 secure="true"
 clientAuth="false"
 sslProtocol="TLS"
 URIEncoding="UTF-8" />

<!-- Define an AJP 1.3 Connector on port 8009 -->
<Connector port="8009"
 address="scalixbook.org"
 enableLookups="false"
 redirectPort="8443"
 protocol="AJP/1.3"
 URIEncoding="UTF-8" />
 (...)
```

These changes make Tomcat listen for encrypted connections. You may now restart Scalix with `/etc/init.d/scalix restart`; restart Tomcat only with `/etc/init.d/scalix-tomcat restart` or do a reboot. Test success of your changes with `lsof -i :8443`:

```
scalix:~ # lsof -i :8443
COMMAND  PID USER   FD    TYPE DEVICE SIZE NODE NAME
java    1739 root   10u   IPv4   4950        TCP *:pcsync-https (LISTEN)
scalix:~ #
```

Or point your Browser to `https://scalixbook.org:8443`, replacing scalixbook.org with your server name. You should receive the Tomcat testpage. Add `/sac` to the URL and you will see the Scalix admin console.

# Configuring Apache2 for SSL Redirection

While we have successfully configured Tomcat, we now have to prepare Apache for http redirection to https, so that users addressing http are automatically redirected to https. For this purpose, Apache also needs a SSL certificate:

- Create a TLS/SSL key:

```
openssl req -new -x509 -newkey rsa:1024 -days 3650 -keyout \
privkey.pem -out server.pem
```

- Remove the passphrase:

```
openssl rsa -in privkey.pem -out privkey.pem
```

- Merge private key and public key into a single file.

```
cat privkey.pem >> scalix-apache.pem
```

- Copy this file to /etc/ssl/certs/.

- Make Apache listen on port 443, too: Add listen 443 to the Apache's config file listen.conf.

- Add the mod_rewrite module by adding rewrite to this line in your server's config in /etc/sysconfig/apache2:

```
# Added by Scalix installer: proxy proxy_ajp deflate
APACHE_MODULES="actions alias auth_basic authn_file authz_host
 authz_groupfile authz_default authz_user authn_dbm autoindex
 cgi dir env expires include log_config mime negotiation setenvif
 ssl suexec userdir php5 proxy proxy_ajp deflate rewrite"
```

- Edit the file /etc/opt/scalix-tomcat/connector/ajp/instance-scalix.conf:

```
<VirtualHost *:80>
    Include /etc/opt/scalix-tomcat/connector/ajp/app-scalix.*.conf
  <LocationMatch "^/sac/*">
    RewriteEngine on
    RewriteRule ^(.*) https://%{SERVER_NAME}%{REQUEST_URI} [R,L]
  </LocationMatch>
  <LocationMatch "^/webmail/*">
    RewriteEngine on
    RewriteRule ^(.*) https://%{SERVER_NAME}%{REQUEST_URI} [R,L]
  </LocationMatch>
</VirtualHost>

<VirtualHost *:443>
SSLEngine on
SSLCertificateFile /etc/ssl/certs/scalix-apache.pem
Include /etc/opt/scalix-tomcat/connector/ajp/app-scalix.*.conf
</VirtualHost>
```

Another convenient thing is to redirect all http or https access to the Scalix server to webmail. This will not affect the admin console. Simply place a file like the following in the document root of your Web server:

```
<html>
<head>
<title>Redirect</title>
<meta http-equiv=refresh content="0; url=https://scalixbook.org/
                                              webmail/">
</head>
<body>
<br>
<p>Redirecting to Scalix Webmail via a Secure Connection... </p>
</body>
</html>
```

# Some More Ideas ...

If you prefer not to do encryption in Tomcat at all, but do it all in Apache, here is an example that is reported to work on CentOS 5. For other RHEL4 derivatives, you will need mod_jk instead of mod_ajp and mod_proxy. This is a custom vhost definition; it may need to be rolled into the standard Scalix files. Things like /caa and /res can't be rewritten, so there will need for an exclusion rule. This configuration was taken from a DMZ machine; it forwards the requests to the real Scalix server.

```
<VirtualHost *:80>
        ServerAdmin <address>
        ServerName mail.domain.com

        RewriteEngine on
        RewriteRule ^(.*) https://mail.domain.comconcurrent.
                                       co.za:443$1 [R,L]

</VirtualHost>

<VirtualHost *:443>
        ServerAdmin <address>
        ServerName mail.domain.com
        ErrorLog logs/mail.domain.com-error_log
        CustomLog logs/mail.domain.comconcurrent.co.za-access_log
                                                      common

        RewriteEngine on
        RewriteCond %{REQUEST_METHOD} ^(TRACE|TRACK)
        RewriteRule .* - [F]

        SSLEngine on
        SSLCipherSuite ALL:!ADH:RC4+RSA:+HIGH:!SSLv2
```

```
SSLCACertificateFile /etc/pki/tls/certs/ca-bundle.crt
SSLCertificateFile /etc/pki/tls/certs/localhost.crt
SSLCertificateKeyFile /etc/pki/tls/private/localhost.key
<Location />
        SSLOptions +StdEnvVars
        AddOutputFilterByType DEFLATE text/xml text/html
                                              text/css
        AddOutputFilterByType DEFLATE application/x-javascript
        Order Allow,Deny
        Allow from all
</Location>
<IfModule mod_setenvif.c>
SetEnvIf User-Agent ".*MSIE.*" nokeepalive ssl-unclean-
                                          shutdown \
downgrade-1.0 force-response-1.0
</IfModule>
<IfModule mod_log_config.c>
CustomLog logs/ssl_request_log \
  "%t %h %{SSL_PROTOCOL}x %{SSL_CIPHER}x \"%r\" %b"
</IfModule>
Alias /mail /usr/share/squirrelmail
ProxyPass /api ajp://scalix.domain.comconcurrent.co.za:
                                          8009/api
ProxyPass /m ajp://scalix.domain.com:8009/m
ProxyPass /m ajp://scalix.domain.com:8009/m
ProxyPass /webmail ajp://scalix.domain.com:8009/webmail
ProxyPass /Scalix http://scalix.domain.com/Scalix
ProxyPass /omhtml http://scalix.domain.com/omhtml
</VirtualHost>
```

The following table shows more ideas and concepts that will help to make your Scalix server even more secure. Unfortunately, describing them in detail is beyond the scope of this book.

| Action | Function |
| --- | --- |
| Tripwire (http://sourceforge.net/projects/tripwire) | Intrusion detection, notices unwanted file changes. |
| Change greetings of the servers (SMTP, IMAP, POP, Apache, Tomcat) | No version number may be displayed. Attackers have to find out what kind of server is running here. (Security by obscurity?) |
| Change ports of servers | Redirect ports from unusual ports using Stunnel. |

| Action | Function |
|---|---|
| AppArmor (http://www.novell.com/de-de//linux/security/apparmor), SElinux (http://www.novell.com/de-de//linux/security/apparmor) and (http://selinux.sourceforge.net) etc. | Restrict access to resources, files, hardware etc. with policy-based software. Hardly works with Scalix, advanced configuration skills are needed. |
| Run servers as non-root user | A compromised server does not offer root-privileges to the attacker any more. Works with Tomcat and Apache on Scalix. |
| Deny root-logins for SSH | If you have several admins logging in as root, you can trace who acquired root privileges by su. This is not possible with normal root logins. |

There are many more possible ideas that help securing a Scalix server. The Scalix Wiki and Forums are the best place to look for guidelines.

# Summary

In this chapter, we have learnt how to secure a Scalix server. Firewalls and OpenVPN do a very good job, but there are some quirks where the admin has to pay attention. Stunnel works flawlessly, whereas https redirection does not survive updates and cannot be recommended, but it helps understanding the structure of the Scalix web server.

# 10
# Backup and Restore

In this chapter, we will discuss how to backup and restore a Scalix mail server. Besides a complete backup by copying and synchronizing the whole server, the administrator can make a backup of /var/opt/scalix directory and restore this by simple copy. Scalix also offers special tools to export and import single mailboxes, and there are several scripts available that do automated backups of all or single mailboxes. For large environments, LVM snapshots and SEP sesam, a proprietary backup software, can be used.

## Saving /var/opt/scalix

The simplest backup that an administrator can do is to copy and save the directory /var/opt/scalix with all of its subdirectories. On a single Scalix server, this will save all mailboxes, calendar data, public folders, directories, and system configuration. Because the Scalix servers continuously creates, moves, and links files below this subdirectory, it is absolutely recommended to stop the Scalix server before copying. Otherwise, a restore may produce errors and we may end up with lost or corrupted data. Thus, the easiest full backup of the Scalix server is the following procedure:

- Stop all running Scalix services.
- Copy /var/opt/scalix recursively to a different location and make sure that all permissions and ownerships are preserved.
- Restart all Scalix services.
- The command omshut and omon accomplish this job for us. To stop and restart the Scalix server, try the following commands:

```
scalix:/ # omshut
Disabling 14 subsystem(s).
scalix:/ #
```

Now, the Scalix services are down. On most systems, it is a good idea to stop also the Scalix database server and Scalix Tomcat:

```
scalix:/backup # /etc/init.d/scalix-postgres stop
Stopping scalix-postgres service (scalix):        done
scalix:/backup # /etc/init.d/scalix-tomcat stop
Stopping Tomcat service (scalix)Using CATALINA_BASE:   /var/opt/
scalix/sx/tomcat
Using CATALINA_HOME:   /opt/scalix-tomcat
Using CATALINA_TMPDIR: /var/opt/scalix/sx/tomcat/temp
Using JRE_HOME:
                                                  done
```

Now it is safe to copy the directory /var/opt/scalix to a safe place. You can replicate this Scalix server by simply setting up an identical server and copying the contents of your backup to /var/opt/scalix of the new server. Don't forget to stop the Scalix services on this host too, with omshut. Once your backup is done, omrc restarts all services:

```
scalix:/ # omrc
Scalix 11.1.0.10849

Copyright (C) 2002-2007 Scalix Corporation.  All rights reserved.
(...)
                    RESTRICTED RIGHTS LEGEND
Use, duplication, or disclosure by the U.S. Government is subject to
(...)
Enabling 8 subsystem(s).
Directory Relay Server      Started
(...)
Archiver                    Started
omrc : Scalix started
scalix:/ #
```

The omshut command simply tells about the stopped services, whereas the omrc command lists copyright and license information as well as the started services. The following sequence of commands is a full backup of your Scalix server:

```
scalix:/ # mkdir /backup/var_opt_scalix
scalix:/ # omshut
Disabling 14 subsystem(s).
scalix:/ # /etc/init.d/scalix-postgres stop
Stopping scalix-postgres service (scalix):        done
scalix:/backup # /etc/init.d/scalix-tomcat stop
Stopping Tomcat service (scalix)Using CATALINA_BASE:   /var/opt/
scalix/sx/tomcat
```

```
(...)
                                                                done
scalix:/ # tar -czpf /backup/var_opt_scalix/2007_06_24.tar.gz /var/
opt/scalix
tar: Removing leading `/' from member names
scalix:/ # /etc/init.d/scalix-postgres start
Starting scalix-postgres service (scalix):
done
scalix:/ # /etc/init.d/scalix-tomcat start
Starting Tomcat service (scalix)Using CATALINA_BASE:   /var/opt/
scalix/sx/tomcat
Using CATALINA_HOME:   /opt/scalix-tomcat
Using CATALINA_TMPDIR: /var/opt/scalix/sx/tomcat/temp
Using JRE_HOME:

 done
scalix:/ # omrc
Scalix 11.1.0.10849
(..)
```

First, a directory called /backup/_var_opt_scalix is created. This is where we will store the compressed Scalix data. Then, services are stopped, and the tar command is invoked.

tar -czpf creates (-c) a new, compressed (due to the -z parameter) file archive at the location specified after the parameter -f. The -p switch makes tar preserve user permissions on the directories and files that are stored, which is necessary for a successful Scalix backup. The second path listed is the directory that is supposed to be stored in the tar.gz file. It is a good idea to add the date of the full backup in the filename.

# Restoring /var/opt/scalix

Restoring a full backup to your Scalix server is as easy. The only difference is in the parameter with which tar is invoked: -x is used for extraction. The sequence of commands thus looks like this:

```
scalix:/ # omshut
Disabling 14 subsystem(s).
scalix:/ # /etc/init.d/scalix-postgres stop
Stopping scalix-postgres service (scalix):         done
scalix:/backup # /etc/init.d/scalix-tomcat stop
Stopping Tomcat service (scalix)Using CATALINA_BASE:   /var/opt/
scalix/sx/tomcat
(...)
                                                                done
scalix:/ # tar -xzpf /backup/var_opt_scalix/2007_06_24.tar.gz
scalix:/ # /etc/init.d/scalix-postgres start
```

```
Starting scalix-postgres service (scalix):
done

scalix:/ # /etc/init.d/scalix-tomcat start
Starting Tomcat service (scalix)Using CATALINA_BASE:    /var/opt/
scalix/sx/tomcat
Using CATALINA_HOME:    /opt/scalix-tomcat
Using CATALINA_TMPDIR: /var/opt/scalix/sx/tomcat/temp
Using JRE_HOME:

 done
scalix:/ # omrc
Scalix 11.1.0.10849
(..)
```

If you plan to use a "backup similar backup" strategy, you should do restores on a regular basis. It is a very good idea to keep an identical Scalix machine and restore current backups to this machine. Such testing is the best preparation for a real disaster recovery.

# Incremental Backups to a Different Machine

Rsync (`http://samba.anu.edu.au/rsync`) is a tool for synchronizing directories and files. It can be used on a local machine and to and from remote servers over a network connection. One of its biggest advantages is that it supports incremental backups and SSH connections to remote servers. Using `rsync`, the administrator can save bandwidth and storage, while using safe, encrypted connections. This backup process is also very simple:

- Stop Scalix and all its services.
- Invoke `rsync` with the archive switch `-a`.
- Restart Scalix services.

The command `rsync -avz /var/opt/scalix /backup/rsync` does a local incremental backup of `/var/opt/scalix` to `/backup/rsync/scalix`:

```
scalix:/ # rsync -avz /var/opt/scalix /backup/rsync/
(...)
scalix/sx/webmail/log4j.properties
scalix/sx/webmail/swa.properties
scalix/sx/webmail/swa.properties.bak
sent 109309996 bytes   received 175444 bytes   3589686.56 bytes/sec
total size is 206054028   speedup is 1.88
scalix:/ #
```

If invoked for the second time, only changes will be copied. The additional parameter `-e ssh user@host` lets `rsync` use SSH to copy the backup data to the remote SSH host, logging in with the specified user's credentials, asking for the remote user's password.

Obviously, entering the SSH key is not very handy for automated backups. But SSH offers a strategy with which safe password-less logins are possible — public key authentication. For this purpose, the user who wants to log in without a password creates a SSH key pair on his client. While the private key remains on the SSH client, the public key is copied and appended to the file `~/.ssh/authorized_keys` on the SSH server. It is a very good idea to add a special user for backup purposes. In the following example, this user is called `mailbackup`.

- Generate a SSH key pair:

    ```
    scalix:/ # ssh-keygen -t rsa
    Generating public/private rsa key pair.
    Enter file in which to save the key (/root/.ssh/id_rsa):
    Enter passphrase (empty for no passphrase):
    Enter same passphrase again:
    Your identification has been saved in /root/.ssh/id_rsa.
    Your public key has been saved in /root/.ssh/id_rsa.pub.
    The key fingerprint is:
    b3:a1:2e:77:51:67:6e:7c:21:3e:a3:a1:61:48:17:3f root@scalix
    scalix:/ #
    ```

- Copy the key to the SSH server:

    ```
    scalix:/ # scp ~/.ssh/id_rsa.pub 10.123.10.2:/home/mailbackup/
                                            .ssh/authorized_keys
    The authenticity of host '10.10.10.2 (10.10.10.2)' can't be
                                                established.
    RSA key fingerprint is 3b:60:59:24:f8:51:62:39:41:af:fd
                                                :c0:5d.......
    Are you sure you want to continue connecting (yes/no)? yes
    Warning: Permanently added '10.123.10.2' (RSA) to the list of
                                                known hosts.
    Password:
    id_rsa.pub

                                    100%   393      0.4KB/s
                                          00:00

    scalix:/ #
    ```

- Verify the password less login:

    ```
    scalix:/ # ssh mailbackup@backupserver
    Have a lot of fun...
    mailbackup@backupserver:~>
    ```

- Now try to backup the Scalix message store with the full `rsync` command:

```
scalix:/ # rsync -avz -e ssh /backup/rsync/
        mailbackup@10.10.10.2:/home/mailbackup
building file list ... done
(...)
sent 112170487 bytes  received 187290 bytes  253915.88 bytes/sec
total size is 206054028  speedup is 1.83
scalix:/ #
```

You now have a full backup of your Scalix mail store on the remote machine.

If invoked for the second time, `rsync` only transfers the differences:

```
scalix:/ # rsync -avz -e ssh /backup/rsync/ mailbackup@10.10.10.2:/
                                            home/mailbackup
building file list ... done
sent 157491 bytes  received 20 bytes  35002.44 bytes/sec
total size is 206054028  speedup is 1308.19
scalix:/ #
```

Please note that for a complete restore you will have to take care of the correct permissions in the directory structure.

# Exporting/Importing Single Mailboxes

Scalix comes with several tools that make single mailbox backups possible. Two of them are sxmboxexp and sxmboximp. The first program is used to store mailbox data to a single file, which can be restored to the Scalix server with the second command. The following table shows the most important options of the export command:

| sxmboxexp Options | |
| --- | --- |
| -a, --archivefile | Back up the user's mail store to this file. |
| -u, --user <username> | The name of the user whose storage is to be backed up. |
| -x, --exclude <folder-id> | Exclude these folders from the backup. |
| c, --config [Y \| N] | Back up this user's configuration. |
| -p, --public | Back up the user's public folders. |
| -f, --folder <folder-id> Folder selection for export | Identify single folders for backup. |
| -h, --help, | Show brief help |

The usage of sxmboxexp is very straightforward: The command:

```
scalix:/ # sxmboxexp -u "Norbert Graf" -a /backup/NorbertGraf.mbox
```

will backup the complete mail store of the user Norbert Graf to the file /backup/NorbertGraf.mbox.

# Automated Backups to File

The backup command can easily be automated, so that up-to-date backup copies of the user's mail store are always available. In the Scalix wiki, there is a good example for the usage of sxmboxexp with a cronjob (http://www.scalix.com/wiki/index. php?title=HowTos/BackupScript_Mbox_Style). The short script called sxbackup looks like this:

```
#! /bin/bash
echo "[`date`]"
echo "Mailbox Backup Starting."
MBOXDIR="/backup/mailboxes"
if [ -d $MBOXDIR ]; then
    echo "Found Backup Directory. Using It."
else
    echo "Creating Backup Directory ${MBOXDIR} to backup mailboxes."
    mkdir ${MBOXDIR}
fi
for i in $(omshowu -m all | cut -d "/" -f 1 | sed -e 's: $::g' -e 's/
/\//g'); do
    user=`printf "$i" | sed -e 's:/: :g'`
(...)
    echo ${user}
    if [ -a $MBOXDIR/$i.mbox ]; then
        echo "Existing backup found.  Removing before creating new
backup."
        rm ${MBOXDIR}/${user}.mbox
    fi
    echo "Backing up user [${user}]"
    sxmboxexp -u "${user}" -a ${MBOXDIR}/"${user}".mbox --listlevel
folder -F
done
echo "Mailbox Backup Complete."
echo "[`date`]"
```

simply creates one file per user, storing all user's mailboxes in the directory /backup/mailboxes. A suitable cronjob like:

```
0 1 * * 6 /backup/scripts/mailbox_backup.sh > /var/log/mailbox_
backup[`date '+%m.%d.%Y'`].log
```

makes sure that the backup is run once every week. Add this line to your /etc/crontab file to have it run automatically.

An example run looks like the following:

```
scalix:/home/mfeilner # /sbin/sxbackup
[Sa Jun 23 16:57:36 CEST 2007]
Mailbox Backup Starting.
```

```
Creating Backup Directory /backup/mailboxes to backup mailboxes.
sxadmin
(..)
Markus Feilner
Backing up user [Markus Feilner]
# Archive file     : /backup/mailboxes/Markus Feilner.mbox
# Archive contents : Markus Feilner
# Archive date     : 2007-06-23 16:57:36

F-0000000001     Inbox
F-0000000002     Outbox
F-0000000003     Sent Items
F-0000001089     Deleted Items
F-0000001139     Calendar
F-0000001140     Contacts
F-0000001141     Drafts
F-0000001142     Notes
F-0000001143     Tasks
(...)

# Number of folders : 10
# Number of messages: 52
# Total item size    : 35441Kb
Norbert Graf
Backing up user [Norbert Graf]
(...)
Mailbox Backup Complete.
[Sa Jun 23 16:57:40 CEST 2007]
scalix:/home/mfeilner #
```

The script uses omshowu to receive all users available on the Scalix server, and stores every user's mail and groupware data like Calendar, Contacts, and more to a file in /backup/mailboxes:

```
scalix:/backup/mailboxes # ls -l
total 84488
-rw-rw---- 1 root scalix 86356685 2007-06-23 16:57 Markus Feilner.mbox
-rw-rw---- 1 root scalix    44463 2007-06-23 16:57 Norbert Graf.mbox
-rw-rw---- 1 root scalix    16060 2007-06-23 16:57 sxadmin.mbox
-rw-rw---- 1 root scalix     2643 2007-06-23 16:57 sxqueryadmin.mbox
scalix:/backup/mailboxes #
```

This test system obviously has four users.

# Importing Data with sxmboximp

Again, the next step is the restore process. Importing from a file created with sxmboxexp is done with the simple command:

```
scalix:/backup/mailboxes # sxmboximp --archive Norbert\ Graf.mbox
```

The administrator has restored Norbert Graf's mail store. For testing purposes, it is a very good idea to add a dummy user like Restore Test and restore the backed up data to this user's mailbox:

```
scalix:/backup/mailboxes # sxmboximp --archive Norbert\ Graf.mbox --
user "Restore Test"
```

Log in to the Web mailer as the dummy user and check for success:

Here are the most important options from the sxmboximp command:

| sxmboximp | |
| --- | --- |
| -a, --archivefile <file> | Import from the specified file. |
| -u, --user <username> | Restore to this user's account. |
| -x, --exclude <folder-id> | Exclude this folder for this restore process. |
| -s, --subfolder | Include subfolders. |
| -c, --config [Y \| N] | Import the user's configuration files. |
| -h, --help | Show brief help. |

sxmboxexp and sxmboximp are tools that are based on the HP OpenMail tools, omcpoutu and omcpinu. These commands are still available, together with detailed man pages.

# Backup Tools for Large Environments

Here, we see some of the methods used in large environments for creating backups:

## Logical Volume Management (LVM) Snapshots

Logical Volume Management is a technology that adds a virtual layer between your hard disks' partitions and your data. It is a three-layer model, consisting of logical volumes, volume groups, and physical volumes. Several hard disks or partitions are grouped to a "volume group", in which several logical volumes exist. To the operating system, the logical volumes appear like partitions and may contain file systems.

LVM is very handy in many situations, and a lot of admins also use it in small setups. Volumes can be resized, and moved between disks and hard disks can be added and removed. Snapshots of file systems allow "on-the-fly"- live-copies of an entire file system and the system can store single files that are bigger than single partitions or disks. All of this can be done during normal operation—unmounts, remounts or reboots are not necessary.

Setting up LVM is a three-step process:

- Initialize your disks for usage with LVM
- Create Volume groups containing the disks
- Create logical volumes in the volume groups

Administration and configuration of LVM is done with the following tools:

| Logical Volume Management - Tools | |
|---|---|
| pvdisplay, pvcreate | Display physical volumes and initialize disks for LVM |
| vgdisplay, vgcreate, vgextend, vgreduce, vgscan | Display, create, extend, reduce, and scan for volume groups |
| lvdisplay, lvcreate, lvextend, lvreduce | Display, create, extend, and reduce Logical Volumes |

Setting up Logical Volume Management is the recommended setup for large Scalix installations. Interested administrators will find a detailed description in the administration handbook, and even more details in the LVM HOWTO at the Linux Documentation project's website: (`http://tldp.org/HOWTO/LVM-HOWTO/index.html`).

One special feature of LVM are logical volume snapshots. Explaining LVM snapshots would go too far into details here, therefore a superficial explanation might say: When a LVM snapshot is taken, all write access to a volume is stopped, "buffered", and written to disk later, so that a live backup of arbitrary running services can be done. The usage of LVM snapshots is described in detail in `http://tldp.org/HOWTO/LVM-HOWTO/snapshots_backup.html`.

If you are using a SUSE distribution, you can have YaST configure your logical volumes:

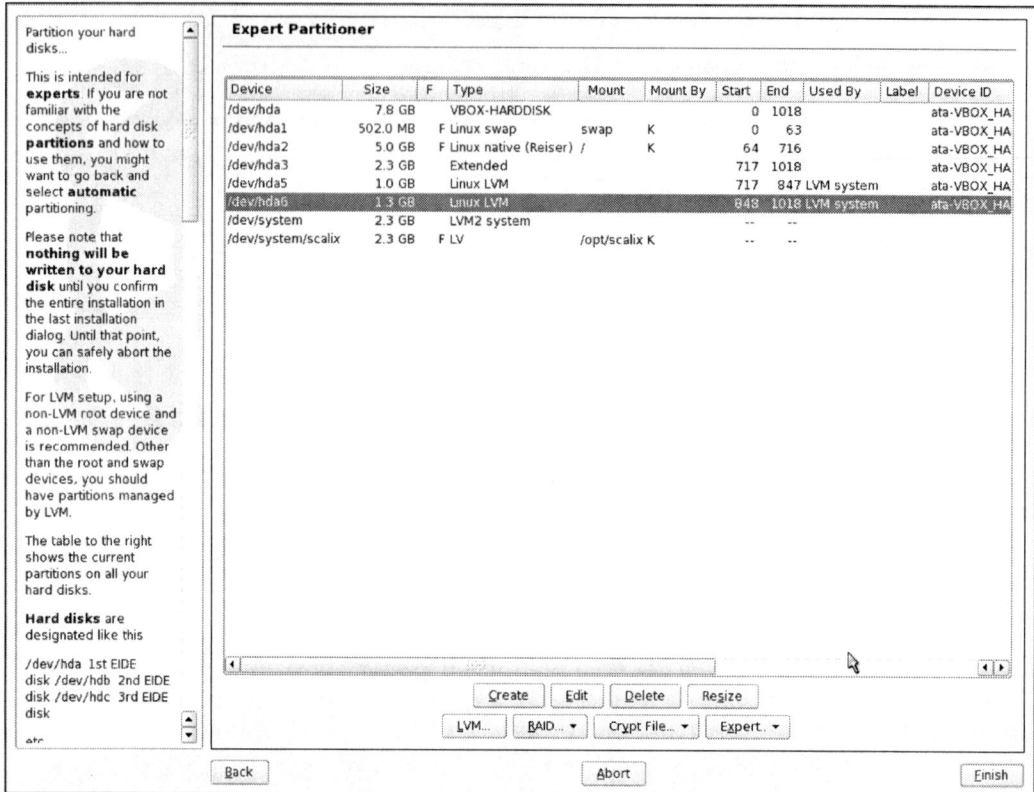

# Sxbackup from the Scalix Admin Resource Kit

Another useful pre-configured backup tool from the Scalix resources is sxbackup. It is part of the admin resource kit, and beginning with Scalix version 11.3, it is even part of the install. Otherwise, it can be found here: `http://www.scalix.com/wiki/index.php?title=Admin_Resource_Kit`.

The Scalix Administration handbook contains details to this tool, too. Sxbackup is able to use Logical Volume Management to do a snapshot and rsync or tar to store the backup. After downloading and extracting the file, a guided setup is available. Change to the directory you extracted sxbackup to and type `/setup`.

```
This script configures complete tar archive type or incremental to
remote using rsync type Scalix Server backups. Please refer to the
sxbackup.pdf for more information. Would you like to setup your
backups now?

              < Yes  >                    <  No  >
```

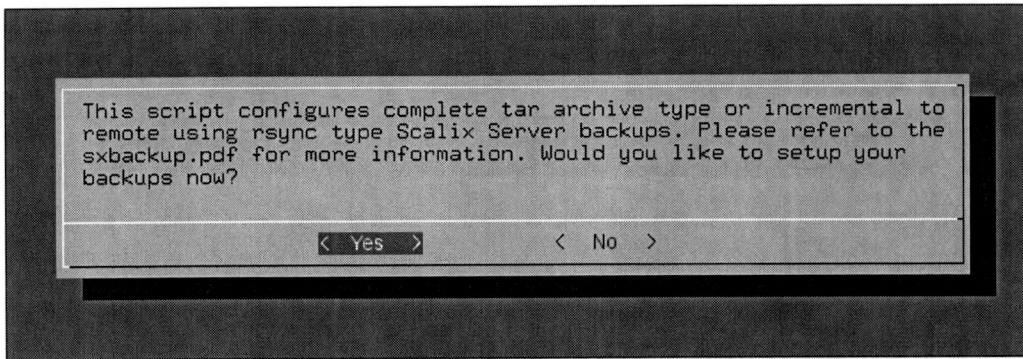

Sxbackup setup then asks for your LVM and rsync data. The sxbackup archive provides brief documentation in `sxbackup.pdf`.

# Single Mail Restore with SEP sesam

In large environments, the proprietary backup software SEP sesam (`http://www.sep.de`) may be the ideal choice for a Scalix server. SEP consists of a backup server and several client software packages, like groupware connectors or database engines. One of them is a Scalix connector called "SEP sesam module for Scalix", available from (`http://download.sep.de/db_modules/scalix`). It is designed for large scale networks and offers several high-end features like:

- Single mail restore
- Search for mails in the backup
- Snapshot-backups
- Full backup and restore of the server for disaster recovery
- Graphical user interfaces for administration and setup

Extensive documentation can be found here (`http://wiki.sepsoftware.com/wiki/index.php/Scalix_doc`). The SEP client software is included with a vast amount of Linux distributions, including openSUSE and Red Hat. According to rumours, there will be an integration of the Scalix server with Scalix in the forthcoming versions including one free "SEP sesam One" server. The online module that includes single mail restore will, however, only be available to the Sysadmin user, and not the groupware users.

SEP for Scalix comes with a fully-featured GUI client, from where an administrator can start, stop, and configure automatic and manual backups. After its start, click on **Create New** to arrange a new task.

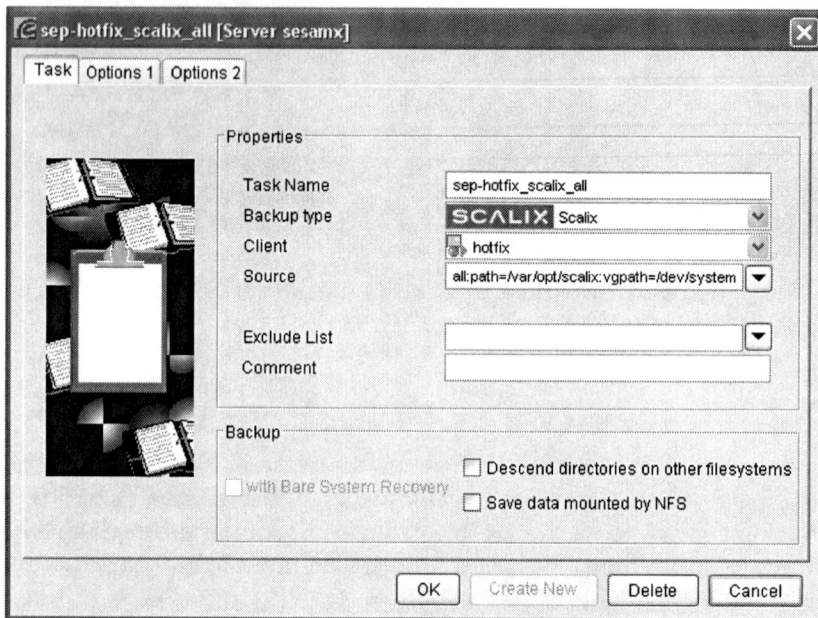

Choose a task name and a valid source. If you choose Scalix as the backup type, then this will be automatically done for you. Click on **Ok** to proceed. In the next dialog, select the Scalix source on the server and click on **Ok**.

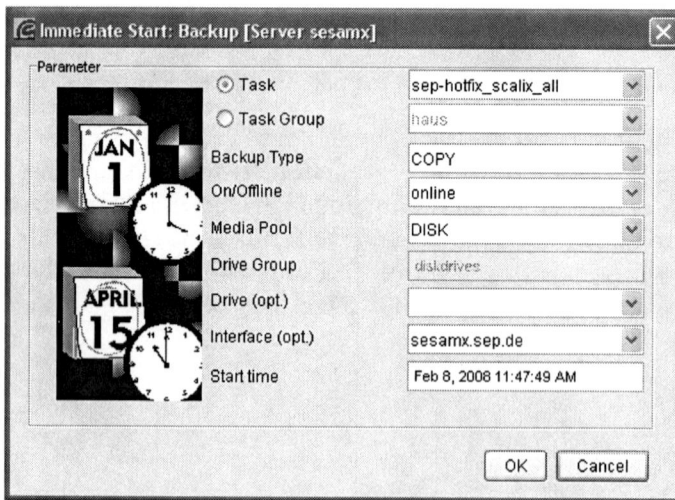

If you want, you can start the backup right away. SEP supports online and offline backups and media pools. Configure this dialog your preferences, enter a start time in the appropriate field and click on **OK** to start. In the SEP client GUI, you are able to control all the tasks you have scheduled.

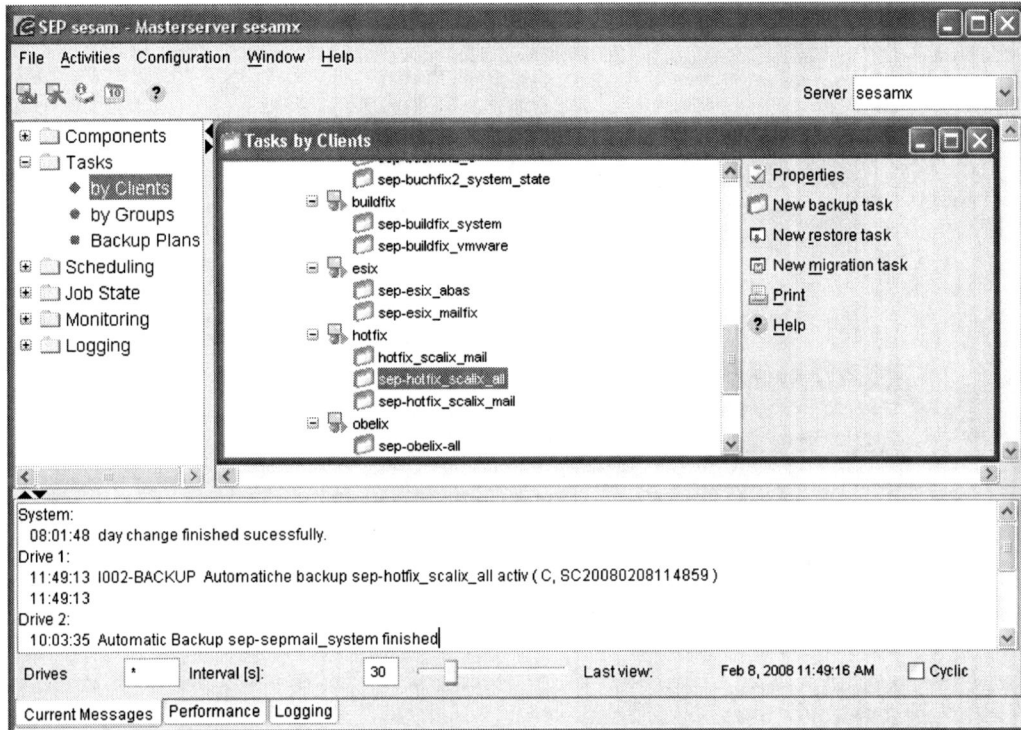

The tree on the left helps you to sort your tasks either by clients and groups, events, or job state. Click on the entry **Clients** to see the current state of all scheduled backup jobs and change settings.

By selecting **Job State - Backups**, the current state of the each backup job can be observed. The **Monitoring** tab shows the current state of each running backup job:

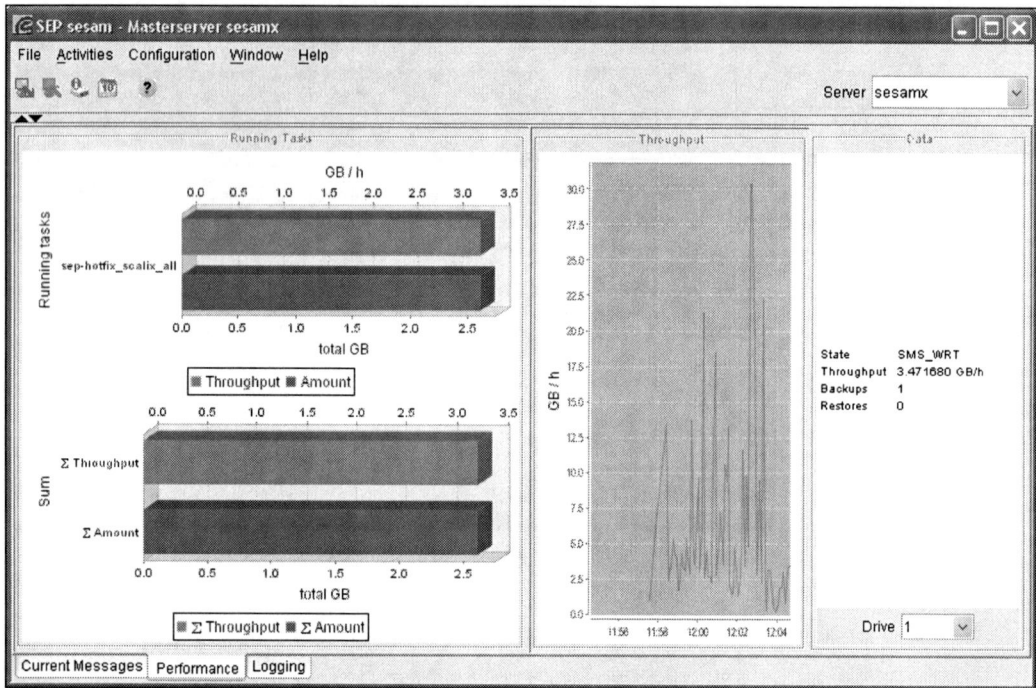

On of the most important features of the SEP backup software is the ability to do a single mail restore for a variety of mail servers including Scalix. The following image shows a single Mailbox in the **Mailbox view**. Scalix enables the user, by switching to **File view** to search by hand or automatically with the **Search** button for the missing emails.

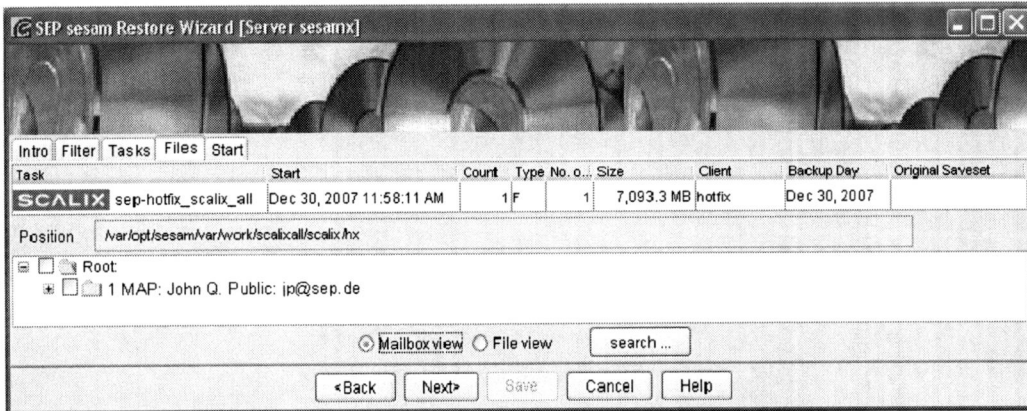

# Summary

In this chapter, we learned how to do full, incremental or single mailbox backups of our Scalix server. Both Scalix backup tools and Linux system tools were used to backup and restore the Scalix server data to a local directory and other servers, including the basic architecture of a SEP backup server.

# Scalix Directory Integration

In this chapter, you will learn how to administrate Scalix in sync with data stored in remote directories. This chapter starts with an explanation of how Scalix delivers its information in LDAP-style and rounds up with a guide on how to integrate Scalix with an external Microsoft Active Directory.

## Integrating with an External LDAP Directory

In Chapter 1, we learned that LDAP stands for Lightweight Directory Access Protocol, a defined way of accessing information stored in a directory. The Scalix directory, however, is based on the x.500 standard, which differs from the LDAP standard. Scalix comes with a special daemon offering connectivity to the Scalix directory server. An interface enables LDAP clients to connect to this daemon and ask for information stored in the Scalix directory.

A simple LDAP client installed on almost every Linux system is the command line tool ldapsearch. Because the Scalix LDAP server allows read access to everyone, without authentication, the command ldapsearch -h localhost -p 389 -x lists the directory information of your Scalix users and more. While the parameter -h is followed by the hostname or IP of your Scalix machine, -p is not necessary except if you have changed the LDAP port. The option -x enables simple authentication instead of some SASL method. A very detailed man page may help you with the details of your distribution's implementation of ldapsearch.

Here is an example output of ldapsearch on our test server:

```
mfeilner@scalix:~> ldapsearch -h localhost -p 389 -x | more
# extended LDIF
#
# LDAPv3
# base <> with scope subtree
# filter: (objectclass=*)
```

```
# requesting: ALL
#
# ScalixUserAdmins, Scalix
dn: cn=ScalixUserAdmins, o=Scalix
cn: ScalixUserAdmins
objectClass: top
objectClass: distributionList
objectClass: mhsDistributionList
objectClass: scalixDistributionList
surname: ScalixUserAdmins
mhsORAddresses: S=ScalixUserAdmins/OU1=scalix/CN=ScalixUserAdmins
omInternetAddr: ScalixUserAdmins@scalix.scalixbook.org
mail: ScalixUserAdmins@scalix.scalixbook.org
rfc822Mailbox: ScalixUserAdmins@scalix.scalixbook.org
omAddress: ScalixUserAdmins /scalix/CN=ScalixUserAdmins
omMailnode: scalix
omCn: ScalixUserAdmins
omGlobalUniqueId: 0900000044158664-891.17.891.88
omLocalUniqueId: 160
(...)
# Norbert Graf, Scalix
dn: cn=Norbert Graf, o=Scalix
cn: Norbert Graf
c: US
objectClass: top
objectClass: person
objectClass: organizationalPerson
objectClass: mhsUser
objectClass: scalixPerson
surname: Graf
givenName: Norbert
mhsORAddresses: S=Graf/G=Norbert/OU1=scalix/CN=Norbert Graf
omInternetAddr: "Norbert Graf" <Norbert.Graf@scalixbook.org>
mail: Norbert.Graf@scalixbook.org
rfc822Mailbox: Norbert.Graf@scalixbook.org
omAddress: Norbert Graf /scalix/CN=Norbert Graf
omMailnode: scalix
omCn: Norbert Graf
omGlobalUniqueId: 1510000044158664-891.17.891.88
omLocalUniqueId: 353
omParentDl: 256
omParentDl: 192
omParentDl: 160
omParentDl: 224
omUlClass: Full
--More--
(...)
```

As you can see, there is detailed information on the user Norbert Graf including his email address, Scalix user name, and mailbox. You can easily use this information for synchronization scripts that import the data into your LDAP-server or for other services that need the input and provide LDAP compatibility.

# The Scalix LDAP Server

The Scalix LDAP server is controlled by the commands omon and omoff, whose man page provides detailed information on its usage. After changes to its configuration, the server must be restarted. The command omoff -a slapd stops the Scalix server, and with omon -a slapd it is started. Disabling the server may take a while (in the background), if you try to restart it too early, you will receive the following error:

```
scalix:/ # omoff -a slapd
Disabling 1 subsystem(s).
scalix:/ # omon -a slapd
omon : [OM 4824] Cannot start up subsystem LDAP Daemon,
       delayed shut down pending, 1 minute(s) left.
scalix:/ # omon -a slapd
Enabling 1 subsystem(s).
scalix:/ #
```

> Use omoff -w and it will wait for the service to shut down before displaying the shell, use -d0 if you don't want to wait.

Scalix's slapd configuration is done in the following three configuration files:

*   ldap.attribs — on our example server, the full path is: /var/opt/scalix.
    org/sx/s/sys/ldap.attribs. This defines the mapping of the LDAP
    attributes to the internal x500 directory attributes.
    ```
    (...)
    2.5.4.7      l,locality,localityName,2.5.4.7,OID.2.5.4.7
    2.5.4.8
      st,state,stateOrProvince,stateOrProvinceName,2.5.4.8,OID.2.5.4.8
    2.5.4.10     o,organization,organizationName,2.5.4.10,OID.2.5.4.10
    2.5.4.11
        ou,organizationalUnit,organizationalUnitName,2.5.4.11,OID
        .2.5.4.11
    2.5.4.6      c,country,countryName,2.5.4.6,OID.2.5.4.6
    2.5.4.9      street,streetAddress,2.5.4.9,OID.2.5.4.9
    (...)
    ```

Every line contains one pair of directory attributes, the OID strings of the x500-style Scalix directory and the LDAP representation. RFC 1779 will help you if you need to change things here, and there are many useful comments in this file. A simple advice: Don't change anything here unless you are absolutely sure about what you are doing.

- `slapd.conf`, on our system `/var/opt/scalix.org/sx/s/sys/slapd.conf` contains the configuration of the LDAP server. This file follows the configuration of the OpenLDAP server and provides a lot of comments to each possible parameter.

- `dit.cfg`, or `/var/opt/scalix.org/sx/s/sys/dit.cfg` in our example holds configuration parameters for those who want to change standard directory values. If, for example, an admin wants to change the default objectclasses for Scalix users, the option `PERSON_CLASSES` in this file is the right place to do so:

```
#
# Person Classes.  A white-space separated list of
     objectclasses that
# correspond to ordinary Scalix users.  This set of
     objectclasses is
# used when no explicit objectclass is given for an entry
     in an Scalix
# directory.
#
PERSON_CLASSES=top person organizationalPerson
     mhsUser scalixPerson
```

# Preparing a LDAP Server for Password Management

This procedure is explained in detail in the Scalix documentation and the Scalix wiki, its current link is (`http://www.scalix.com/wiki/index.php?title=HowTos/Using_OpenLDAP_for_password_management`), but this page and the configuration found there are subject to constant changes and may be outdated. The following is what worked on Scalix 11 on our test servers. Please note that this paragraph is only an introduction, a short overview of the to-dos that will not work if you do not know what you are doing.

Integrating external LDAP passwords is basically done in 3 steps:

- Install and configure an (Open-)LDAP server
- Configure PAM
- Configure Scalix to use the external passwords

First, you will need a LDAP server ready to authenticate users. If you are running SLES 9 or 10, there probably is an LDAP server, running and configured correctly. If not, there are YaST modules to set it up and administrate it: Just activate the button **Use LDAP** during installation when you configure user management:

After this, the **normal** Yast user management dialogs will use this server's LDAP back end for user configuration:

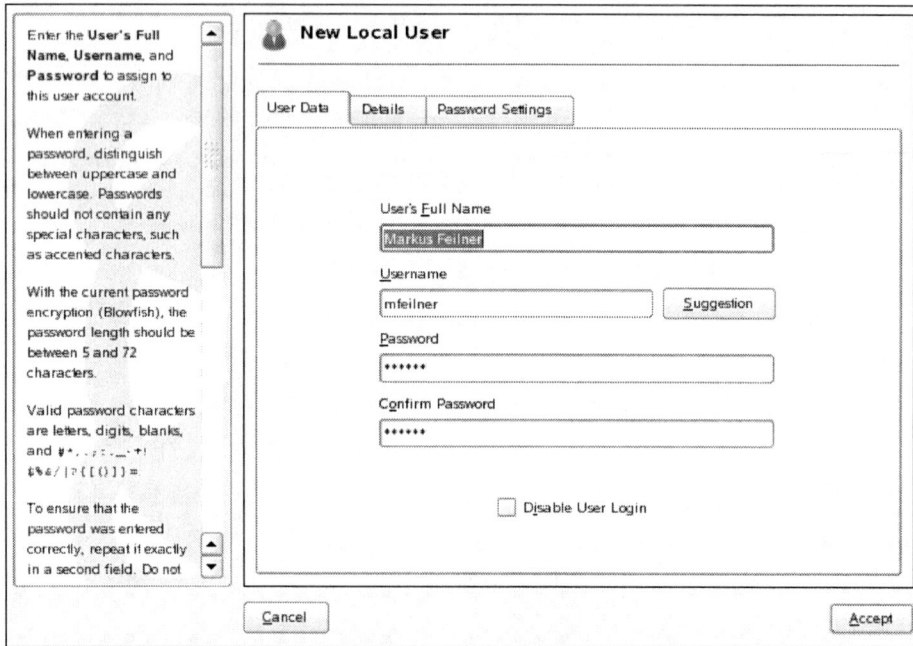

Note that this will only work if you have OpenLDAP and the YaST modules for LDAP connectivity installed. If you have troubles with that, have a look at: (`https://secure-support.novell.com/KanisaPlatform/Publishing/471/3000394_f.SAL_Public.html`).

On other platforms or if you want to do this manually: Install OpenLDAP-server, and make sure that the configuration of `/etc/openldap/slapd.conf` includes the following directives pointing to the necessary LDAP schemas:

```
include        /etc/openldap/schema/core.schema
include        /etc/openldap/schema/cosine.schema
include        /etc/openldap/schema/nis.schema
include        /etc/openldap/schema/inetorgperson.schema
```

Then change the suffix of your server to the values in the same file. Enter credentials for your administrator (don't type a plain text password here—use encryption!). After that, start your server with the init script `/etc/init.d/slapd start`. Check functionality with a call of `ldapsearch -x -h localhost` and control the correct entry for your domain name and administrator's data in the output.

Then generate the following file `import.ldif` and load it into the directory:

```
dn: dc=scalixbook,dc=org
dc: scalix
objectClass: top
objectClass: domain

dn: ou=People,dc=scalixbook,dc=org
ou: People
objectClass: top
objectClass: organizationalUnit

dn: uid=mfeilner, ou=people, dc=scalixbook, dc=org
objectclass: top
objectclass: person
objectClass: organizationalPerson
objectClass: inetOrgPerson
uid: mfeilner
userPassword: {SSHA}xxxxxxxxxxxxxxxxxxxxxxxx
cn: Markus Feilner
sn: Feilner
gn: Markus
```

Import can be done with the command `ldapadd` and its parameter `-f` (read from file). In the standard setup, you have to authenticate to your directory for write access. This is done with the parameter `-D`, followed by the administrator account:

```
ldapadd -x -D "cn=Manager, dc=scalixbook,dc=org" -W -f import.file
```

After importing the above data, the output should show the user's data. In the next step, add this user to your Scalix directory (either with the admin console or the `omaddu` command). Make sure that the Scalix user ID matches the LDAP UID field.

# Configuring Scalix for LDAP Authentication

As a second task, Scalix has to be configured to use the LDAP server. Configure the file `/etc/ldap.conf` on your Scalix server to use the external LDAP server by default. Enter hostname, LDAP base, and credentials for the LDAP bind here. Then change to the directory `/var/opt/scalix/sx/s/sys/pam.d` and change or create the following files:

- For Outlook, SWA and Mail authentication: `ual.remote`
- For example, Mozilla Mail and authenticated SMTP in general: `smtpd.auth`
- For POP3 clients: `pop3`
- For SWA and SAC: `omslapdeng`

Enter these lines to the first three files of this list, and make sure that the template lines by Scalix are not active:

```
auth sufficient om_ldap
auth sufficient om_auth
auth required pam_deny
account required om_auth
password required om_auth
session required om_auth
```

In a nutshell: PAM tests if account and username exist, if the user is allowed to log in, and if the password supplied is correct. As a fallback mechanism, if LDAP fails, a check against the Scalix directory is supplied too. So if your LDAP connection fails to work, there will still be authentication for true Scalix user accounts.

Scalix still needs to know the whereabouts of the LDAP server: edit /var/opt/ scalix/sx/s/sys/pam.d/omslapdeng and paste the following:

```
host=ldap.scalixbook.org
search=subtree
base=ou=people,dc=scalixbook,dc=org
filter=uid=%s
tls=off
```

Please replace host and domain name with your values.

That's all, you can now test the LDAP connectivity with whatever client you configured your system for. For example, if you edited the ual.remote file, then you may use Outlook and enter an LDAP user's credentials in the setup dialog. Simply by editing the right file and putting PAM directives in the right order, you can create a complex authentication scenario.

# Active Directory Integration

If you have an Active directory environment, Scalix Enterprise Edition can be integrated and administrated from your Windows server with only a few steps. All you need for this setup is a Windows 2003 server with a full installation of Microsoft's Active Directory—and a valid Scalix license. For your testing, there is a 60-day trial on the Scalix website, which is unlimited in function and serves well for test scenarios. Download the Enterprise Edition, and you will find the Windows software in the package.

Three steps are necessary to have Active Directory manage your Scalix users and their mailbox configuration:

- Install the Active Directory extensions provided by Scalix.

- Install the Windows Management Console GUI extensions provided by Scalix.

- Make the Scalix server synchronize its database with Active Directory on a regular basis.

> Technically, this is all you need the Scalix license for. All of the rest is accessible in the Community Edition also. If you want to and know how, you can extend the Active Directory schema yourself. Not an easy task, though.

The following guide will walk you through these steps. Please note that single-sign-on authentication for your users can be provided with Kerberos Authentication. However, this setup would go beyond the scope of this book, and it is dealt with in detail in the Scalix Setup Guide on the Scalix website.

# Installing the Active Directory Extensions

In the software directory of the Enterprise edition, you will find a .msi file that contains the installer. A simple double-click on it will install the extensions. After successful installation, you will find a file named ScalixForestPrep.exe in the subfolder Scalix below C.:\Program Files. By executing this file in a shell with the option **Install your Active Directory tree** the Scalix branch is being populated. Don't worry, if there is not much feedback: If you are successful, all you will receive is a **update successful**. Again, please note: Your changes won't have an effect on all your servers immediately.

After initial ADS extension and populating the forest, you have to add a first user.

# Create a New Scalix-ADS User

Just follow the normal procedure in Active Directory, like you normally do. One way to do so is adding a user via the context menu in the Active Directory management software:

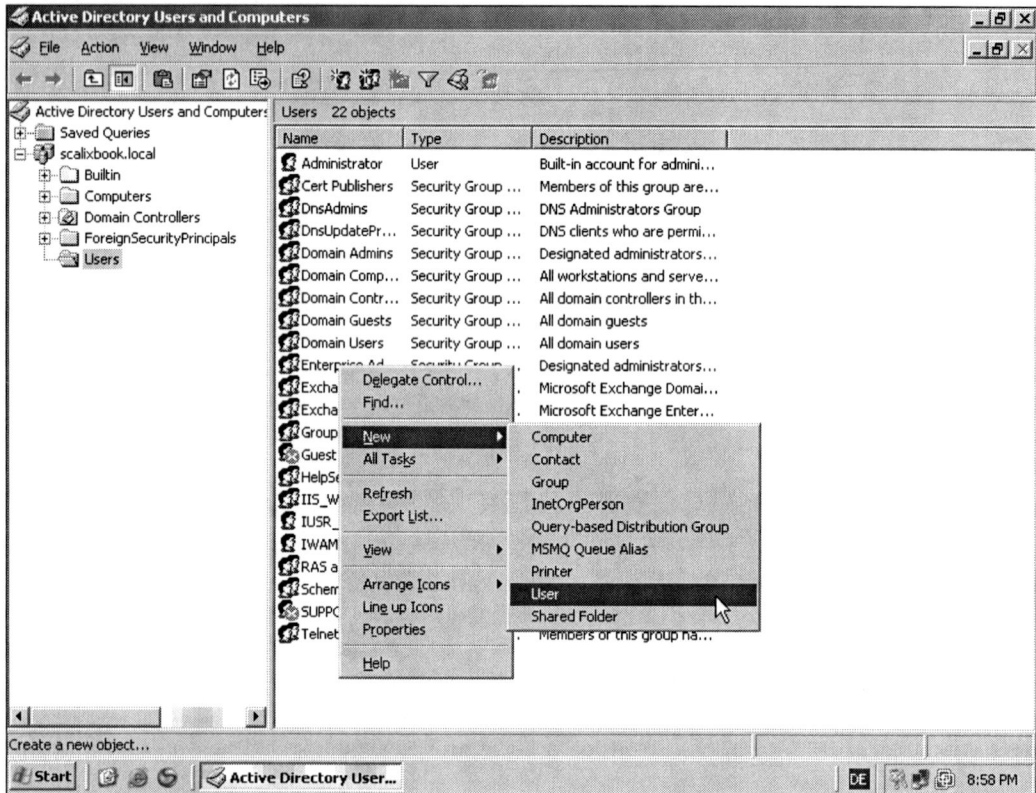

Type username and credentials and click on **Next** to proceed. The third window in this series of dialogs may seem new to you:

Enter your Scalix server's data and click on **Next**. Confirm the last dialog window with the button **Finish**, and your user is instantly added to your Active Directory's user database with a complete set of Scalix Mail settings. Please keep in mind that due to limitations of ADS, it may take a while until all your Windows servers will know of his existence.

# The Scalix ADS Extensions

But the Scalix ADS toolset has more to offer. There are a whole set of parameters that can be set from within the User Management of Active Directory. Select the new Scalix user and open his properties dialog:

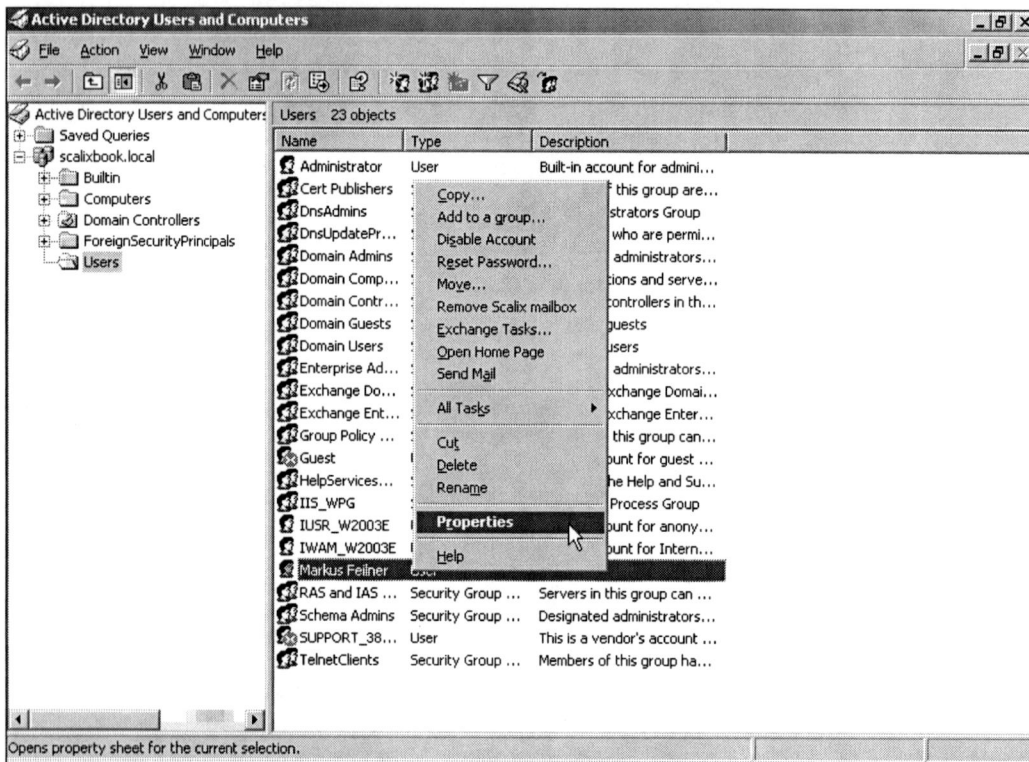

The Scalix extensions have added two new tabs. On the first tab **Scalix General** the administrator sets the mailnode responsible for this user, his email addresses, and the mailbox type (Standard or Premium):

**Markus Feilner Properties**    ? | X

| Member Of | Dial-in | Environment | Sessions | Remote control |

| General | Address | Account | Profile | Telephones | Organization |

| Terminal Services Profile | COM+ | Scalix General | Scalix Advanced |

Home Mailnode: scalix01

Email Address

○ Use server generated email addresses (Recommended)

● Specify email addresses manually

markus.feilner@scalixbook.org
info@scalixbook.org

[ Add Email ]    [ Edit email ]    [ Remove ]

Mailbox Type: Scalix Premium user ▼

[ OK ]    [ Cancel ]    [ Apply ]

The second tab **Scalix Advanced** offers language, mailbox limits, administrative access, and the possibility of hiding this user's entry.

**Markus Feilner Properties**    ? | X

| Member Of | Dial-in | Environment | Sessions | Remote control |

| General | Address | Account | Profile | Telephones | Organization |

| Terminal Services Profile | COM+ | Scalix General | Scalix Advanced |

Scalix Server Message Language: Default ▼

Mailbox Limits

Maximum Mailbox Size: 100 MB.

☑ Send warning on outgoing mail when near limit

☐ Reject incoming mail when over the limit

☑ Send mail to the user when over the limit

To grant this user administrative access, select the following checkbox:

☐ Enable Administrator capabilities

To hide this entry from being displayed in the system addressbook, select the following checkbox:

☐ Hide User Entry

[ OK ]    [ Cancel ]    [ Apply ]

# The Management Console Extension

The Microsoft Management Console (MMC) is a part of Windows since 2000. It offers centralized administration for the Windows administrator. Software vendors can add modules to this platform, and so did Scalix. In your software directory, you will find another .msi file called ...Aduc_GUI_....-msi. Double-click on it to have the MMC module installed.

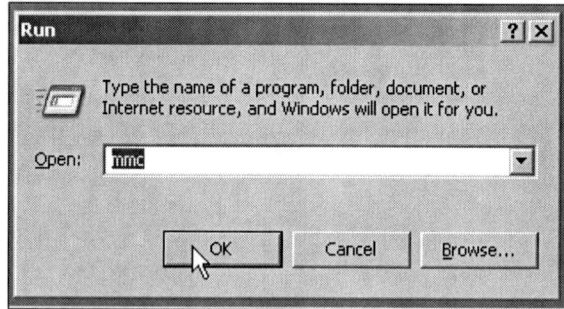

After the installation, execute the command mmc to start the Management Console. You'll see an empty box, where you can load external "snap-ins".

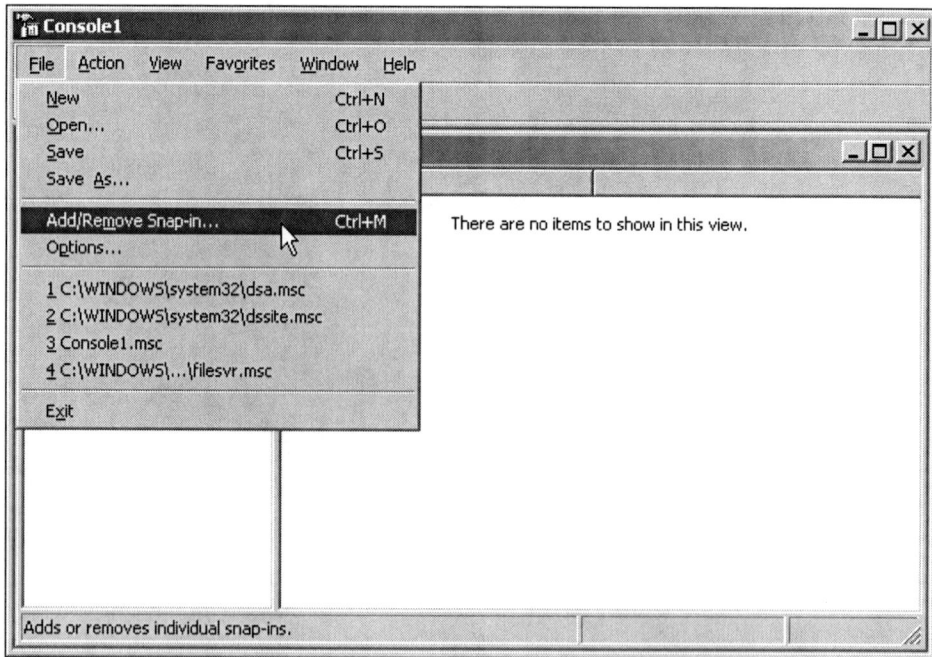

Select **Add/Remove Snap-In** from the main menu to add the Scalix MMC snap-in. In the following dialog, click on the **Add** button.

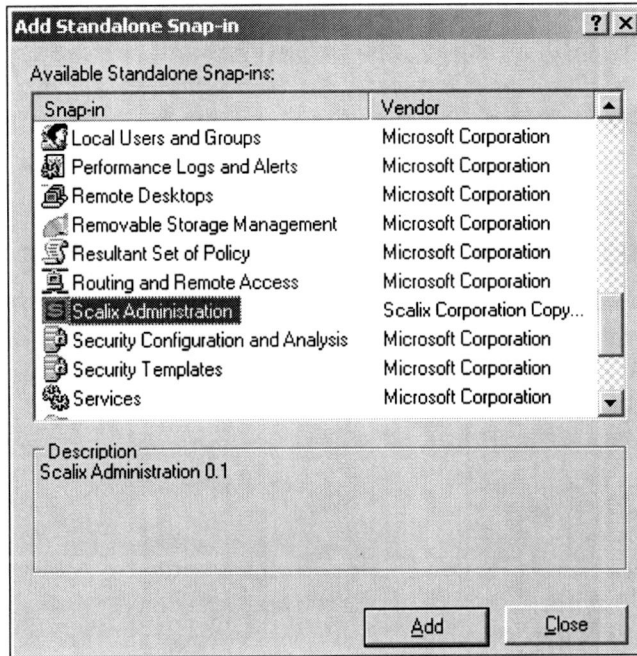

You'll see a list of available plug-ins. Select the Scalix plug-in and click on **Add**.

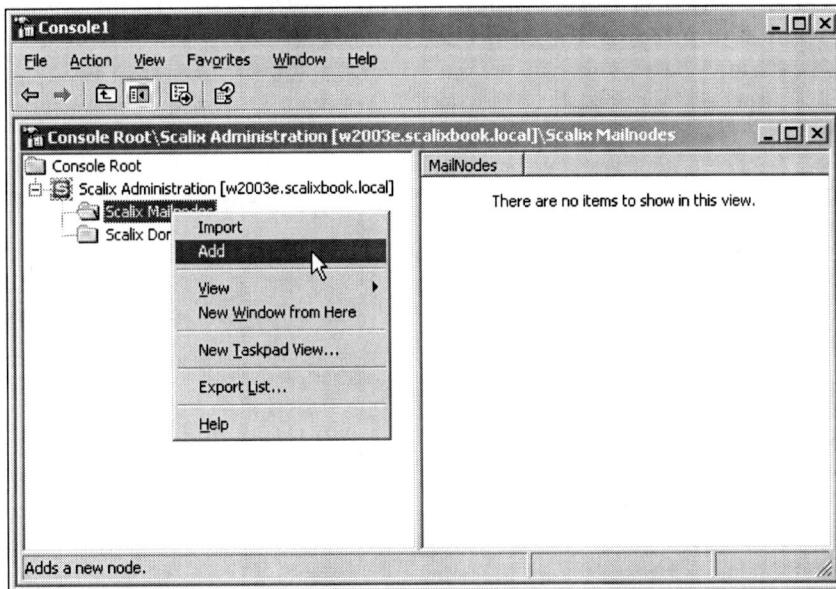

You are now able to manage your mailnodes and domains from within the Microsoft Management Console: You can add, change, and delete mailnodes, create new users, groups, and mailboxes.

The only thing that is still missing is the synchronization with the Scalix server, which is done by omldapsync. Once configured, omldapsync has to be run by a cron job on a regular basis and will keep the Scalix directory in sync with your Active Directory.

# Activating Synchronization Agreements

Tell omldapsync to use the Windows Active Directory as a source for a so-called "synchronization agreement". This connection is a one-way synchronization: Active Directory's settings are the master, Scalix directory serves only as a slave configuration.

Enter:

```
omldapsync -i AD_SX1
```

where AD_SX1 is the name that you choose for this so-called synchronization agreement. Scalix can have more than one of these agreements and supports several different external directory standards. You'll find concise information on this program in its man page.

After entering the above command, omldapsync offers twelve different actions. To create a sync agreement with ADS, enter 1 and hit return. Enter the hostname of your Windows' domain controller, the Administrator's LDAP dn, your Scalix host data and credentials, and pass decisions on the synchronization strategy. I won't go into detail here. Following is a simple example that works on our test servers. The Scalix setup GUID is a very detailed help for this purpose, too.

Please note we have scalixbook.local as domain, because we do not recommend putting an ADS server in the wild Internet.

```
scalix01:~ # omldapsync -i AD_SX1
2007-06-26 14:04:57 STATUS: Interactive for AD_SX1 started ########
Common tasks menu for syncid AD_SX1
0. Display this menu
1. Configure the LDAP dir sync settings
2. Force a complete (re)load of the directory
3. Update the directory after some changes
4. Accept previous error and update directory
5. Skip previous error and update directory
6. Update the directory and prompt for error
```

```
7. Modify all sync records from the directory
8. Delete all sync records in the directory
d. Toggle debug mode from current setting <0>
n. Toggle test mode from current setting <>
q. Quit
INPUT: Please enter an option (0):1
2007-06-26 14:04:58 STATUS: Configuration of AD_SX1 started ########
INPUT: Select sync agreement type to create (21): 11
2007-06-26 14:05:47 INFO: create file AD_SX1/sync.cfg ...
###########################################################
# NOTE: Some remote LDAP attributes are reserved by Scalix.
# If these have already been used, change the defaults now.
# Otherwise, accept the defaults presented inside brackets.
INPUT: value for SCALIXHIDEUSERENTRY (scalixHideUserEntry):
INPUT: value for SCALIXMAILBOXCLASS (scalixMailboxClass):
INPUT: value for SCALIXLIMITMAILBOXSIZE (scalixLimitMailboxSize):
INPUT: value for SCALIXLIMITMAILBOXSIZE (scalixLimitMailboxSize):
INPUT: value for SCALIXLIMITOUTBOUNDMAIL (scalixLimitOutboundMail):
INPUT: value for SCALIXLIMITINBOUNDMAIL (scalixLimitInboundMail):
INPUT: value for SCALIXLIMITNOTIFYUSER (scalixLimitNotifyUser):
INPUT: value for EX_SCALIX_MAILBOX (scalixScalixObject):
INPUT: value for EX_SCALIX_MAILNODE (scalixMailnode):
INPUT: value for EX_SCALIX_MSGLANG (scalixServerLanguage):
INPUT: value for EX_SCALIX_ADMIN (scalixAdministrator):
INPUT: value for EX_SCALIX_MBOXADMIN (scalixMailboxAdministrator):
###########################################################
INPUT: Edit config file now y/n (n):y
INPUT: Use vi to edit y/n (n): n
JAVA_HOME[/usr/java/j2sdk1.4.2_02]:/usr/java/jre1.5.0_11
EX_HOST[]:w2003e.scalixbook.local
EX_LOGON[cn=Export Admin,cn=users,dc=your_org,dc=com]:cn=Administrator
,cn=users,dc=scalixbook,dc=local
EX_PASS[]: ******
IM_HOST[]:scalix01.scalixbook.local
IM_CAA_URL[1]                                                    :http://
scalix01.scalixbook.local/caa/
IM_CAA_KEYSTORE[]: (leave this empty)
IM_CAA_NAME[user_name@your_domain.com]:sxadmin
IM_CAA_PASS[]: *****
EX_BASE1[cn=users,dc=your_org,dc=com]:cn=users,dc=scalixbook,dc=local
IM_OMADDRESS[/internet,tnef]: (leave this empty)
INPUT: Compare old config to new y/n (n):y
INPUT: Replace old config with new y/n (?):y
INPUT: Attempt to test data extraction now y/n (n): y
```

If this worked out fine, you will receive the following feedback:

```
STATUS: Configuration of AD_SX1 completed ########
2. Force a complete (re)load of the directory
```

The last sentence indicates that an initial synchronization is about to take place. If you want to start the sync agreement manually later, type:

```
omldapsync -u AD_SX1
```

Enter this command as a cron job on your scalix system to have the scalix database updated automatically.

## Synchronizing Contacts with Active Directory

If you need to synchronize your Scalix Addressbooks with the Microsoft directory's adressbook, you will find concise information here in the Scalix wiki: http://www.scalix.com/wiki/index.php?title=HowTos/AD-Contact-Sync.

## Summary

After a brief look on Scalix' LDAP tools, you have learned in this chapter how to integrate an external LDAP directory with Scalix and how to configure Scalix's LDAP server. Then, we integrated the Scalix Administration tools for Active Directory, with the help of which a Windows Admin can almost entirely manage Scalix.

# 12
# HA and Multi-Server Setups

This chapter starts with questions that you have to ask yourself before you set up any multi-server environment with Scalix. After that, we see two examples of how a High Availability (HA) setup might look. The first example deals with the expensive, proprietary systems and uses the Enterprise Edition to setup an Active/Active cluster. The second example, however, describes in brief what you need to do to set up an Active/Passive Cluster with Backup functions, when you use the Community Edition. After that, a brief look at mail routing and directory synchronization rounds up common tasks in multi-server setups.

## Multi-Server Setups

Before you start installing several Scalix servers, you have to make some decisions:

- Which architecture will your setup have? Does a HA cluster make sense?
- Which server will have what kind of role? Which server will be the master?
- Where do you want to install the Scalix Admin Console (SAC)?
- How should directory synchronization work between your machines?
- Think about the hardware. If you are running a HA cluster, you may need twice as many resources on a single system in case of a failover.
- How should outgoing mail be routed?

After having made decisions on each of these questions, you can proceed with your installation. With Scalix, there are several ways to install a multi-server environment. Probably the easiest way is to spread the Scalix components over several hosts for load-balancing purposes. Another reasonable setup is a multi-server environment with DNS-subnets and Scalix mailnodes responsible for those. And then there are Failover Clusters. Let's discuss two common setups.

# The Common "Simple" Two-Node Cluster

Our first example describes probably the most common commercial Scalix HA-Setup : A cluster with two nodes, both running an active Scalix instance and a passive, failover instance for the other node's active instance. In this setup, each node can take over the other server's instance and provide access to groupware data for both instances' users. Each of the four Scalix instances will have its own virtual IP, which is managed by the cluster software. A concise how-to is currently under development in the Scalix Wiki. Its growing length shows that this is not at all a "simple" task (`http://www.scalix.com/wiki/index.php?title=HowTos/ Setting_up_for_High_Availability_How-To`). You will need deep knowledge of Linux and of the Red Hat Cluster Suite (RHCS). Describing this setup in detail would go beyond the scope of this book, but the following outline may provide a roadmap for setting up an HA Scalix cluster. For this setup, you will need an enterprise-level clustering solution like the Red Hat Cluster Suite as a basis. Furthermore, only the Scalix EE Enterprise Edition offers the support for such an active/active cluster. Thus, you will need at least an evaluation license of EE, plus a valid license for RHCS. After you have organized the operating system and the EE, you have to accomplish the following steps:

- Set up your Red Hat cluster. Install two instances and add a dedicated storage for the Scalix instances to each of the cluster nodes. Use Logical Volume Management (LVM) for the storage devices. Check the DNS and network connectivity between the nodes and run failover tests. Prepare mount points for two Scalix instances on each of the nodes' filesystems. (The Scalix Wiki suggests `/var/opt/scalix/m1` and `/var/opt/scalix/m2` as example directories.) Add a Scalix service to the cluster software's setup and check if it has been successfully activated.

- Install Scalix EE instances. Use the `--instance` and `--hostname` parameters to specify the instance and the hostname you want to install. Repeat this step for each of the instances you need.

- Choose one of the Scalix instances for the Admin instance. Deactivate the Scalix components caa and sac on the instances that are not running the admin server. The program `/opt/scalix-tomcat/bin/sxtomcat-webapps` takes add and del options, thus a `/opt/scalix-tomcat/bin/sxtomcat-webapps --del hostname caa sac` will do the job for you. In the next step, rerun the Scalix installer (don't forget the `instance` and `hostname` parameters) and select **Reconfigure Scalix Components**. Enter the fully-qualified hostname of your Scalix instance that runs the Admin console in the **Scalix Management Agent** dialog.

- Set the Tomcat shutdown port on all but one of the instances to a different value. The default is 8005. The command `/opt/scalix-tomcat/bin/sxtomcat-modify-instance -p 8006 mail2` sets this port to 8006. Don't use duplicates, but restart Tomcat after this reconfiguration.

- Disable the automatic start of the Scalix services on all nodes, because these will be controlled by the cluster manager software.

- Register the Scalix nodes on all instances in `/etc/opt/scalix/instance.cfg`. Create a merged file that contains the combined content of all of your instances.

- Adapt your Apache configuration according to the steps in the Scalix Wiki. Every Tomcat-based application unfortunately needs the instances specified. Therefore, you have to do a lot of small steps of work here.

- Integrate the Scalix services in your RHCS setup and bring the nodes up.

- Run failover tests over and over again. Disconnect either server and check for its availability.

Despite the fact that this setup is fairly complex, it is probably the most common Scalix Cluster setup. If you decide to set up your Scalix servers this way, it may be a good idea to contact a Scalix consultant, because you may spend many hours trying to setup Tomcat and RHCS.

# The "Cheap" Active-Passive Cluster

But after the shock of the "simple" cluster setup, there is a reward for all the readers who were not terrified and are still here. The described setup is only the beginning. Scalix and OpenMail were developed especially for multi-server-environments, thus there is really no limit to your creativity once you have a setup running. The bitter pill is the license. For a real multi-server-setup, only a valid license key activates the necessary Scalix functions. You will need the expensive Enterprise edition. But one solution that proved handy in many small enterprises is an active-passive setup with an open-source operating system and the Scalix Community Edition.

In this setup, two servers are installed absolutely identically (except for the IP and hostname). Just install your basic Scalix system twice. Add a cronjob that uses `rsync` to synchronize the `var/opt/scalix` directory like we did in the Backup chapter.

Here you may find the biggest weakness of this "cheap" setup: You will always have a (let's hope it's only a small) difference of the mail store between the two servers. The amount of the delta differs from the time span elapsed since your last `rsync`. If you have no problem with that, this may be a nice setup for you.

Test your setup and both servers. Basically, that's all. Now you have a "manual" cluster which an administrator activates in case of failure on the main Scalix server. And, even better: we already have a full backup on this disk! Perhaps you want to add a tape drive and backup this disk to tape every now and then.

If you are firm with scripting, a free cluster software like Heartbeat (LinuxHA) may prove helpful to automate the failover. There are only some services to be stopped and started on both machines, and I consider Heartbeat easier to learn than RHCS. You may want to try DRBD to synchronize your file system with the active node. There is a lot of helpful open-source software available, as long as you confine yourself to an active-passive cluster.

# Mailrouting in the Enterprise Edition: omaddrt

Enough of clusters, let's deal with a network of Scalix mail servers: A central part of such a multi-server setup is Mail Routing. If you plan to install several Scalix servers in a parallel setup, you have to decide how they should route emails to the Internet. There is a broad variety of setups for this purpose, and all of them include setting rules for the routing of mail. In the following setup, a Scalix server is told to route mail for two other machines, one of them in Zurich, the other one in Munich via the appropriate servers. There are three commands that help you set up mail routes: omshowrt, omaddrt, and omdelrt.

Since omaddrt is the most important program for your setups, here are the most important options it can be given:

| Options for omaddrt | | |
|---|---|---|
| -m | O/R-address | The O/R Address pattern that is supposed to be routed. |
| -q | queue | The name of the delivery service queue where messages are supposed to be added. SMINTFC is the Sendmail Interface input queue. |
| -i | route-info | Adds additional routing information. |
| -d | rule-set | A ruleset can be associated to the rule specified. It is defined in a file under /var/opt/scalix/rules/, and the name of the file should be identical with the name specified here. |
| -R | filename | Specifies a file where the omaddrt command is added to after being executed. This may prove handy for tracking of configuration changes. |

Don't worry if you do not understand all options at once, we will do an example right away. But first, let's have a look at our mail routes in place with omshowrt:

```
scalix:~/ # omshowrt -q all
UNIX        internet                                    MIME
UNIX        internet,tnef                               TNEF
LOCAL       scalix
scalix:~/ #
```

This is the standard setup after installation. Now let's install the two routes for our Swiss and Bavarian branches:

```
scalix:~/ # omaddrt -m munich,mailnode -q SMINTFC -i scalix@munich.
scalixbook.org
omaddrt : Route successfully added
scalix:~/ # omaddrt -m zurich,mailnode -q SMINTFC -i scalix@zurich.
scalixbook.org
omaddrt : Route successfully added
scalix:~/ #
```

It seems the two routes were successfully added. Let's control that with omshowrt:

```
scalix:/var # omshowrt -q all
UNIX        internet                                    MIME
UNIX        internet,tnef                               TNEF
SMINTFC     munich,mailnode                             scalix@
munich.scalixbook.org
LOCAL       scalix
SMINTFC     zurich,mailnode                             scalix@
zurich.scalixbook.org
scalix:~/ #
```

Simple, isn't it? If you want to keep track of your changes to the mail routing table, just add a -R to the command line and specify a filename:

```
scalix:~/ # omaddrt -m munich2,mailnode -q SMINTFC -i scalix@munich.
scalixbook.org -R munich
omaddrt : Route successfully added
scalix:~/ # ls -l
insgesamt 4
-rw-rw-r-- 1 scalix scalix 78 2007-07-25 21:49 muenchen
scalix:~/ # cat munich
omaddrt -m "munich,mailnode" -q "SMINTFC" -i "scalix@munich.
scalixbook.org"
scalix:~/ #
```

Just try and practice typing rules, you can use the `omdelrt` command to delete them later on:

```
scalix:~/ # omdelrt -m munich2,mailnode
omdelrt : Route successfully deleted
scalix:~/ #
```

Please note that before the new routing rules are applied, you have to restart the router daemon with `omoff` and `omon`:

```
scalix:~/ # omoff -d0 -w route
Disabling 1 subsystem(s).
Service Router            Stopped
scalix:~/ # omon route
Enabling 1 subsystem(s).
scalix:~/ #
```

For more complex setups, especially with regard to domain name rewriting by the Sendmail SMTP relay, have a look in the `smtpd.cfg` file in your `/var/opt/ scalix/.../sys/` directory. This well-documented file offers quite a few interesting and helpful options. (Don't forget to restart the SMTP Relay after editing this file, use `omoff-d0 smtpd` and `omon smtpd` for that. If you need more assistance, take a look in the Scalix documentation and the manual pages.

# Keeping Directories Synchronized

As soon as you are running several Scalix directory servers in your multi-server environment, you will come across the topic of keeping these directories at the same level of information. If your user account is changed on the master server, every other server in your network must be informed of the change. Scalix magically fulfills this need, but how does this work? As always, there are some small tools that create import and export agreements for the Scalix directory servers:

- `omadds`: It stands for **add a directory synchronization agreement**. It adds a local synchronization agreement for import (`-i`) or export (`-e`) and allows an abundance of options. For example, you can export all your data, but keep back the phone numbers and specify many more details.

- `omdelds`: It deletes directory synchronization agreements and proves especially worthwhile when you are testing.

- `ommodds`: It allows changing of an active synchronization agreement. Its options are almost as abundant as are those of `omadds`.

- `omshowds`: Of course there is again another `om-` tool that simply shows the synchronization agreements.

Let's do some examples. First, we will tell our Scalix server to add/import its directory contents from the Munich machine. Because we specify a time with the -t switch, this will not take effect before January, 1st 2009. After the `omaddds` command, a `omshowds -i 1` shows the first synchronization agreement with incoming directory data.

```
scalix1:/ # omaddds -i -m +DIRSYNC/munich -t "090101 00:00"
Added a Directory Synchronization import agreement and default
Directory-wide
data to the Directory.
scalix1:/ # omshowds -i 1
SYNCHRONIZING DIRECTORY        : **
EXPORT OR ADDRESS              : +DIRSYNC /munich
DS-STRT-AT                     : 090101 00:00
DS-PERIOD                      : 15
DS-IR-FLG                      : N
scalix1:/ #
```

In the second example, we establish an export agreement to allow the Zurich machine to import the directory data from the host `scalix2`. Can you imagine the complex scenarios this may lead to!

```
scalix2:/ # omaddds -e -m +DIRSYNC/zurich
Added a Directory Synchronization export agreement to the Directory.
scalix2:/ #
scalix2:/ # omshowds -e 1
SYNCHRONIZING DIRECTORY        : **
IMPORT OR ADDRESS              : +DIRSYNC /zurich
DS-EL-FLG                      : N
scalix2:/ #
```

Again, `omshowds` is used to list agreements, this time the first outgoing agreement is questioned.

If you want to have the directory synchronization performed at service start, then add these two lines to `/var/opt/scalix/sx/s/sys/general.cfg`:

```
DS_CUST_SEND_REQ_NOW=TRUE
DS_CUST_MSGQ_TIMEOUT=2
```

Restart the Directory synchronization service to make these changes active:

```
omoff -d 0 -w dirsync; omon dirsync
```

There are also specific tools for synchronization of public folders between Scalix servers, they are called `omaddbbsa`, `omdelbbsa`, `omlistbbsa`, and `ommodbbsa`. All of them are used in a similar style like `omadds`. For more information, have a look at the excellent man pages of all the above mentioned programs.

# Summary

In this chapter, we have learnt which steps need to be taken to setup an Active/Active cluster with RHCS and the Scalix Enterprise edition. The chapter showed how an Active/Passive cluster providing backup storage can also be done with the community edition, and finished with mail routing and directory synchronization issues.

# 13
# Defeating Spam and Viruses

In this chapter, you will learn how to integrate measures against spam and viruses in Scalix. Both Clamav and Spamassassin are used, and hints for integrating commercial software is included. After that, we will learn about Scalix's own methods of avoiding incoming spam.

## Commercial or Open Source?

There are several commercial tools for spam and virus filtering, like Sophos, McAfee, Trend Micro, and many others. The open-source community also offers two software packages that integrate flawlessly with Scalix: Spamassassin and Clamav. Because the process of configuration is similar for all of these, the following chapter shows how to set up the free programs. Following the guidelines on the next few pages, an administrator can easily make his Scalix server spam- and virus-resistant with any solution he might choose. The only thing that he must take care of is to make the individual binary of the virus scanner chosen executable for the Scalix user, normally by executing `chmod a+rx` on that file. In order to find out which file this is, please refer to the documentation of the anti-spam product.

## Scalix Virus Scanning—How It Works

Every Scalix system is capable of rule sets that define how to process incoming messages. After receiving a new message, the service router tests these and executes commands on the email. Normally, if a spam or virus is detected by an external command, the router deletes that email or may quarantine the message by moving it to a special folder. Such rules are stored in the file rules. In this directory, (for our example domain scalixbook.org, this is located in: `/var/opt/scalix/sx/s/rules`), a special file has to be created that contains the routing rule for the spam or virus check. This new file has to be called `ALL-ROUTES.VIR`. While files in this directory normally apply only to one Scalix routing configuration, the anti-virus rule set must be executed for all of them. With an external mapper script, the Scalix router will have the virus scanner check the mail. After the check, the scanner returns a result to the service router , which will then decide how to proceed with the message.

Thus, the integration of an anti-virus software on a Scalix server is done in four steps:

- Installing the AV software like Clamav.
- Preparing the service router for virus checking.
- Integration and configuration of the mapper script.
- Restarting the service router and testing the configuration.

# Installing Clamav

Clamav is a free and very active open-source-software project. Up-to-date versions of this virus scanner can and should be downloaded from its homepage (http://www.clamav.net), the stable release contains signatures of more than 150,000 viruses. There are two databases that need to be kept on a recent status on your system, main.cvd and daily.cvd. The latter contains daily updates of signatures. On SUSE systems, the rpms are available in the package management, on our openSUSE 10.1, Clamav 0.91.1 and Clamav-db 0.91.1 can be installed easily with YaST. If you have older versions in your repository, go to the website and download the new ones. A cron job that retrieves updated databases may also prove to be a good idea.

If you download the software from the website, a simple rpm *-i clamav...rpm* and *rpm -i clamav-db...rpm* installs it into your system. On openSUSE 10.1, some additional packages need to be installed, rpm will tell you the details. For some other systems, the Clamav server daemon, clamd, may be contained in an extra package. During installation, a new user and group called vscan (for Virus Scanner) are created. You have to add this user to the group Scalix on your system by changing the following entry in /etc/group:

```
scalix:!:104: vscan
vscan:!:105:
```

If needed, adjust your Clamav configuration to your needs, the configuration file is /etc/clamd.conf. On some systems, it may be clamav.conf, which has to be changed. Scalix needs the config in /etc/clamd.conf. If you happen to have a system like this, rename the file and make sure that Clamav uses this as its configuration file. For this, you will need to edit clamd.conf and possibly /etc/init.d/clamd.

The Clamav server, `clamd`, is started with:

```
scalix:~ # rcclamd start
Starting Clam AntiVirus daemon                          done
scalix:~ # netstat -atulpen | grep clam
tcp        0      0 127.0.0.1:3310            0.0.0.0:*
LISTEN      65          17257       3849/clamd
scalix:~ #   scalix:~ # rcclamd start
```

As you can see, the admin can control by using netstat if `clamd` has started properly. Telnet is also possible. Clamav by default uses port 3310.

# Setting Up Scalix for Virus Control

In the rules directory, create a file with at least this content:

```
VIRUS-UNCLEANED=1 ACTION=REJECT NDN-INFO=!ndninfo.txt
```

This line is enough to tell the service router not to accept infected mails, and reject them with the non-delivery-notification specified in `ndninfo.txt`. There are several options allowed in this rules file. Possible actions, for example, include: ALLOW, REJECT, DISCARD, DEFER, and RETURN. The Scalix administration guide holds detailed information on that if you need more input. Scalix suggests setting up anti-virus routing including the non-delivery notification. However, as most viruses today come from botnets and infected Windows PCs, it may be better to leave out the last option in the mentioned configuration for the rule file.

Now, restart the service router and don't forget to wait a little between the two commands:

```
scalix:~ # omoff -s sr
scalix:~ # omon -s sr
```

If you want to only have the prompt return when the SR is off, do `omoff -w sr` and `omon -w sr`. The next step is copying the scan file `omvscan` from the example directory to the rules directory and making it executable:

```
scalix:~ # cp /var/opt/scalix/sx/s/rules.eg/omvscan.map /var/opt/
scalix/sx/s/rules/
scalix:~ # cd /var/opt/scalix/sx/s/rules/
scalix:/var/opt/scalix/sx/s/rules # chown root omvscan.map
scalix:/var/opt/scalix/sx/s/rules # chmod 555 omvscan.map
scalix:/var/opt/scalix/sx/s/rules #
```

If you are interested in more details, open the file omvscan.map with an editor like vi or emacs. You are shown the mapper script that connects Scalix with the different virus scanner engines available, namely McAfee, Trend Micro, and Clamav. I recommend reading this well-documented script. It is worth taking a little time over, and gives a deeper insight in the processes involved around the "Scalix Server Router Virus Scanning Protocol Client", even more than the Scalix documentation. If you do not find the file in the above path, take a look in /opt/scalix/examples/general/omvscan.map.

The mapper is configured by a file named omscan.cfg.

```
scalix: # cp /opt/scalix/template/release.sys/omvscan.cfg /var/opt/
scalix/sx/s/sys/
```

On Scalix 11, it is located in /opt/scalix/template/release.sys/omvscan.cfg; copy it to the ~/sys directory of your installation. Open it with an editor:

```
# $RCSfile: omvscan.cfg,v $
#
#          Configuration for Service Router Generic anti-virus
scanning.
#
# Notes:
#          Each line in each section should be a valid assignment
#          to an environment variable in the bash shell.
#          Do not re-use variable names in different sections.
[GENERAL]
ANTI_VIRUS_ENGINE="ClamAV"
OMAV_LOGFILE=$(omrealpath '~/logs/omvscan.log')
# 0 is off, 1 is ERRORS, 2 is ERRORS & WARNINGS, 3 is same as 2 +
DEBUG
OMAV_LOGLEVEL=0

[Trend Micro InterScan VirusWall]
TREND_ENGINE=/opt/trend/ISBASE/IScan.BASE/vscan
TREND_SCAN_OPTIONS='-p/etc/iscan -v0 -za'
TREND_CLEAN_OPTIONS='-p/etc/iscan -v0 -za -c'
TREND_LOGPFX=$(omrealpath '~/tmp/trendvs.log')
TREND_USE_LOCKING=no
TREND_LOCK_FILE=trendvs.lock

[McAfee Virus Scan]
MCAFEE_ENGINE=/usr/local/bin/uvscan
MCAFEE_SCAN_OPTIONS='--secure --noboot --mime'
MCAFEE_CLEAN_OPTIONS='--secure --noboot --mime --norename -c'
MCAFEE_LOGPFX=$(omrealpath '~/tmp/mcafee.log')
MCAFEE_USE_LOCKING=no
MCAFEE_LOCK_FILE=mcafee.lock

[ClamAV]
CLAMAV_ENGINE=/usr/bin/clamdscan
```

```
CLAMAV_SCAN_OPTIONS='--stdout'
CLAMAV_CLEAN_OPTIONS='--stdout'
CLAMAV_LOGPGX=$(omrealpath '~/tmp/clamav.log')
CLAMAV_USE_LOCKING=no
CLAMAV_LOCK_FILE=clamav.lock
```

The first block [GENERAL] has three options, one of them, ANTI_VIRUS_ENGINE, specifies the virus scanner Scalix is supposed to use, and which is configured in the following lines. These contain three paragraphs, one for each virus scanner that Scalix supports. The last block is relevant for Clamav, so check the paths and options, if they correspond to the Clamav version of your distribution and your preferences. Again, the Scalix administration guide has concise information on each of the options described.

That's all, you can now proceed to test your Clamav setup. Some checks that may be useful are:

- Check if Clamav is running and whether it is started automatically on boot.

- Download the virus test files from the Clamav website or from http://www.eicar.com and send them to (and from) your Scalix server.

- Turn up the logging detail level, for example with the command omconflvl router 15 and restart the service router. Check the log files for problem, failure or error notifications. A successfully rejected infected mail will show an entry saying **VIRUS-UNCLEANED**.

- Don't forget to turn down the log level again after you have confirmed Clamav-Scalix works fine. Otherwise, you will get huge log files.

# Scalix Anti-Spam

As with the anti-virus software, there is also some free anti-spam software available. Beside commercial products, the free software project Spamassassin is one of the best available solutions. It is integrated in most distributions, rpms are available and they install flawlessly with YaST. On openSUSE 10.1, eleven dependencies, mostly Perl libraries, are installed with Spamassassin and after that it is ready to be used. Perl-based rulesets check each incoming mail, comparing the text with patterns from libraries. Furthermore, there is an abundance of tests that can be combined to powerful anti-spam measures. However, checking incoming mail is only half the way. A lot of spam can be avoided by checking sender/recipients/IPs and DNS data before the mail server accepts the mail. In the last year, techniques like greylisting came up, and there are many vendors in the market who sell out-of-the-box anti-spam appliances.

As Scalix uses Sendmail as SMTP server, setting such mail restrictions can be very tedious. Other mail servers like Postfix offer more and better possibilities for filtering mail; and spam filtering is a process that costs a lot of resources and needs permanent updates of libraries, tests, and programs. Thus, I recommend setting up a dedicated Postfix-Amavis-Spamassassin mail relay for all incoming mail. The Postfix spam filter can integrate peer-to-peer network technologies like Vipul's Razor and similar, which is very complicated with Sendmail. And by separating Spam filtering and Scalix, both performance and efficiency in your mail network will be increased, and the Scalix server can concentrate on its proper work—groupware.

Nevertheless, Scalix directly supports Spamassassin, and the following paragraphs briefly show how to set this up. For all the readers who want to dig in deeper into the secrets of Sendmail configuration and access restriction, I recommend the official Scalix documentation in the server setup guide and both the Sendmail and Spamassassin howtos at `http://www.tlpd.org`.

First, let's make a backup of our old SMTP server configuration of Scalix:

```
scalix:/var/opt/scalix/sx/s/sys # cp smtpd.cfg smtpd.cfg.org
scalix:/var/opt/scalix/sx/s/sys #
```

Now, open the `smtpd.cfg` file in your favourite editor. Again, you'll find a well-documented, helpful file for Scalix administration and configuration. Beside the configuration of mail relaying, there are many options that control the behavior of Scalix's SMTP server. For Spamassassin, simply add the lines:

```
SMTPFILTER=TRUE
RELAY accept 127.0.0.1
```

at the end of the file and save it. These two lines simply tell Scalix to use a mail filter and to accept connections only from the localhost.

Now comes the ugly part: We have to change the Sendmail configuration. Unfortunately, the Sendmail syntax is rather complicated, and explaining what we are doing here would go beyond the scope of the book.

```
(...)
# delimiter (operator) characters (old $o macro)
O OperatorChars=.:%@!^/[]+
(...)
```

If your installation has a = in this line, remove it. Then, search for the line containing `InputMailFilter`:

```
(...)
# Input mail filters
#O InputMailFilters
(...)
```

Change this line to:

```
O InputMailFilters=Spamassassin
```

and add the following lines directly below it:

```
(...)
#Milter options
#O Milter.LogLevel
O Milter.macros.connect=b, j, _, {daemon_name}, {if_name}, {if_addr}
O Milter.macros.helo={tls_version}, {cipher}, {cipher_bits}, {cert_
subject}, {cert_issuer}
O Milter.macros.envfrom=i, {auth_type}, {auth_authen}, {auth_ssf},
{auth_author}, {mail_mailer}, {mail_host}, {mail_addr}
O Milter.macros.envrcpt={rcpt_mailer}, {rcpt_host}, {rcpt_addr}
(...)
```

Search for the section MAIL FILTER DEFINITIONS, which is usually empty and add the lines:

```
Xspamassassin, S=local:/var/run/spamass-milter/spamass-milter.sock,
F=, T=C:15m;S:4m;R:4m;E:10m
```

That's it so far! With these lines, we have basically told Sendmail to use Spamassassin for checking incoming mail. However, there are still many possible configuration options left. Spamassassin can be configured in /etc/mail/spamassassin; the Scalix smtpd.cfg file offers many possible settings against unwanted mails and spoofing; and last but not least there is a Sendmail macro file that can be used to generate a detailed individual configuration for all those who understand it. And then there is spamass-milter ().

At last, it's time for some checks to make sure Spamassassin is working with Scalix:

- Check your run level script configuration. Is Spamassassin being started at boot?

- Check with tools like ps, top, netstat, and telnet whether Spamassassin is running

- Check the files in /var/log, namely mail.info and mail.err, for errors and information from spamd. This daemon will report a **clean message** or **detected spam**, depending on the result of the scan.

# Authentication and Relay Control

You may agree that spam usually comes from unauthorized persons. Scalix provides some options in its `smtpd.cfg` file where the administrator can adjust who is allowed to send mail under which circumstances, using the Scalix server. Because there seems to be an abundance of options, the following lines give a short overview over the most important ones in `smtpd.cfg`. Speaking generally, there are events and actions triggered by events. Based on patterns, the Scalix server triggers a suitable action when an event occurs.

- Allowed events are: SUBMIT, ANONYMOUS, AUTH_SUCCESS, AUTH_MISMATCH, RELAY, ORIGINATOR, and RECIPIENT. The command SMTPFILTER completes this list.

- Possible actions taken can be of: Accept, Defer, Discard, Header, Reject, and all of them with the string `Log_` as a prefix, that cause the action to be logged.

- The available patterns are: An IP address, e.g. 123.234.132.231, an IP subnet and mask like 123.234.200.0/255.255.240.0, a hostname, for example spammer.scalixbook.org, the end of a domain like .spammer.net, the start of a domain, 123.234. The keyword ALL matches all hosts.

Although there may be several entries for each event in the config file, only the first action specified will be executed, all of the following are ignored.

Most of the actions and events should be self-explanatory, only notable is the header directive: It adds an extra header to the mail processed, if the conditions triggered the specified event. The following example shows how to allow a certain host to relay mail:

```
RELAY Accept scalixbook.org
RELAY Reject ALL
```

If you want to allow a single host to send mail:

```
SUBMIT Accept scalixbook.org
SUBMIT Reject ALL
```

There are many combinations possible, the ORIGINATOR keyword could be used to block and log unwanted mail from a known spammer making annoying advertising for books:

```
ORIGINATOR Log_Reject mfeilner@feilner-it.net
ORIGINATOR Accept ALL
```

An administrator who wants to protect a colleague from receiving mail could use this:

```
RECIPIENT Log_Reject mfeilner@scalixbook.org
RECIPIENT Accept ALL
```

And last but not least, there is a easy solution to integrate DNS-servers like Spamcop that deliver information on known spammers. In this case, a special DNS query to a server is run by Scalix to determine whether the relevant server (mostly the origin of a mail) is known for sending spam.

```
SUBMIT Log_Reject DNSBL,bl.spamcop.net,ALL
```

After such changes, don't forget to restart your smtpd service with `omoff -d0 smtpd` and `omon smtpd`.

# Summary

In this chapter, we have prepared Scalix for spam and virus filtering by Clamav and Spamassasin. The configuration files involved are the same when proprietary mail filter programs are used. The central configuration file of the Scalix server, `smtpd.cfg`, offers a huge variety of rules for mail relaying, authentication, and submission. For the admin who needs more, there is the Sendmail configuration. In these files, anything that Sendmail is capable of, is possible, but their syntax is very complicated

# Bibliography

## Links Used Throughout the Book:

## Chapter 1

1. "The History of Electronic Mail" by Tom Van Vleck
   http://www.multicians.org/thvv/mail-history.html

2. "Reflections on the 25th Anniversary of Spam" by Brad Templeton
   http://www.templetons.com/brad/spam/spam25.html

3. RFC 196 — "A Mail Box Protocol":
   http://www.faqs.org/rfcs/rfc196.html

4. Techtarget definition of RFCs:
   http://whatis.techtarget.com/definition/0,,
   sid9_gci214264,00.html

5. "The First Network Email" by Ray Tomlinson
   http://openmap.bbn.com/~tomlinso/ray/firstemailframe.html

6. RFC 469 — "Network Mail Meeting Summary":
   http://tools.ietf.org/html/469

7. J.C.R. Licklider, Albert Vezza, "Applications of Information Networks", Proc
   of the IEEE, 66(11), Nov 1978, as quoted by Dave Crocker:
   http://www.livinginternet.com/e/ei.htm.

8. RFC 733 - Standard for the format of ARPA network text messages:
   http://tools.ietf.org/html/733

9. The Top 50 RFCs:
   http://www.faqs.org/rfc-pop1.html

10. Howard Rheingold, on the very first mailing list:
    `http://www.rheingold.com/vc/book`

11. X.400 message handling services:
    `http://www.itu.int/rec/T-REC-X.400/en`

12. Citadel BBS:
    `http://www.citadel.org`

13. A history of MS Exchange:
    `http://blogs.brnets.com/michael/archive/2005/02/07/347.aspx`

14. MAPI definition at techtarget.com:
    `http://searchexchange.techtarget.com/sDefinition/0,,sid43_gci214084,00.html`

15. Microsoft's MAPI documentation:
    `http://msdn.microsoft.com/library/default.asp?url=/library/en-us/mobilesdk5/html/mob5oriMessagingAPIMAPI.asp`

16. Openchange Projekt:
    `http://www.openchange.org`

17. Wikipedia on MIME:
    `http://en.wikipedia.org/wiki/MIME`

18. Permanent Message Header Field Names List by the IANA:
    `http://www.iana.org/assignments/message-headers/perm-headers.html`

# Chapter 2

19. "And now announcing the General Protection Fault award "winners" for 1999 ", Nicolas Petreley on Infoworld:
    `http://www.infoworld.com/articles/op/xml/00/01/17/000117oppetreley.html`

20. "Closing down OpenMail: It's not about profit", Nicolas Petreley on Linuxworld
    `http://www.itworld.com/App/325/lw-03-penguin_2`

21. HP's Press Release on closing down OpenMail:
    `http://www.hp.com/softwarereleases/releases-media2/discon/B2298-80060.htm`

22. HP's Press Release on selling OpenMail to Samsung:
    `http://www.hp.com/hpinfo/newsroom/press/2001/011113a.html`

23. "Samsung Contact: More compatible with Outlook than Exchange?" Robin 'Roblimo' Miller on Linux.com:
    `http://trends.newsforge.com/article.pl?sid=02/11/01/1827249&tid=138&tid=29&tid=30&tid=31`

24. Samsung Contact retreats from its mail server:
    `http://samsungcontact.com/documents/Samsung%20Contact%20Announcement%20Letter.pdf`

25. "Xandros acquires open-source email vendor Scalix", Chris Preimesberger on desktoplinux.com:
    `http://www.desktoplinux.com/news/NS8461099683.html`

26. The License of the Scalix Community Edition:
    `http://www.scalix.com/community/opensource/licensing.php`

27. The Scalix Ecosystem—Add-ons and related Software projects:
    `http://www.scalix.com/enterprise/ecosystem/applications.php`

28. Scalix Community Resources on the Web:
    `http://www.scalix.com/community/resources`

# Chapter 3

29. Scalix CE Downloads:
    `http://www.scalix.com/community/downloads/index.php`

# Chapter 4

30. PuTTY SSH Client for Windows:
    `http://www.chiark.greenend.org.uk/~sgtatham/putty/download.html`

31. NoMachine:
    `http://www.nomachine.com`

32. FreeNX:
    `http://freenx.berlios.de`

# Chapter 7:

33. Nagios open source monitoring system:
    `http://www.nagios.org`

34. Nagios Documentation:
    `http://www.nagios.org/docs`

35. Scripts for the integration of Scalix with Nagios:
    `http://downloads.scalix.com/ark/scalix-nagios.tar.gz`

# Chapter 8:

36. Iptables Netfilter Homepage:
    `http://www.netfilter.org/`

37. SUSEfirewall2 documentation
    `http://en.opensuse.org/SuSEfirewall2`

38. OpenVPN Homepage:
    `http://openvpn.net/`

39. Tinyca2 certificate authority management:
    `http://tinyca.sm-zone.net/`

40. Xca certificate management:
    `http://xca.sourceforge.net/`

41. Squid web proxy:
    `http://www.squid-cache.org/`

42. Stunnel Website:
    `http://www.stunnel.org/`

43. Apache Web server:
    `http://httpd.apache.org/`

44. Tomcat Application Server:
    `http://tomcat.apache.org/`

45. Tripwire open source data integrity tool:
    `http://sourceforge.net/projects/tripwire/`

46. Novell's Apparmor:
    `http://www.novell.com/de-de//linux/security/apparmor/`

47. Security-Enhanced Linux:
    `http://www.nsa.gov/selinux/`

48. SELinux for Distributions:
    `http://selinux.sourceforge.net/`

# Chapter 9

49. Rsync website:
    `http://samba.anu.edu.au/rsync/`

50. Automated Scalix backup scripts:
    `http://www.scalix.com/wiki/index.php?title=HowTos/BackupScript_Mbox_Style`

51. Logical Volume Management howto:
    `http://tldp.org/HOWTO/LVM-HOWTO/index.html`

52. LVM snapshots documentation:
    `http://tldp.org/HOWTO/LVM-HOWTO/snapshots_backup.html`

53. Automated backup scripts from the Admin Resource Kit:
   `http://www.scalix.com/wiki/index.php?title=Admin_Resource_Kit`

54. Proprietary Backup software for Scalix from SEP:
   `http://www.sep.de`

55. SEP download
   `http://download.sep.de/db_modules/scalix/`

56. SEP documentation
   `http://wiki.sepsoftware.com/wiki/index.php/Scalix_doc`

# Chapter 10:

57. Scalix Wiki on OpenLDAP and Password management:
   `http://www.scalix.com/wiki/index.php?title=HowTos/Using_OpenLDAP_for_password_management`

58. How to enable LDAP authentication on SLES9 or SUSE Linux 10.x:
   `https://secure-support.novell.com/KanisaPlatform/Publishing/471/3000394_f.SAL_Public.html`

59. Synchronize your Scalix Addressbooks with the Microsoft directory's addressbook
   `http://www.scalix.com/wiki/index.php?title=HowTos/AD-Contact-Sync`

# Chapter 11:

60. Setting up Scalix for High-Availability (this website is under permanent construction):
   `http://www.scalix.com/wiki/index.php?title=HowTos/Setting_up_for_High_Availability_How-To`

# Chapter 12:

61. Clamav antivirus homepage:
   `http://www.clamav.net`

62. Virus test files:
   `http://www.eicar.com`

63. Linux documentation project, including HOWTOs on Sendmail and Spamassassin:
   `http://www.tlpd.org`

64. Spamassassin milter project:
   `http://savannah.nongnu.org/projects/spamass-milt`

# Acronyms Used

| Abbrevation | Full Description |
|---|---|
| AIX | Advanced Interactive eXecutive |
| AJAX | Asynchronous JavaScript and XML |
| ARPA | Advanced Research Projects Agency |
| ARPANET | Advanced Research Projects Agency Network |
| ASCII | American Standard Code for Information Interchange, alternative USASCII |
| BBS | Bulletin Board Systems |
| BSD | Berkeley Software Distribution |
| BTX | Bildschirmtext (german) |
| CALDAV | Calendar via WebDAV (CALendar Distributed Authoring and Versioning) |
| CCITT | Comité Consultatif International Téléphonique et Télégraphique |
| CDDL | Common Development and Distribution License |
| CLI | Command Line Interface |
| CRM | Customer Relationship Management |
| CTSS | Compatible Time-Sharing System |
| DAP | Directory Access Protocol |
| DEC | Digital Equipment Corporation |
| DLL | Dynamic Link Library |
| DNS | Domain Name System |
| FISH | Files transferred over SHell protocol |
| GroupDAV | Groupware Distributed Authoring and Versioning |
| GTK | GIMP-Toolkit |
| GUI | Graphical User Interface |
| HP UX | Hewlett Packard UNIX |
| HTML | Hypertext Markup Language |
| HTTP | Hypertext Transfer Protocol |
| HTTPS | Hypertext Transfer Protocol Secure |
| IANA | Internet Assigned Numbers Authority |
| ICAL | Icalendar Standard |
| IEEE | Institute of Electrical and Electronics Engineers |
| IETF | Internet Engineering Task Force |
| IMAP | Internet Message Access Protocol |
| IP | Internet Protocol |
| ITU | International Telecommunication Union |
| JRE | Java Runtime Environment |

| Abbrevation | Full Description |
|---|---|
| KDE | KDE Desktop Environment |
| LDAP | Lightweight Directory Access Protocol |
| LVM | Logical Volume Management |
| MAPI | Messaging Application Programming Interface |
| MDA | Mail Delivery Agent |
| MIME | Multipurpose Internet Mail Extensions |
| MIT | Massachusetts Institute of Technology |
| MOTIS | Message Oriented Text Interchange System |
| MPL | Mozilla Public License |
| MSDN | Microsoft Developer Network |
| MTA | Mail Transfer Agent |
| MUA | Mail User Agent |
| MULTICS | Multiplexed Information and Computing Service |
| MX | MX Resource Record, Mail Exchange |
| NRD | 2nd Version of RD |
| NRPE | Nagios Remote Plugin Executor |
| NX | NoMachine's X Proxy Software |
| OSI-Model | Open Systems Interconnection Reference Model |
| PAM | Pluggable Authentication Modules |
| POP | Post Office Protocol |
| PSQL | PostgreSQL |
| RAND | *Research ANd Development* |
| RD | Readmail |
| RFC | Request for Comments |
| RPM | RPM Package Manager, formerly *Red Hat Package Manager* |
| SAC | Scalix Admin Console |
| SDC | System Development Corp. in Santa Monica, California |
| SDL | Simple DirectMedia Layer |
| SDS | Scientific Data Systems |
| SMTP | Simple Mail Transfer Protocol |
| SOAP | Formerly: Simple Object Access Protocol, description was considered misleading and therefore dropped |
| SQL | Structured Query Language |
| SSH | Secure Shell |
| SWA | Scalix Web Access |

| Abbrevation | Full Description |
|---|---|
| TCP | Transmission Control Protocol |
| UAL | User Agent Layer |
| UDP | User Datagram Protocol |
| URL/URI | Uniform Resource Locator/Identifier |
| UUCP | UNIX-to-UNIX-CoPy |
| VCAL | Vcalendar |
| VPN | Virtual Private Network |
| WAP | Wireless Application Protocol |
| WebDAV | Web-based Distributed Authoring and Versioning |
| WWW | World-Wide-Web |
| X.25 | A standardized protocol suite for network connections |
| X.400 | An alternative Mail Standard |
| X.500 | A Directory Standard |
| XML | Extensible Markup Language |
| YAST | Yet Another Setup Tool |

# Relevant RFCs

| RFC # | Title |
|---|---|
| 196 | A MAIL BOX PROTOCOL |
| 469 | Network Mail Meeting Summary |
| 733 | STANDARD FOR THE FORMAT OF ARPA NETWORK TEXT MESSAGES (1) |
| 354 | THE FILE TRANSFER PROTOCOL |
| 385 | COMMENTS ON THE FILE TRANSFER PROTOCOL (RFC 354) |
| 772 | MAIL TRANSFER PROTOCOL |
| 821, 974, 1869, 2821, 1123 | SIMPLE MAIL TRANSFER PROTOCOL |
| 876 | Survey of SMTP Implementations |
| 1047 | DUPLICATE MESSAGES AND SMTP |
| 1090 | SMTP on X.25 |
| 1425, 1651, 1869 | SMTP Service Extensions |
| 1426, 1652, | SMTP Service Extension for 8bit-MIMEtransport |
| 1427, 1653, 1870 | SMTP Service Extension for Message Size Declaration (obsolete by #1653) |
| 1830, 3030 | SMTP Service Extensions for Transmission of Large and Binary MIME Messages |

| RFC # | Title |
|---|---|
| 1845 | SMTP Service Extension for Checkpoint/Restart |
| 1846 | SMTP 521 Reply Code |
| 1854, 2197 | SMTP Service Extension for Command Pipelining |
| 918 | POST OFFICE PROTOCOL |
| 937 | POST OFFICE PROTOCOL - VERSION 2 |
| 1081, 1225, 1460, 1725, 1939, 1957, 2449, 5034 | Post Office Protocol - Version 3 |
| 1730, 1731, 1732, 1733, 2060, 2061, 3501, 4466, 4469, 4551, 5032, 5182 | INTERNET MESSAGE ACCESS PROTOCOL - VERSION 4 |
| 733, 822, 2822 | Internet Message Format |
| 1521, 1522, 1590. 2045, 2046, 2047, 2048, 2077, 2184, 2231, 2646, 3798 | Multipurpose Internet Mail Extensions (MIME) |
| 2015, 3156 | MIME Security with Pretty Good Privacy (PGP), MIME Security with OpenPGP |
| 2251, 2252, 2253, 2254, 2255, 2256, 2829, 2830, 3377, 3771, 4510, 4511, 4512, 4513 | Lightweight Directory Access Protocol (LDAP) |
| 2426 | vCard MIME Directory Profile |
| 4791 | Calendaring Extensions to WebDAV (CalDAV) |
| 3288, 3902, 4227 | Using the Simple Object Access Protocol (SOAP) |

# Index

**users icon, SAC**
  about 94
  address, adding 98
  configuration options 100
  filters, editing 95
  filters, list view 96
  password, changing 94
  user, adding 96-98
  user list, filtering 95

# V

**VCAL** 27
**virus control** 231-233
**virus protection option** 135

# W

**WebDAV** 27
**websites** 239-243
**World Wide Web (WWW)** 13

# X

**X.400** 13
**X.500** 26
**Xandros** 31

# Y

**YaST** 49

## Packt Open Source Project Royalties

When we sell a book written on an Open Source project, we pay a royalty directly to that project. Therefore by purchasing Scalix, Packt will have given some of the money received to the Scalix Project.

In the long term, we see ourselves and you—customers and readers of our books—as part of the Open Source ecosystem, providing sustainable revenue for the projects we publish on. Our aim at Packt is to establish publishing royalties as an essential part of the service and support a business model that sustains Open Source.

If you're working with an Open Source project that you would like us to publish on, and subsequently pay royalties to, please get in touch with us.

## Writing for Packt

We welcome all inquiries from people who are interested in authoring. Book proposals should be sent to authors@packtpub.com. If your book idea is still at an early stage and you would like to discuss it first before writing a formal book proposal, contact us; one of our commissioning editors will get in touch with you.

We're not just looking for published authors; if you have strong technical skills but no writing experience, our experienced editors can help you develop a writing career, or simply get some additional reward for your expertise.

## About Packt Publishing

Packt, pronounced 'packed', published its first book "Mastering phpMyAdmin for Effective MySQL Management" in April 2004 and subsequently continued to specialize in publishing highly focused books on specific technologies and solutions.

Our books and publications share the experiences of your fellow IT professionals in adapting and customizing today's systems, applications, and frameworks. Our solution-based books give you the knowledge and power to customize the software and technologies you're using to get the job done. Packt books are more specific and less general than the IT books you have seen in the past. Our unique business model allows us to bring you more focused information, giving you more of what you need to know, and less of what you don't.

Packt is a modern, yet unique publishing company, which focuses on producing quality, cutting-edge books for communities of developers, administrators, and newbies alike. For more information, please visit our website: www.PacktPub.com.

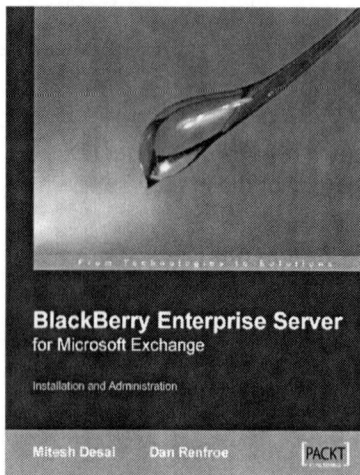

## BlackBerry Enterprise Server for Microsoft® Exchange

ISBN: 978-1-847192-46-2          Paperback: 188 pages

Installation and Administration

1.  Understand BlackBerry Enterprise Server architecture

2.  Install and configure a BlackBerry Enterprise Server

3.  Implement administrative policies for BlackBerry devices

4.  Secure and plan for disaster recovery of your server

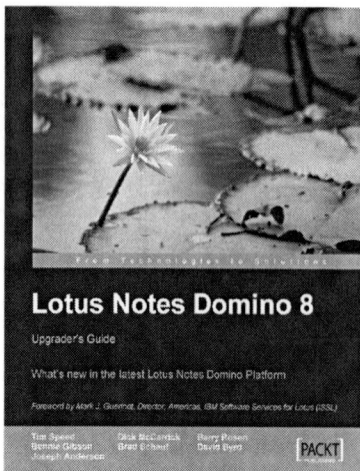

**BlackBerry Enterprise Server**
for Microsoft Exchange

Installation and Administration

Mitesh Desai     Dan Renfroe          PACKT

## Lotus Notes Domino 8

ISBN: 978-1-847192-74-5          Paperback: 250 pages

What's new in the latest Lotus Notes Domino Platform

1.  Upgrade to the latest version of Lotus Notes and Domino

2.  Understand the new features and put them to work in your business

3.  Appreciate the implications of changes and new features

**Lotus Notes Domino 8**

Upgrader's Guide

What's new in the latest Lotus Notes Domino Platform

Foreword by Mark J. Gurevitat, Director, Americas, IBM Software Services for Lotus (ISSL)

Tim Speed     Dick McCarrick     Barry Rosen
Bennie Gibson     Brad Schaut     David Byrd
Joseph Anderson                    PACKT

Please check **www.PacktPub.com** for information on our titles

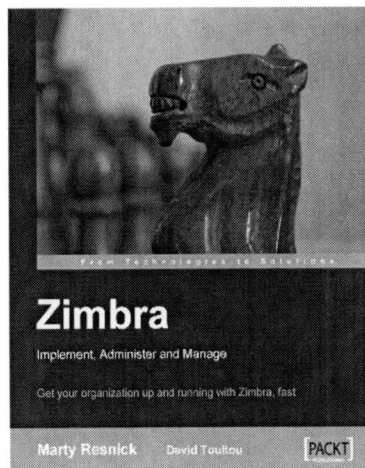

Printed in the United Kingdom
by Lightning Source UK Ltd.
129789UK00001B/195-196/P

9 781847 192769